Cross-Racial Class Protest
in Antebellum
American Literature

Cross-Racial Class Protest in Antebellum American Literature

TIMOTHY HELWIG

UNIVERSITY OF MASSACHUSETTS PRESS
Amherst and Boston

Printed in the United States of America

ISBN 978-1-62534-497-7 (paper); 496-0 (hardcover)

Designed by Sally Nichols
Set in Berthold Walbaum and Fairfield LH
Printed and bound by Maple Press, Inc.

Cover design by Kristina Kachele Design, llc

Cover art: Top: detail from lithograph "Fourpe Tap's Encounter with a Giant Negro," artist unknown, c. 1847. Courtesy of the Yale Collection of American Literature, Beinecke Rare Book and Manuscript Library; Bottom: detail from W. & F. Langenheim, *North-east corner of Third & Dock Street. Girard Bank, at the time the latter was occupied by the military during the riots May 9, 1844*, 1844, oversize half-plate daguerreotype. Courtesy Library Company of Philadelphia.

Library of Congress Cataloging-in-Publication Data

Names: Helwig, Timothy, author.
Title: Cross-racial class protest in antebellum American literature / Timothy Helwig.
Description: Amherst : University of Massachusetts Press, 2020. | Includes bibliographical references and index.
Identifiers: LCCN 2019044405 | ISBN 9781625344960 (hardcover) | ISBN 9781625344977 (paperback) | ISBN 9781613767429 (ebook) | ISBN 9781613767436 (ebook)
Subjects: LCSH: American literature—19th century—History and criticism. | Working class in literature. | Social classes in literature. | Race relations in literature. | African Americans in literature. | Working class writings, American—History and criticism.
Classification: LCC PS217.W66 H37 2020 | DDC 810.9/355—dc23
LC record available at https://lccn.loc.gov/2019044405

British Library Cataloguing-in-Publication Data
A catalog record for this book is available from the British Library.

An early version of chapter one appeared as "Denying the Wages of Whiteness: The Racial Politics of George Lippard's Working-Class Protest," *American Studies* 47, no. 3–4 (Fall–Winter 2006), 87–111. A portion of the Coda appeared as "Crime and American Romanticism," *A History of American Crime Fiction*, ed. Chris Raczkowski (New York: Cambridge University Press, 2017), 56–68.

To Magdelyn

CONTENTS

ACKNOWLEDGMENTS

This project began in the fall of 1996 when I first encountered George Lippard's *The Quaker City* in a graduate seminar with Lori Merish at Miami University of Ohio. She inspired the class with her excitement and brilliance, and I am grateful to her for showing me that studying class and race in antebellum popular literature is serious business. I also owe an incalculable debt to my dissertation adviser at the University of Maryland, Robert S. Levine, for his patient mentorship, his supportive replies to my countless e-mails over the years, his shared love of the Baltimore Orioles, and his friendship. His passion for an historical approach to literature and his engaging and accessible style of academic writing have set a standard that I can only hope to approach. Whenever I find myself lamenting that I am not lucky and never win anything, I stop myself and remember my good fortune in having worked as a graduate student with Lori and Bob.

I am grateful for the short-term research fellowships from the American Antiquarian Society and the Library Company of Philadelphia that enabled me to conduct the initial archival research for this project, and I appreciate the dissertation fellowship from the University of Maryland that helped me to first write out my ideas about the cross-racial strategies in nineteenth-century American print culture. A sabbatical and a summer stipend provided by Western Illinois University were instrumental in helping me complete the manuscript. Special thanks go to the welcoming librarians at the Colchester, Illinois, District Library for giving me access to their lone microfilm machine and a quiet place to work.

I thank editor Brian Halley of the University of Massachusetts Press for his interest in the project and his keen insights throughout the editorial process, production editor Rachael DeShano for her hard work and meticulous attention to detail, and copyeditor Julie Shilling for her great care in improving my manuscript. Any errors that remain are my own. I would also like to express my appreciation to the anonymous readers at the press for their thorough and constructive reviews.

I extend my gratitude to my supportive colleagues at Western, especially Christopher Morrow, Jose Fernandez, Marjorie Allison, Mark Mossman, Bill Knox, David Banash, Kyle Mayborn, and Susan Martinelli-Fernandez. I greatly appreciate the steady friendship of colleagues at other universities, especially Carl Ostrowski, David Anthony, and Ed Whitley, a fellow Maryland Terp. I am deeply grateful for the support of my longtime friends both inside and outside the academy, namely Bryan Love, Helen Hull, Beth Hepler, Judi Ketteler, Betsy Van Schaick, Troy and Jill Ruth, Mike Leichliter, Becky Morrow, Ethan Knight, and the late David Leese and Chuck Martorana.

Finally, I would like to thank members of my family for their encouragement and support. I am grateful to my parents, Dan and Pat Helwig, my older brothers Dan and Ted Helwig, and my cousin Tracey Waite for their love and their curiosity about what I do. Most of all, I would like to thank Magdelyn Hammond Helwig, my wife and best friend, without whose love this book would not have been written. I dedicate this book to her.

Cross-Racial Class Protest in Antebellum American Literature

Introduction

In the first half of *The Empire City* George Lippard introduces a diverse cast of characters as they ride a doomed locomotive from Trenton, New Jersey, to New York City. The popular novel was first serialized from 1849 to 1850 in Lippard's *Quaker City Weekly* story paper. In an aside characteristic of the radical labor advocate's allegorical style, he pauses to discourse on the dreadful force symbolized by the steam engine: "The Nineteenth Century! Yes, with the hot coals burning at its iron heart, with the hot steam swelling every iron vein, it thunders along, hurled by its own mad impulses, and woe to the weak—woe to the helpless, who linger on its iron track. Woe to them! It crushes them down with a shriek, and bathing its iron wheels in their blood, goes shouting and triumphant on its terrible progress."[1] The passage captures the sensationalism and Gothic excess—the shrieking, the wheels slicked with blood—that mark the labor advocate's fiction written on behalf of the antebellum working class, who were not only mangled in horrific accidents inside unsafe factories, as reported in the popular press, but also increasingly disempowered and degraded by the transition from apprenticeships to wage labor, all in the name of industrial progress.

Yet beyond its suspicion of American exceptionalism and triumphalism, Lippard's writing is especially noteworthy for sympathizing with the *multiracial* working poor in the North, for attacking chattel slavery in the South, and for imagining working-class solidarity that transcended racial lines. The train's passengers include many of the oxymoronic villains and unlikely heroes of Lippard's class-accented fiction, and he invites the reader to "discover the representatives of all classes of society, confined within [the train cars'] narrow walls, and borne with lightning speed every moment nearer to the Empire City." A banker schemes to exploit the poor, a senator (a thinly veiled portrayal of Daniel Webster) plots to seduce a virtuous woman, a minister escorts the young parishioner he has ruined to an abortionist, and a South Carolina slaveowner, with the help of his hired bloodhound, pursues two fugitive slaves, his own half brother and half sister. Contrasted with these dubious citizens, the once-proud mechanic John Hoffman, now ex-convict Number Ninety-One, surveys the scene: "I sees a bloodhound from Baltimore, and a bloodhound from New York, crouchin' near the stove in car A, or the next one to this, an' talkin' of a runaway slave, an' a reward of five thousan' dollars fur him, dead or alive!" When his younger companion does not comprehend, Hoffman educates him with a cross-racial economic critique against coarse Southern slavecatchers and corrupt Northern police officers: "Poleese offisser. The one hunts black men, tother white men; both live by suckin' human blood, and a jolly life it must be."[2] By expressing equal disdain toward the heartless agents of "wage" and chattel slavery, Hoffman, his lower status indicated by his dialect, serves as Lippard's idealization of the white working-class "radical democrat," who sympathizes with the oppressed regardless of race.

The Empire City, released as a complete novel around the time the Fugitive Slave Law was passed in September 1850, sympathizes with the fugitive slave siblings Randolph and Esther as they escape slavecatchers, justifies antislavery violence against slaveowners, and depicts cross-racial love through the marriage of Randolph, black, and Eleanor, white, that closes the narrative. Other sensational fiction by Lippard, Augustine Duganne, George Thompson, Ned Buntline, and Harry Hazel features black, white, and racially liminal artisan republican heroes who protect the multiracial working classes and fugitive slaves from the schemes of the wealthy class, who are invariably figured as *white.* Significantly, white-authored city-mystery fiction, the quintessential literary genre of the white working class, shares numerous correspondences with the fiction and nonfiction of early African American literature, a relationship that has not yet been explored extensively in the scholarship about antebellum writing. The early black press and particularly the 1850s writing of Frederick Douglass, William Wells Brown, and Frank J. Webb express concern for the working conditions of Northern blacks (and whites), endorse antislavery violence and resistance to the Fugitive Slave Law, and make appeals to poor Southern whites to become allies against an economic system—chattel slavery—that depresses their opportunities. When we read across the varied genres that circulated in antebellum print culture and consider the city-mystery novels, novellas, short stories, slave narratives, autobiographies, speeches, literary reviews, and editorials in relation to one another, we can identify the cross-racial strategies that manifest broadly in white- and black-authored texts. Foremost through the class-accented discourses of sensationalism, artisan republicanism, antislavery protest, and nativism, white and black authors strive to construct cross-racial class solidarity that would help to counter "wage" slavery in the North and chattel slavery in the South. While Lippard and Douglass are the main protagonists in this historical and comparative study of the cross-racial correspondences in antebellum American literature, all of the authors examined contribute to a fuller and nuanced understanding of the potential for class solidarity that boldly transcended racial difference.

Countering Historical Meta-Narratives of Racial Strife

At the beginning of his 1851 romance *The House of the Seven Gables,* Nathaniel Hawthorne draws a distinction between two types of historical accounting: the official record of events crafted by public authorities and over time established as "facts," and the unofficial but more truthful history of events that shadows the public record as they are handed down from generation to generation. Hawthorne refers to this alternative history as "tradition—which sometimes brings down truth that history has let slip, but is oftener the wild babble of the time, such as was formerly spoken at the fireside, and now congeals in newspapers."[3] Notwithstanding its mild anxiety toward penny papers that Hawthorne is known to have read regularly, this passage's focus on counter-history is indicative of my approach in *Cross-Racial Class Protest in Antebellum American Literature* for the way it calls attention to the subjectivity of our national narratives about class and race, and our need to continue reevaluating the meta-narratives that have accrued about the multiracial working classes prior to the Civil War. Like the "twice-told tales" of the marvelous that entertained and inspired Hawthorne as a boy sitting around the hearth, white-authored sensational fiction, which "congeals in newspapers" of the period's burgeoning popular print culture that is central to this study, constitutes a less recognized but no less truthful counter-history to the prevailing meta-narrative of racial strife between the black and white working classes; moreover, how white-authored sensational fiction influenced and, in turn, was influenced by the newspapers and major works that comprise early African American literature, remains an underexplored relationship in American literary criticism. How white working-class and black authors dared to imagine an elusive and ever-fleeting cross-racial solidarity amidst the emergence of industrial capitalism in the urban northeast and the horrors of chattel slavery in the South is the subject of this book.

Pictorial representations of the sturdy white workingman, sleeves rolled up, circulated in broadsides of the 1830s and 1840s labor movement to promote the interests of the producing classes against the emergent forces of industrial capitalism. The erosion of the artisanship system of labor accelerated in the 1820s with the opening of the Erie Canal and the extension of railroads, which created markets to the West, and with an expanded cheap labor force and a generation of consumers provided by staggering rates of immigration. According to historian Sean Wilentz, "this disruption of the American artisan system of labor ranks as one of the outstanding triumphs of nineteenth-century American capitalism."[4] In the key manufacturing (and publishing) centers of Boston, Philadelphia, and New York City, once-proud artisans, journeymen, and apprentices were reduced to anxious and dependent "wage slaves" in factories marked by unsafe working conditions, and the first unions sprang up through which the producing classes politicked for the rights to the fruits of their own labor. Most famously, the enduring image of a flexed, white, muscular arm with a hand grasping a hammer appeared in a General Trades' Union broadside promoting a rally in New York City in 1836. This pictorial symbol of the proud, even defiant, laborer helped to normalize the American laborer as white, and to inaugurate a longstanding meta-narrative that the white working classes were overwhelmingly hostile toward the free blacks and fugitive slaves alongside whom they lived, worked, and played in increasing numbers in the two decades leading up to the Civil War.

Notable race riots in which white mobs targeted the homes and livelihoods of blacks—the 1826 riots in the Beacon Hill section of Boston; the 1834, 1838, 1842, and 1849 riots in Philadelphia; and the 1863 Draft Riots in New York City—have been meticulously detailed by historians, who often point to job competition and economic depressions, such as the deep one that followed the Panic of 1837, as primary instigators for the violence. Historian Bruce Laurie's investigation of the Philadelphia riot of 1834, which saw the deaths of two blacks and the destruction of two churches and thirty black homes, concludes, "Evidence abounds that whites attacked Blacks (and some employers) in order to muscle their way into jobs on the waterfront and elsewhere." Other prominent studies of the white working class, such as Alexander Saxton's *The Rise and Fall of the White Republic,* David Roediger's *The Wages of Whiteness,* and Noel Ignatiev's *How the Irish Became White,* share the broad cultural narrative that working whites agitated for rights and higher wages in the workplace by denying those same protections to blacks. As Roediger sums up, "White workers could, and did, define and accept their class positions by fashioning identities as 'not slaves' and as 'not Blacks.'"[5]

The problem with any meta-narrative is what it obfuscates, and, in this case, focusing almost exclusively on the hostilities between the white and black working class has three major implications for our understanding of race relations and the popular cultural expressions of the antebellum working class. First, it paints the white working class as a politically reactionary and racist monolith, thereby compounding the demonization of the working poor that for centuries has helped to enable economic inequality and the myth of American exceptionalism to thrive. As historian Nancy Isenberg cautions us in her recent book *White Trash,* "Rationalizing economic inequality has been an unconscious part of the national credo; poverty has been naturalized, often seen as something beyond human control. By this measure, poor whites had to be classified as a distinct breed."[6] If we treat the white working class as a reactionary and racist monolith and overlook the inspiring moments of cross-racial sympathy in its cultural expressions of the antebellum period, we help to sustain the self-fulfilling narrative that American race relations were, are, and will be inevitably hostile.

Second, the meta-narrative obscures from view the lived reality of the multiracial working classes and their coordination of class protest during the antebellum years. Starting with James Oliver Horton in the 1990s, African American historians have mined exceptions to the meta-narrative of persistent racial hostilities among the working classes, positing the free black community as successful actors, not merely victims, within American history. In *Free People of Color: Inside the African American Community,* Horton documents how blacks in Boston found education, employment, and a strong sense of community in black churches, and were active in the Underground Railroad. As Horton points out, multiracial living was more common in the nineteenth-century city than we realize: "African Americans, American-born whites, and immigrants shared neighborhoods, and, although there was some residential clustering, the solid urban racial or ethnic ghetto of the twentieth century had not yet developed." These diverse living arrangements not only promoted cross-racial socializing and understanding but also produced instances of shared class protest. Leslie M. Harris documents a coordinated strike for higher wages by New York's black and white waiters in 1853 and the prolific interaction among the multiracial working class, particularly in the Five Points district: "Black and white workers shared class-based neighborhoods throughout the antebellum period. They participated in social and cultural activities after work in interracial bars and dance halls and sometimes intermarried."[7] The lived experience of the antebellum multiracial working class is more complex than we may realize, and careful consideration of the writing of white and black authors reveals their shared pursuit—rooted in the quotidian of daily life—of an elusive cross-racial class solidarity.

Third, the meta-narrative of hostile race relations prevents us from gaining a full appreciation of the shared strategies of class protest in white-authored popular fiction and black-authored literature of the 1840s and 1850s. One of the earliest genres of novel-writing in America, the white-authored city-mystery emerged out of the class-accented penny press begun in the early 1830s as a result of technological innovations in the steam press, cheap postal rates, and high literacy rates among whites. As communications historian Dan Schiller notes, the penny press provided cheap daily newspapers to the growing masses of the reading public as an alternative to the six-cent papers that were largely mouthpieces of political parties and mercantile interests.[8] The crime reporting and serialized fiction published in penny papers and weekly story papers appealed to working-class readers foremost through the ideology of artisan republicanism, which, as a counter-rhetoric to liberal capitalism, championed the rights of the "producing classes,"[9] and, according to Wilentz, called for an informed citizenry that would subordinate private interest for the greater good. In contrast to liberal capitalism's emphasis on the individual's right to compete in the marketplace and then retreat to the private sphere of family life and domesticity, American republicanism preserved the Enlightenment focus on engaged citizenship and advocated "*equality* under a representative, democratic system of laws."[10] The fact that white-authored sensational fiction's artisan republican class protest often included a critique of chattel slavery demonstrates that working-class appeals to equality were not always limited to the narrow politics of white male suffrage.

Cross-Racial Class Protest in Antebellum American Literature analyzes the shared strategies of class protest in popular and canonical texts by white and black authors, from white-authored sensational fiction to black-authored fiction, slave narratives, autobiographies, published speeches, and newspaper editorials. Even though historians note that racial and ethnic divisions among Northern workers helped to prevent an effective labor movement from materializing prior to the Civil War, there is evidence that white and black authors imagined cross-racial class solidarity in their writing. In addition to class-accented sensationalism, all of the authors in this study employ idiosyncratic combinations of artisan republicanism, antislavery protest, and anti-immigrant and anti-Catholic nativism to insist on the rights of the multiracial and native-born producing classes. Throughout their fiction and nonfiction, white and black authors rely on thrilling incidents, Herculean working-class heroes, effete aristocratic villains, and conspiratorial plots to develop a dual critique of Northern "wage slavery" and Southern chattel slavery. Collectively, these shared representational strategies cultivate and nurture cross-racial sympathy among their multiracial working-class readers. That these discursive efforts to build cross-racial class solidarity have crossed genres—novels, novellas, and short stories on the one hand, and slave narratives, autobiographies, speeches, and editorials on the other hand—is reflective of the decentralized "culture of reprinting" in the antebellum period that literary critic Meredith L. McGill argues was characterized "by a strong appeal to republican values."[11] Given the unpredictable and far-ranging dissemination of fictional and nonfictional texts in antebellum print culture, the propensity in literary studies to focus on cultural representations within isolated genres has helped to obscure from view the stunning appeals in white- and black-authored texts to cross-racial sympathy among the multiracial working classes. Through a comparative approach, this volume documents and analyzes a dynamic cross-racial conversation between white-authored sensational fiction and early African American literature that was rooted in sympathy for the multiracial victims of industrial capitalism in the North and for chattel slaves in the South.

Cross-Racial Possibilities in City-Mysteries

In the spirit of literary critic Lori Merish's *Archives of Labor,* which broadly views "antebellum literature as class dialogue," this volume analyzes the cross-pollination of working-class protest in white- and black-authored literature. In her recovery study of popular narratives by, for, and about working-class women, Merish argues that white women working in Northern cotton mills, which received shipments of cotton picked by Southern slaves, inevitably drew on the discourses of race and slavery to represent their labor experience. In a chapter analyzing literary depictions of New England factory women, Merish details how, amidst the influx of Irish immigrant women to the mills, the perceived "compromised whiteness" of the native-born mill women did not lead simply to reductive expressions of racism, but rather "marked new possibilities of interracial class solidarity in mill women's texts." Through meticulous research of the writing of the mill women themselves, Merish finds compelling evidence of white women writers "reaching for a more effective medium of 'sympathy' between white and black female laborers."[12] In contrast to the work of Roediger and Ignatiev, who see racial hostility as being foremost in white workers' reactions to increasing job competition from African Americans, Merish allows for an equally plausible reaction to reduced labor power by white workers: gestures toward solidarity and sympathy that could transcend racial lines. In keeping with Merish's discoveries regarding working-class women's writing, this volume locates and examines the recurrent expressions of cross-racial sympathy in white-authored sensational fiction not as incidental or exceptional, but as purposeful and instrumental in inspiring working-class readers toward labor reform and antislavery agitation.

Other literary critics have explored the malleability of race and the potential for cross-racial identification among the working classes in popular cultural forms of the antebellum period. In *Love and Theft,* literary critic Eric Lott argues that blackface minstrelsy simultaneously encouraged and discouraged an identification between white and black working-class men. Within minstrelsy's propensity to exploit, appropriate, and denigrate blackness to entertain the plebeian classes, Lott insists disenfranchised whites would also identify and sympathize with the representations of blackness they witnessed on stage as minstrel performers poked fun at the professional middle classes and expressed desire for the preindustrial past of unalienated labor.

According to Lott, part of minstrelsy's appeal to white working-class men lay in its construction of black masculinity: "To wear or even enjoy blackface was literally, for a time, to become black, to inherit the cool, virility, humility, abandon or *gaité de coeur* that were the prime components of white ideologies of black manhood." With race increasingly figuring class identity and interracial living becoming a staple of life in the urban northeast, it is little wonder that white authors of sensational fiction would invest in cultural "blackness" and integrate a host of dynamic black characters designed to appeal to white working-class readers. While this study's focus on the cross-racial sympathy proliferating in white-authored sensational fiction is indebted to Lott's insights about the racial ambivalence inscribed in working-class forms, Lott viewed Lippard's city-mysteries as largely implicated in racist discourse. "Lippard certainly shared the racism of much of the antebellum labor movement, and in his novel *The Quaker City* . . . he uses race as a metaphor for corruption."[13] As we will see, Lippard's city-mystery writing often privileges cross-racial sympathy over racist rhetoric, and *The Quaker City* includes one of the popular genre's most progressive representations of blackness.

White-authored city-mysteries, which promised to expose widespread corruption and crime in northeastern cities, drew liberally on the Gothic and sensational modes to mount their class protest. In *Love and Death in the American Novel,* Leslie A. Fiedler asserts that American fiction is "a gothic fiction, nonrealistic and negative, sadist and melodramatic—a literature of darkness and the grotesque in a land of light and affirmation." Fiedler's assessment of our national literature is reflected in city-mysteries' propensity not only to represent urban crime through excessive depictions of horror and terror but also to make those representations function thematically as a counter-narrative to American exceptionalism. Furthermore, Fiedler's characterization of the European Gothic novel that influenced early American literature captures the city-mysteries' primary strategies of class protest: "Most gothicists were not only avant-garde in their literary aspirations, but radical in their politics; they were, that is to say, anti-aristocratic, anti-Catholic, anti-nostalgic." Although city-mystery writers expressed nostalgia for yeoman agrarianism that preceded the emergence of industrial capitalism, they used artisan republicanism and figured Northern capitalists as greedy "merchant princes" and slave-owners as dissipated "aristocrats," and, when it served their dual critique of "wage" and chattel slavery, employed nativist discourse that imagined Catholic conspiracies emanating from Vatican City. White-authored sensational fiction's class critique through the Gothic mode echoes Cathy N. Davidson's observation in *Revolution and the Word* that "the Gothic created its own symbolic space where the hierarchies of a traditional society and the excesses of individualism could both be called into question."[14]

City-mysteries rely frequently on class-accented sensationalism to drive home their labor reform message and antislavery protest. Literary critic Nina Baym defines antebellum sensational fiction aptly as "the highly wrought, the heavily plotted, the ornately rhetorical, the tremendously exciting, and the relentlessly exterior." Baym's definition is reflected in city-mysteries' emphasis on thrilling and remarkable incident, such as popular white authors like Lippard relying more on allegory than verisimilitude to document the grave threats to the republic. For literary critic Michael Denning, sensationalism merges with artisan republicanism in city-mysteries to express class conflict. Denning's *Mechanic Accents: Dime Novels and Working-Class Culture in America* remains the foundational text in the study of city-mystery fiction, as he documents its broad appeal to the masses through inheritance plots, secret societies of workers, and the figure of the Mechanic Hero. For Denning, city-mystery writers, whom he refers to anachronistically as "dime novelists," "shared the vocabulary and rhetoric of an artisan republicanism; in an ideological universe that continued to be shaped by battles over the meaning of republicanism and the legacy of the revolution, the urban craftworkers had given a peculiar mechanic accent to the discourses, rituals and iconography of the Republic."[15] The black and white cast of working-class protagonists that proliferate in city-mystery fiction, I argue, complicates historian David Roediger's claim that the white working class invested deeply in the psychological "wages of whiteness" and routinely denigrated people of color. In fact, as we will see, white-authored sensational fiction harnessed the rhetorical strategies and tropes from slave narratives, encouraged cross-racial identification among Northern workers, and elicited sympathy for all oppressed peoples in the North and the South.

In another influential study of city-mystery fiction, David S. Reynolds in *Beneath the American Renaissance* documents the genre's "radical democratic" energies: "the central conflict is between various oxymoronic oppressors (the reverend rake, the Christian slaveholder, the churchgoing capitalist, and so forth) and some version of the likable pariah, who embodies the embittered vindictiveness of lower-class or disenfranchised groups."[16] These oxymoronic characters appear in the scene from Lippard's *The Empire City* featured at the opening of this book: the banker is not merely providing a service but scheming to steal people's money, and the once-proud mechanic-turned-criminal is more honest and likable as he expresses contempt for slavecatchers and corrupt officers of the law. Although Reynolds finds the "radical democratic" energies compromised more often than not by city-mysteries' tendency to indulge in sensationalism and voyeurism for their own sake and is more interested in studying popular novels as fodder for the great imaginative works of canonical writers like Herman Melville, Nathaniel Hawthorne, and Walt Whitman, Reynolds's groundbreaking scholarship about the life and writing of George Lippard helped to establish the importance of city-mystery fiction to American literary history. Reynolds also identifies the latent potential for cross-racial sympathy in the role reversals involving black characters in Lippard's *The Quaker City*, yet helps to establish the longstanding scholarly view that "Lippard was more concerned with the white slavery in northern factories than with black slavery on southern plantations."[17] While Lippard as a labor advocate naturally devoted more attention to labor reform in the North, I will show that his insistence on combining the fights to end "wage" and chattel slavery, which he expressed in passionate editorials in his weekly story paper, is rearticulated in his sensational fiction and is echoed by Frederick Douglass in the early 1850s.

Sensationalism, as a primary class-accented discourse that traversed city-mystery fiction and early African American literature, produces moments of cross-racial sympathy in ways that are similar to and distinct from sentimental fiction, another prolific mode of popular antebellum writing that is often marginalized by modernist aesthetics. Literary critic Jane Tompkins, whose *Sensational Designs* helped to recuperate popular fiction from "twentieth-century critics [who] have taught generations of students to equate popularity with debasement" and "emotionality with ineffectiveness," argues that popular novels, like the sentimental *Uncle Tom's Cabin,* are worthy of study precisely because of their ability to speak to a mass readership and their desire to impact the world. In conventional understandings of the sentimental novel, which literary critic Julia A. Stern explains is marked by "an affective atmosphere and moral ideology," it appeals to readers' emotions, such as sympathy, through such tropes as motherhood and domesticity. Literary critic Naomi Greyser explains that sentimentalism's appeal to sympathy "comes through where rhetors concern themselves with emotionally *reaching* audiences and enlisting sympathetic reception."[18] The sentimental novel's effort to impact readers and effect social change through sympathy for others is shared by sensational city-mysteries, but in the latter's effort to evoke cross-racial sympathy in readers, the male-authored Gothic city-mysteries of this study appeal to the material suffering of the poor while at the same time distrusting the middle-class platitudes traditionally associated with sentimentalism.

David S. Reynolds notes that Lippard "relentlessly parodies the sentimental-domestic ethos" in ironizing the middle-class home as an ineffective refuge from a public sphere replete with corrupt commerce and politics. Shelley Streeby shows that "Lippard depicts the world of sentimentality as feminized, emasculating, and bourgeois, while he describes his own sensational style . . . as a more masculine and realistic form of representation."[19] Although the strategies of cross-racial protest in Lippard's and others' city-mysteries rely on building sympathy for the oppressed, their sensational writing focuses on the materiality of human experience and thereby encourages readers to identify across racial lines in ways that are more indicative of empathy than sympathy. Whether it is the Herculean body of a black laborer ripped open by a bullet in Augustine Duganne's *The Knights of the Seal* or the tortured and mangled bodies of captured runaway slaves in William Wells Brown's *Clotel,* the sensational and graphic depictions of bodily destruction were intended to elicit both horror and a less emotional understanding in white working-class readers of physical suffering that transcended racial lines. Moreover, as part of their cross-racial class protest, city-mystery writers privileged the succoring of the poor's physical needs over their spiritual needs rather than the reverse, a charge they often leveled against evangelicals and missionaries. Like Rebecca Harding Davis would in her 1861 short story about working-class Welsh immigrants, "Life in the Iron-Mills," Lippard introduces Quaker characters who balance their attention to the material and the spiritual. In his 1848 *Memoirs of a Preacher: or, the Mysteries of the Pulpit,* Lippard pays homage to Quaker abolitionist Lucretia Mott, and in his 1854 serial fiction *Eleanor; or, Slave Catching in the Quaker City,* he uses a Quaker abolitionist, Elijah Carwin, as his mouthpiece for critiquing the Fugitive Slave Law.

While literary critics have identified the working-class accents of city-mysteries, they have not explored fully how those accents have been used in the service of appealing to the black working class and protesting the Fugitive Slave Law and chattel slavery. For example, black, white, and racially liminal artisan heroes, emasculated and dehumanized in the industrial marketplace, struggle against the machinations of the "upper ten," who are in league with Southern slaveowners, slavecatchers, and newly arrived immigrants. The popular genre's racially ambivalent critique of "wage" slavery in the North and its economic critique of chattel slavery in the South converge to encourage cross-racial class solidarity and cross-racial sympathy with the oppressed. Moreover, city-mystery fiction shares a wealth of correspondences with early African American literature: the white-authored genre draws on tropes from slave narratives, endorses justified anti-slavery violence, appeals to poor whites to join the cause to end chattel slavery, and privileges the concerns of native-born whites and blacks at the expense of newly arrived European immigrants and Catholics. Although the appeals of city-mysteries did not produce significant labor reform in the antebellum years or avert the Civil War, they share with early African American literature a profound commitment to social justice and a hope to form a more perfect Union.

Working-Class Accents of Early African American Literature

Just as white-authored city-mysteries borrow tropes and polemical strategies from African American literature, African American writers employ sensationalism, artisan republicanism, and nativism to mount a dual critique of chattel slavery in the South and labor practices in the North. They employ the expressed Gothic horrors of chattel slavery, the suspenseful experiences of fugitive slaves, and the thrilling and heroic stand of charismatic black characters against violent race prejudice in the North; the artisan republican critique of dissipated slaveowners who enjoy the fruits of others' labor and live amidst imported luxuries; and the native-born appeals to the rights of free blacks to make a home in America and reject colonization schemes—all of which correspond with the dual critique of "wage" and chattel slavery in sensational fiction. Moreover, in a mutual effort to build cross-racial sympathy, the writing of Frederick Douglass and William Wells Brown represents poor whites as potential allies in the fight to end chattel slavery and as being capable of overcoming their race prejudice; and it condemns the middle-class propensity to demonize the rural white poor as "white trash." My analysis of the working-class tropes and strategies in black-authored texts provides a corrective to scholarship that privileges the middle-class values of racial uplift in the study of early African American literature.

While artisan republicanism constitutes a shared mode of class protest, African American writers' celebration of "free labor" ideology could undermine cross-racial class solidarity. Historians Eric Foner and Jonathan Glickstein have explained that "free labor" appeals, articulated frequently in the 1850s by abolitionists, can be understood fundamentally as pro-capitalist, which would conflict with the labor concerns of white city-mystery writers and potentially alienate their working-class readers.[20] In *Free Soil, Free Labor, and Free Men,* Foner argues that antebellum appeals to free labor celebrated the equal opportunity to compete in the marketplace, the ability to rise in status from wage worker to small business owner, and the self-reliance of the hard-working individual. According to Foner, free labor ideology posited the North as "a dynamic, expanding capitalist society, whose achievements and destiny were almost wholly the result of the dignity and opportunities which is afforded the average laboring man."[21] Artisan republicanism, which emphasized the concerns of ordinary laborers in the workplace and pride in craftsmanship, is not antithetical to free labor's appeals to the common man. As this volume will show, it is wrong to assume that most labor advocates were indifferent or hostile to the plight of chattel slaves. "Given the large number of artisans who signed abolitionist petitions, we should not let the evangelicalism of the abolitionist leaders obscure that portion of the anti-slavery constituency whose roots lay in Enlightenment rationalism and republican notions of equality and liberty, rather than in Christian benevolence."[22] A number of white labor advocates, including city-mystery writers George Lippard and Augustine Duganne, protested chattel slavery as part of a broad critique of inequality in the republic.

African American writers like Frederick Douglass, William Wells Brown, and Frank J. Webb made free labor arguments against chattel slavery, pointing out, for instance, that black slaves and the white poor alike stagnated under a hierarchical slave economy, but that does not mean they blindly embraced the perception of leading white abolitionists like William Lloyd Garrison that labor and capital were not at odds in the North. Douglass's fiction and nonfiction of the 1850s in particular devoted attention to the realities of Northern race prejudice and the economic plight of the multiracial working classes. In Douglass's writing, artisan republicanism and free labor converge in shared respect for the virtue of honest labor and class-accented resistance to chattel slavery. If African American historian George M. Fredrickson is right that "for many abolitionists human perfectibility meant little more than the attainment of conventional middle-class attributes,"[23]

Douglass's writing offers an important challenge to middle-class ideologies that ignored the working classes.

Chapter Outline: Cross-Racial Correspondences

Chapter one, "Black and White Artisan Heroes," analyzes the trope of the racially diverse and hyper-masculine honest laborer appearing in white- and black-authored literature of the 1840s and 1850s. I show that popular white authors like Lippard, Duganne, and Thompson rely on white, black, and racially ambiguous working-class heroes to develop their artisan republican critique of the wealthy classes, who are figured typically as duplicitous, effete, and greedy, and implicated in both capitalism and chattel slavery. I then turn to tracing the correspondences with Frederick Douglass's writing, particularly *The Heroic Slave,* which echoes white-authored popular fiction in its artisan republicanism, its stalwart black hero, and its appeal to cross-racial understanding among the multiracial working classes. In all of these white-authored and black-authored texts, the honest laborer, as a vehicle of artisan republicanism, becomes an Everyman with whom white and black readers can identify.

Chapter two, "The Class Accents of Antislavery Reform," examines how the passage of the Fugitive Slave Law of 1850 accelerated representations of cross-racial alliances in white- and black-authored fiction. I show that the writing of Lippard and Duganne, who spoke at antislavery meetings in Philadelphia, shares Douglass's growing conviction that the efforts to end "wage slavery" in the North and chattel slavery in the South are not mutually exclusive. Additionally, I trace how Douglass's defense of antislavery violence and appeals to cross-racial class solidarity in the early 1850s corresponds with Lippard's novels *The Empire City* and *New York,* which feature black and white vigilantes resisting slavecatchers and meeting violence with violence. The chapter then provides the first comparative analysis of how William Wells Brown's novel *Clotel* and Lippard's novel *New York* employ the Thomas Jefferson and Sally Hemings affair to indict socioeconomic inequality and to imagine cross-racial love and friendship as an alternative to racial enmity. The chapter concludes with an analysis of Lippard's last serialized work of fiction, *Eleanor; or, Slave Catching in the Quaker City*. Written while Lippard lay on his deathbed suffering the symptoms of tuberculosis, *Eleanor* brings together all of the white-authored and black-authored strategies of class and racial protest to mount a powerful critique against the Fugitive Slave Law.

Chapter three, "The Cross-Racial Appeal of Nativism," analyzes the correspondences between African American literature's and city-mysteries' measured employment of anti-immigrant and anti-Catholic nativism. While the early black press, William Wells Brown's *Clotel,* and Frank J. Webb's *The Garies and Their Friends* harness anti-immigrant nativist rhetoric and mount populist appeals to the native-born status of African Americans in order to counter colonization efforts endorsed in abolitionist novels like Harriet Beecher Stowe's *Uncle Tom's Cabin* and Sarah Josepha Hale's *Liberia,* sensational white writers like Augustine Duganne and Ned Buntline promote the interests of the native-born working classes by denigrating newly arrived immigrants as villains or henchmen, at times unwittingly splintering class solidarity and reinforcing middle-class values. Next, as Protestant ministers in the 1850s "condemned 'rum, Romanism, and slavery' as the three evils cursing the nation," Lippard's *New York* and Duganne's *The Tenant-House* employ anti-Catholic nativism and conspiracy to develop their attacks on "wage slavery" and chattel slavery, a strategy that has faint but discernible correspondences with the early black press, including Douglass's *My Bondage and My Freedom* and *Frederick Douglass' Paper.*[24]

Chapter four, "Cross-Racial Sensationalism in the Black and Popular Presses," uses a case study method to reveal class-accented correspondences between Frederick Douglass's newspapers and a weekly story paper in Boston, the *Star Spangled Banner.* I begin by tracing the African American community's growing acceptance of reading popular novels in editorials published in *Freedom's Journal,* the *Weekly Advocate* and the *Colored American,* and the *North Star.* I then turn to analyzing their positive reviews of white-authored sensational novels, including *Frederick Douglass' Paper*'s positive consideration of Emerson Bennett's urban novel *Ellen Norbury,* and its extensive treatment of Mary Hayden Green Pike's abolitionist novel *Ida May.* I show that the favorable treatment of urban sensationalism coincides with Douglass's efforts to establish a multiracial industrial college and thereby improve the lived conditions of Northern blacks. The *Star Spangled Banner,* meanwhile, exemplifies the diversity of racial representations in the cheap press directed at working-class readers. Sympathetic representations of working-class blacks in the *Star Spangled Banner*'s serialized sensational fiction and short sketches ran alongside racist and demeaning caricatures of blacks, creating a bewildering juxtaposition of messages that include gestures toward cross-racial sympathy.

CHAPTER ONE

Black and White Artisan Heroes

To appeal to their primarily—but not exclusively—white working-class readers, prolific white authors of sensational fiction George Lippard and George Thompson relied on multiracial protagonists of the producing classes and built an artisan republican critique of "wage slavery" and economic inequality. Although demographic evidence of precisely who read antebellum city-mysteries is scant, African American novelist William Wells Brown lamented in 1863 that the sensational penny paper the *New York Herald* "gets a larger support from the colored people than *Douglass' Monthly, The Anglo-African,* and *The Pacific Appeal* put together."[1] Through "twice-told tales" of economic exploitation, these popular authors regularly featured parallel plot lines of a working-class black man and a working-class white man struggling against the wealthy classes figured as white. Hyper-masculine black and white mechanic heroes resist the machinations of perverse, effete, and dissipated white aristocrats, members of the "upper ten," who are implicated in Northern "wage slavery" and Southern chattel slavery. These formal elements, largely overlooked in the scholarship about city-mysteries until very recently, produced striking moments of cross-racial sympathy among the black and white working classes.

Cross-racial correspondence between white- and black-authored literature is particularly evident in city-mystery writers' reliance on the slave narrative to figure the plight of their white and black artisan heroes. The slave narrative, a form that enjoyed increased popularity when Frederick Douglass's narrative appeared in 1845, coincided with the practice of white authors of sensational fiction figuring their class concerns through the dehumanizing effects of chattel slavery. Appearing in May 1845, Douglass's narrative sold 13,000 copies in five editions in the first year alone and 30,000 copies by 1850, impressive numbers for the period.[2] Lacking basic knowledge of their parentage, exploited by cutthroat businessmen, monitored by prison officials depicted as "overseers," and resisting their "wage enslavement" through brains and brawn, city-mysteries' racially diverse artisans echo Douglass's heroic flight from slavery and path toward manhood. Moreover, like Douglass's self-representation as a self-educated and resourceful leader among men, the representations of black male characters that populated city-mysteries of the 1840s and early 1850s generally eschewed or at least complicated the romantic racialism that plagued even the most well-intentioned abolitionist fiction of the period; they appeared far more often as class-accented symbols of sturdy masculinity than as the obsequious, pious, and sentimental figures in novels like *Uncle Tom's Cabin*. The fact that heroic free blacks and sympathetic fugitive slaves appeared frequently in city-mystery fiction constitutes a significant yet underexplored correspondence with early African American writing.

As class became increasingly articulated through race in popular forms like blackface minstrelsy, city-mystery writers leaned heavily on what cultural critic W. T. Lhamon Jr. calls the "charisma" of blackness to appeal to their white working-class readers. In his analysis of the racial ambivalences of blackface minstrelsy of the 1830s and 1840s, Lhamon Jr. argues that white working-class audiences of blackface "were choosing to see themselves in terms of blackness and to align themselves with ciphers of rootlessness and transgression" against the stolid middle classes. Consistent with critical reconsiderations of blackface minstrelsy that highlight its potential for engendering cross-racial sympathy within white working-class audiences, this chapter analyzes how city-mysteries, as an emergent popular literary form of the period, mock the upper classes through racially ambivalent images inscribed with what Eric Lott calls "the tones of racial sympathy."[3] In other words, although city-mysteries' representations of blackness could include the demeaning caricature associated with minstrelsy, my analysis of the white-authored popular genre extends beyond a reductive reading that sees only racism to reveal instances of cross-racial identification and sympathy. Lippard's and Thompson's celebration of the dignity and swagger of "Herculean" working-class masculinity embodied in both black and white characters corresponds with the trope of the proud and defiant laborer deserving of his wages that is evident in much of Frederick Douglass's writing, including his 1845 slave narrative, the 1853 novella *The Heroic Slave*, and his 1855 autobiography *My Bondage and My Freedom*.

Of course, white authors depicting the multiracial working classes as "wage slaves" draws a false and disingenuous comparison between capitalist exploitation in the North and chattel slavery in the South, something white and black abolitionists were quick to point out. In "Not to be Trusted," an 1848 editorial in the *Liberator,* William Lloyd Garrison bristles, "We are sick of the wretched clamor about 'Wages Slavery,' as comparable with 'Chattel Slavery' . . . To represent the condition of the laboring classes of the North as equally to be deplored with that of the Southern slaves, and the first to be improved, is to insult the human understanding, and to deal largely in falsehood." In 1853, William Wells Brown pauses in his novel *Clotel* to lament, "Some American writers have tried to make the world believe that the condition of the laboring classes of England is as bad as the slaves of the United States."[4] Therefore, it is essential to keep in mind the limits of city-mystery fiction's strategies of class protest to build cross-racial sympathy and mount antislavery protest, even as we trace the varied and rich cross-racial correspondences that circulate among white-authored sensational fiction and black-authored literature.

Devil-Bug, a Black Hero for the White Working Class

Arguably, no popular author of antebellum sensational fiction expressed cross-racial economic critique more overtly than labor advocate George Lippard. During his short life from 1822 to 1854 in Philadelphia and its environs, Lippard penned the best-selling novel *The Quaker City; or,*

The Monks of Monk-Hall in 1845, which was not outsold in America until the publication of *Uncle Tom's Cabin* in 1852; he printed his own weekly story paper infused with labor and, at times, antislavery politics, the *Quaker City Weekly,* from 1848 to 1850; he founded the semi-secret society the Brotherhood of the Union, which he declared "proscribes no race, no sect,"[5] to promote the interests of multiracial mechanics and their families;[6] and he published at least twenty class-inflected novels that view the American past and present as a series of wars between republican and anti-republican forces. Lippard was most beloved for his romantic chronicling of the battles of the American Revolutionary War, and less known for his novels set during the Mexican War. He was most inspired to write about what he saw as the Class War between labor and capital in the industrial North. Lippard, who, like Edgar Allan Poe, struggled with poverty for most of his adult life, writes succinctly in his story paper, "The world is divided into two great nations, the Rich and the Poor. All other distinctions of class or race are idle and inexpressive."[7] But unlike Poe, whose writing eschewed the didactic in favor of the aesthetic, Lippard came to the militant view that literature had the responsibility to expose corruption and improve society, declaring, "Our Idea of a National Literature, is simply: that a literature which does not work practically, for the advancement of social reform, or which is too dignified or too good to picture the wrongs of the great mass of humanity, is just good for nothing at all."[8] Lippard succumbed to tuberculosis and followed his wife and two children to the grave in 1854, but not before completing the serialized *Eleanor,* his most ardent antislavery novel. Lippard's sensational fiction stands out not only for its popularity but also for its daring insistence on linking the fights to end "wage" and chattel slavery.

Published as a complete novel in 1845, just two years after Eugène Sue's novel of social exposé, *The Mysteries of Paris,* completed its serialization, Lippard's *The Quaker City* utilizes the racially ambivalent artisan republican rhetoric of "wage slavery" and employs charismatic black characters to make a powerful cross-racial economic critique of the upper classes. Through a series of forgery and inheritance plots, Lippard's novel, which sold 60,000 copies in its first year, critiques the capitalist greed of Northern bank directors and merchants who are implicated in Southern chattel slavery, rails against corrupt politicians who fail to uphold the republican principles of the founding fathers, and exposes the self-serving paternalism of the professional middle class and hypocritical moral reformers. Through the character of the grotesque Devil-Bug, the dwarfish, one-eyed, black doorkeeper of Monk-Hall who witnesses and orchestrates the nocturnal debauchery of Philadelphia's elite (the so-called Monks), *The Quaker City* dramatically ushers in urban sensationalism's reliance on sympathetic African American characters for its class protest. If labor historian Bruce Laurie is right that there were fewer labor strikes in the 1840s than the 1830s because laborers were "fragmented and disorganized," it is all the more significant that popular white writers like Lippard and Thompson worked to imagine cross-racial class solidarity amidst rising racial and ethnic division.[9]

Despite Lippard's popularity among the masses, critics have been reluctant to view *The Quaker City* as mounting an effective class critique of the wealthy classes. Michael Denning notes the dearth of (white) working-class characters, and argues that the novel's seduction plot is compromised by the narrator's voyeurism and by featuring a middle-class young woman: "For the most part, Lippard's seduction tales do *not* involve poor girls." David S. Reynolds acknowledges *The Quaker City*'s "role reversal and black humor" that challenge middle-class norms, and yet laments that the novel's sensationalism "becomes an end in itself."[10] Despite Lippard's claim in his preface to the 1849 edition that he "determined to write a book which should describe all the phases of a corrupt social system, as manifested in the city of Philadelphia," Denning's criticism of the city-mystery genre would seem on the surface to apply to *The Quaker City*: "The narrative elements [Karl] Marx identified in Sue—the depiction of workers as passive victims, a world made up of the elite and the lumpen, and the quasi-aristocratic supermen heroes—prevent the emergence of an active working-class protagonist, a mechanic hero."[11] And yet, I argue, critics have not been looking in the right place to properly assess the novel's working-class expression. Although *The Quaker City* lacks the well-developed white mechanic heroes that we find in much of Lippard's subsequent writing, the most memorable characters—Devil-Bug and his hyper-masculine underlings, Glow-Worm and Musquito—are class-accented black characters that complicate prevailing racial stereotypes through their combination of "brains and brawn" and become dynamic vehicles of class protest.

The racially marked tenant of Monk-Hall and arguably the novel's hero, Devil-Bug is ubiquitous in the text as he plays host to the corrupt "Monks," and he figures in the resolution of nearly every subplot. Although Reynolds links "likable criminal" Devil-Bug with the radical democratic energies running through antebellum popular culture, critics have written little about the character's blackness and use of the class-inflected rhetorical devices of blackface minstrelsy. Historian Noel Ignatiev claims, "Lippard shared the common white labor-radical stance of pretending sympathy for the black slave while at the same time stressing the greater wrong done the white wage worker." Literary critic Dana D. Nelson, arguing that the novel dramatizes the dangers of race-mixing and social climbing, reads Devil-Bug's "tawny cheeks" and "swarthy visage" as stoking middle-class anxieties about "the irregular and hybrid results of a forfeited pure group ideal."[12] Both of these claims are complicated by the mounting evidence that Lippard wrote Devil-Bug as a black character who embodies the exploitation of the white and the black wage worker, and one who delivers the novel's class protest to working-class readers. In other words, I contend that Devil-Bug's blackness is what enables the novel's imagined fraternity of white—*and black*—working men, predicated on their shared economic grievances. My June 2010 discovery in the archives of the Historical Society of Pennsylvania of the surviving playbill for the novel's dramatic adaptation, which was never performed in Philadelphia in 1844 due to the threat of violence, lists Devil-Bug as African American. Among the characters listed for the second act, the playbill reads: "Devil Bug, the Door-keeper of Monk Hall, a Negro, deeply dyed in crime," to be played by Mr. Jordan.[13] Combined with Lippard's suggestive characterization within the pages of the novel of Devil-Bug as black, the playbill confirms that Lippard conceived of Devil-Bug as an African American, a fact that is essential for appreciating the novel's cross-racial class protest. Upon Devil-Bug's "stout and muscular frame, with the heavy body, knotted into uncouth knobs at the shoulders," rests the class critique of the best-selling novel *The Quaker City.*[14]

In his descriptions of Devil-Bug, formally named Abijah K. Jones, Lippard suggests strongly that his novel's hero is black. As for the doorkeeper's family background, the reader learns the little that Devil-Bug knows: "Born in a brothel, the offspring of foulest sin and pollution, he had grown from very childhood, in full and continual sight of scenes of vice, wretchedness and squalor. From his very birth, he had breathed an atmosphere of infamy . . . No mother had ever spoken words of kindness to him; no father had ever held him in his arms. He had come into the world without a name."[15] Based on Lippard's depictions of race-mixing in urban brothels and his occasional indulgence in temperance rhetoric's sensational treatment of amalgamation, Lippard leaves open the possibility of Devil-Bug's black heritage by linking his childhood to brothels. Devil-Bug's lack of basic knowledge about his heritage also calls up the trope of broken families in slave narratives. Frederick Douglass's slave narrative, published the same year as *The Quaker City,* famously opens with his lack of "accurate knowledge of [his] age" as well as the identity of his father, and he describes how little he knows about his mother, whom he saw not "more than four or five times in [his] life."[16] In this context, Devil-Bug's ability in the novel to self-fashion a strong sense of identity, even a misanthropic one that delights in revenge and takes the devil for its name, stands as a heroic act that resonates with Douglass's path to manhood.

Devil-Bug's physical attributes resonate with his two black henchmen, Glow-Worm and Musquito, who share the musculature and clothing of the other black and white working-class heroes of Lippard's writing: "From either side of the fire-place, as [Devil-Bug] spoke, emerged a tall Herculean negro, with a form of strength and sinews of iron . . . Their attire was plain and simple. Each negro was dressed in coarse corduroy trowsers, and a flaring red flannel shirt."[17] Embodying the raw strength of the honest laborer illustrated in the General Trades' Union's broadside of 1836, Glow-Worm and Musquito are fiercely loyal to Devil-Bug and easily subdue rakish criminals when called on. Their red flannel shirts, the signature garb of Bowery B'hoys who comprised lower-class fire companies and, according to historian Sean Wilentz, evinced working-class consciousness,[18] are worn by a litany of black and white working-class characters across the city-mystery genre, subtly building cross-racial solidarity. Although Devil-Bug's outfit is not detailed in the novel, a wood engraving by popular illustrator F. O. C. Darley for the 1845 edition of the novel shows Devil-Bug—identifiable because he has the use of only one eye—dressed similarly to his henchmen and with similarly shaded skin (see figure 1). The shading and plain clothes in Darley's illustration link Devil-Bug to his black henchmen, who are depicted in sharp contrast to the richly clad white characters at the center of the novel's seduction plot.

Indicative of city-mysteries' broad strategy of representing the working classes as multiracial, Lippard's fellow Philadelphia city-mystery writer and labor advocate Augustine Duganne incorporates the senseless killing of a "Herculean" black laborer into *The Knights of the Seal; or, The Mysteries of the Three Cities,* an 1845 novel that the abolitionist newspaper the *National Era* would review in 1850. Underscoring the convergence of city-mystery writing and antislavery sentiment, Duganne regularly published in 1847 labor poems written expressly for the *National Era* with titles such as "Working Men" and "The Song of Toil." Probably on account of this established relationship with the newspaper, the *National Era* calls *The Knights of the Seal* "a clever production" but questions Duganne's "moral sense" as a writer "who minutely investigates and boldly unveils the mysteries of vice and crime."[19] It is surprising the review by a leading abolitionist newspaper was not more favorable to *The Knights of the Seal,* which features the fugitive slave-girl Florine, who is pursued by lascivious politicians and judges figured as "bloodhounds," and includes the murder of a virtuous black artisan who exudes the pride and strength of the labor movement.

Figure 1. "Frontispiece wood engraving," F. O. C. Darley, delineator, from George Lippard's 1845 edition of *The Quaker City; or, The Monks of Monk-Hall: A Romance of Philadelphia Life, Mystery, and Crime,* published in Philadelphia by T. B. Peterson and Brothers. Courtesy of the American Antiquarian Society.

In an effort to terrorize a desperate and penniless expelled college student named Paul Gaskill to do his bidding, the villain, Rivingsby, forces the young man to witness the murder:

> Then, sinking his eyes to the point which occupied the attention of his companion, Gaskill beheld, standing at the junction of two streets that slanted to the water's edge—with his broad breast, from which the flannel shirt had blown back, exposed naked to the sun—a tall, athletic negro. He seemed to have just emerged from his labor in one of the innumerable alleys that penetrated the rows of houses, and stood there—his arms folded on his waist, his bosom bare, cooling himself in the fresh breeze that blew from the water—a perfect type of the Herculean negro laborer . . . 'A fine mark,' laughed Rivingsby, as he pulled the trigger of the pistol, while at the very moment the bells of the city pealed out the hour of one. The negro staggered a moment—threw his arms wildly upward—and fell dead to the earth.

Although the black laborer serves a minor plot point, Duganne's lingering description of the powerful physique encourages his white and black working-class readers to identify and sympathize with the laborer, who is violently struck down by a depraved white criminal in broad daylight. The fact that Gaskill's whiteness is compromised as he is exploited repeatedly by various wealthy criminals—his features having become "bronzed and hardened" at sea—creates a subtle link to the murdered black laborer. Invoking the rhetoric of slavery, Gaskill vows to follow a virtuous path: "I swear—to give up my future to repentance; to thwart the schemes of those of whom I have been the *slave,* and to rescue, even if it be by my own sacrifice, the victims of that arch-fiend, Bellingham."[20] While less overt and developed than the cross-racial identification found throughout *The Quaker City,* Duganne's linking of violence against the "Herculean" free black laborer and the white "slave" Gaskill gestures toward sympathy for the multiracial working classes. That Lippard dedicated the first edition of *The Quaker City* to Duganne is indicative of their shared socioeconomic concerns.

Devil-Bug is a complex mix of "brawn" and "brains," by which Lippard challenges the elitist division of physical and mental labor that Stephen Rice has shown was then emerging among the professional middle class "in terms that were difficult to resist and favorable to their class interests."[21] In terms of "brawn," the dwarfish Devil-Bug prefigures Edgar Allan Poe's racially ambiguous and class-accented Hop-Frog, whose compact strength is located in the upper body: "With [Devil-Bug's] long arms and bony fists, the slim legs and massive feet, all gave you the idea, of a Sampson, stunted in his growth; a giant whom nature had dwarfed from the regular proportion of manly beauty, down into an uncouth image of hideous strength."[22] "Hop-Frog," Poe's last story published during his lifetime, in 1849, and one of his most allegorical tales, features the dwarfish title character who, kidnapped "from some barbarous region" and forced to perform as a jester for a cruel monarch, exacts murderous revenge through an ingenious plot that results in the king and his ministers being burned alive. In describing the enslaved jester, Poe writes, "Although Hop-Frog, through the distortion of his legs, could move only with great pain and difficulty along a road or floor, the prodigious muscular power which nature seemed to have bestowed upon his arms, by way of compensation for deficiency in the lower limbs, enabled him to perform many feats of wonderful dexterity."[23] Poe's description of Hop-Frog echoes Lippard's description of the "distorted" Devil-Bug, who "was a strange thickset specimen of flesh and blood, with a short body, marked by immensely broad shoulders, long arms and thin distorted legs."[24] Devil-Bug shares not only the deformity and unusual upper-body strength of Hop-Frog, but also the spirit of class critique against the anti-republican upper classes.

In a recent analysis of Poe's tale, literary critic Paul Gilmore considers the suggestive similarities between Hop-Frog and the diminutive American actor Harvey Leach, who performed as a baboon at P. T. Barnum's American Museum in the 1840s. For Gilmore, "the figure of the freakish other offered Poe a vehicle both for commercial success and for allegorical revenge against the Bostonians . . . to satirize what Poe saw as the hubris and hypocrisy of a Northern, anti-slavery, literary elite."[25] I contend that Lippard's Devil-Bug is another likely source for Hop-Frog, as both class-accented characters are racially marked and resist the aristocratic elite. One can hear in the jest Hop-Frog makes as he prepares to light the king and his seven ministers on fire—that he "shall soon find out who they are"[26]—Devil-Bug's gleeful catch-phrase as he concocts plans of revenge, "I wonders how that 'ill work!"[27] Poe's decision to publish "Hop-Frog" in the *Star Spangled Banner,* a weekly story paper that, as I show in chapter four, included tales featuring cross-racial class protest, suggests that Poe may very well have had Lippard's charismatic spokesman for the multiracial working classes in mind.

Since the 1980s, critics of antebellum culture have identified and analyzed the potential for cross-racial sympathy inscribed within the racist representations of blackface minstrelsy. A popular form that emerged in the 1830s among the Northern working classes, blackface preserved its class accents into the early 1850s, at which point, W. T. Lhamon Jr. argues, "entrepreneurial control absorbed and dampened the implicit critique youths in blackface were making of upright mercantile style." Sean Wilentz discusses blackface's subversive appeal to white workers: "In the blackface burlesque, the minstrels turned from racist humor to mocking the arrogance, imitativeness, and dimwittedness of the upper classes in 'permissible' ways, as in a kind of carnival." Alexander Saxton contends that as antislavery sentiment spread in the North and the West, antislavery expressions entered blackface and challenged the myth of the benign plantation. But it is Eric Lott who argues most persuasively that as the racial images on the minstrel stage became a "kind of metonym for class . . . one occasionally finds in this imagery the tones of racial sympathy."[28] In *The Quaker City,* Lippard builds cross-racial solidarity through black Devil-Bug, whose mockery and burlesque of the professional middle class would have appealed to working-class readers familiar with these tropes from blackface minstrelsy.

In what amounts to a dark comedy of class vengeance, Devil-Bug is most sardonic when he is torturing hypocritical members of the middle class. As the misanthropic doorkeeper of Monk-Hall, who witnesses the debauchery of "lawyers from the court, doctors from the school, and judges from the bench"—the same people who ostracize him in public—Devil-Bug is a righteous punisher in the Class War. The novel's primary seduction plot follows the efforts of Byrnewood Arlington—a junior partner of an importing house that is implicated in chattel slavery through "a large purchase in cotton from a rich planter"—to avenge his sister Mary's seduction and sham marriage to rakish aristocrat Gus Lorrimer in Monk-Hall. To assist Lorrimer, Devil-Bug imprisons Byrnewood in the tower room, and through Devil-Bug's mockery of middle-class domesticity, the wronged brother recognizes his own hypocrisy. Delivering wine laced with opium and a plate of chicken to Byrnewood, along with an iron furnace with which to suffocate him, Devil-Bug performs the part of an obsequious servant and speaks ironically in the third person: "Yer humble servant thought you might be hungry, so he sent you suffin' to eat. Thought you might be cold; so he brung you some coals to warm yesself."

Left alone, Byrnewood muses on his own foibles. "And yet I, I, wronged an innocent girl, because she was my father's servant. Great God! Can she, have a brother to feel for her ruin?"

Devil-Bug watches from an aperture in the faux bookcase as Byrnewood staggers violently from the fumes filling up the sealed room, and he sings a lullaby to the dying man: "'By-a-baby, go to sleep'—that's a good feller."

The sensational juxtaposition of Byrnewood flailing around the manufactured domestic space, "a resort for meditation and study . . . speaking a pleasant tale of fireside joys and comforts,"[29] underscores the white merchant's hypocrisy and mocks the superficial comforts of domesticity that are made possible by the hidden labor of others.

Devil-Bug's other acts of torture against middle-class hypocrites draw on the burlesque and class inflections of blackface minstrelsy. Lhamon Jr.'s explanation of working-class whites' fascination with early black culture resonates with Devil-Bug's outsider status and would appeal to Lippard's readers: "Their identification displays their condition as that of the lowest and least powerful in the city in order to shock and confound the middle-class proprieties. They identify with blacks to bring themselves together and to explain to themselves how others disdain them." While working to bury alive a semi-conscious Byrnewood in Monk-Hall's basement, Devil-Bug mocks him with a racially coded allusion to black culture: "Oh, groan, little children groan, as the nigger wot plays on the banjo ses, but it won't help you the least circumstance!" Devil-Bug's torture of corrupt Reverend F. A. T. Pyne also ironizes the middle class: Tied down to a bed as if he were on the rack, Pyne is nearly tickled to death by Devil-Bug and his two henchmen, who are referred to as "a couple o' first rate lawyers." The comedy of Devil-Bug playing the "pianey" on Pyne's feet is juxtaposed with a description of the reverend's horrific attempt to drug and rape his own stepdaughter, a teenager who turns out to be Devil-Bug's daughter; the fact that Pyne is a shrill nativist who orders his congregation to fire their "pagan" Catholic servants is evidence of Lippard's efforts to preserve class solidarity in the face of the deadly sectarian riots that struck Philadelphia in 1844, which I discuss in chapter three. The irreverence of Devil-Bug is on display in his preparations to slice the throat of Byrnewood's business partner, the white merchant Luke Harvey: "There was a great deal of the philosopher in Devil-Bug. Never a doctor of all the school, with his dissecting knife in hand and the corpse of a subject before him, could have manifested more nerve and coolness than the savage of Monk-Hall . . . Then as if to show that his spirits were not depressed by the solemnity of the operation, he laughed merrily to himself, and hummed the catch of some dismal song." Devil-Bug mocks professionally trained doctors in this morbid scene, and the juxtaposition between solemnity and mirth calls up Frederick Douglass's famous corrective to white readers about slave-songs in his slave narrative. Douglass explains, "[Slaves] would sometimes sing the most pathetic sentiment in the most rapturous tone, and the most rapturous sentiment in the most pathetic tone."[30] In this cross-racial correspondence, Lippard and Douglass seek to educate the white middle class about the harsh realities of their constituents, respectively the multiracial working classes and chattel slaves.

Whereas Devil-Bug mocks the professional classes with his black humor, he performs his most subversive act of class protest when he dupes the wealthy classes and sacrifices himself for his daughter Mabel. In the inheritance plot, the girl's mother, Ellen, was seduced by wealthy merchant Albert Livingstone and then gave birth to a child. A year later, that child having died unbeknownst to Livingstone, Ellen gave birth to a second child—Mabel—whom Devil-Bug sired. In hopes of presenting Mabel as the daughter and heiress of the wealthy Livingstone, Devil-Bug kills the forger Gabriel Von Gelt in order to protect Livingstone's fortune; he slays the confidence-man and cult leader Count Ravoni, who has mesmerized Mabel for his own nefarious purposes; and he sets fire to Livingstone's country estate, killing the merchant and his adulterous wife, Dora. With Livingstone out of the way, Mabel's identity as Livingstone's daughter falsely established, and the police closing in on Monk-Hall, Devil-Bug performs the ultimate self-sacrifice by standing in the path of a rock he has ordered his two henchmen to roll onto Von Gelt's corpse. Though he will not live to see it, Devil-Bug has duped all of the city's wealthy citizens by placing his daughter Mabel among them. Just prior to his suicide, Devil-Bug reflects, "Ha! The g-a-l shall roll in wealth, dress in silks an' satin's, and be a lady all her life, old Devil-Bug's daughter, with the mark o' the red snake on her right temple! It's all settled . . . ho, hoo! Old Devil-Bug's daughter among the grandees o' th' Quaker City!"[31]

Devil-Bug's last jest points to the limits of the text's expression of artisan republicanism, as he gleefully catapults his daughter into the echelons of the upper classes. With a father's love and the acquired knowledge that the system is rigged against the disenfranchised, Devil-Bug acts not to change the system but only to manipulate it to his own advantage. Nevertheless, the end of Devil-Bug's storyline has implications for American exceptionalist ideology. Given that Devil-Bug is figured as black in the novel and thus his daughter Mabel who has "dark eyes" and "long black hair" is multiracial, her marriage to Luke Harvey and sudden wealth provide her with a secure future free of economic want and racial oppression.[32] Lippard's novel presents America at a crossroads in 1845: Will it become a true republic, idealized through Mabel's experience, in which anyone, regardless of origins of class or race, can realize economic mobility, or will it devolve into a corrupt and class-stratified monarchy marked by the abject suffering of the multiracial poor?

In light of Devil-Bug's characterization as black, it is fitting that the climax of the novel's cross-racial class protest comes through his eyes. In a scene cited by numerous scholars as a sign of Lippard's working-class allegiances, Devil-Bug's dream—or nightmare—vision of America in 1950 yokes artisan republicanism and antislavery rhetoric. In his Gothic vision, Devil-Bug witnesses a nation that has succumbed to anti-republican forces in the Class War and ensconced a monarch, ensuring the degradation of the multiracial working classes:

> Then came the slaves of the city, white and black, marching along one mass of rags and sores and misery, huddled together; a goodly tail to the procession of the King. Chains upon each wrist and want upon each brow. Here they were, the slaves of the cotton Lord and the factory Prince; above their heads a loom of iron, rising like a gibbet in the air, and by their sides the grim overseer.[33]

Lippard's artisan republican critique of "wage slavery" leads to cross-racial sympathy that does not privilege the plight of white workers over black workers in the North or chattel slaves in the South. Historian Eric Foner reminds us not to conflate labor advocates' hostility toward abolitionism, which they viewed as indifferent to the harsh working conditions in the North, with their response to chattel slavery. "Inherent in the notion of 'wage slavery,' in the comparison of the status of the northern laborer with the southern slave, was a critique of the peculiar institution as an extreme form of oppression . . . The entire ideology of the labor movement was implicitly hostile to slavery."[34] The fact that Lippard's critique of "wage slavery" in 1845 is multiracial and extends to a critique of chattel slavery is a significant expression of the cross-racial economic critique that would become a staple of popular city-mysteries over the next decade.

Black Sampson: "He was a Negro and yet a Hero!"

In lamenting the lack of assertive white working-class heroes in Lippard's city-mysteries, Michael Denning contends, "Lippard was more successful in imagining a mechanic hero set in the past . . . Lippard was able to depict the mechanic as an autonomous and heroic agent in his tales of the Revolution."[35] While it is true that Lippard's the Mechanic Hero of Brandywine is a class-accented rebel fighting against the anti-republican British forces during the American Revolution, he is not autonomous but designed to resonate with the preceding sketch of Black Sampson, constituting a veritable diptych that can be understood best through comparative analysis. The "twice-told tales" of black and white working-class heroism in Lippard's 1847 compilation of Revolutionary War sketches, *The Legends of the American Revolution "1776." Or, Washington and His Generals,* build cross-racial identification through artisan republican rhetoric. The fact that such black and white character pairings would become a central mode of class protest in the city-mystery genre of the late 1840s and early 1850s is a measure of Lippard's influence.

Lippard's Black Sampson and Mechanic Hero of Brandywine mirror each other in their working-class accents: both men are humble producers who are not bloodthirsty but reluctantly go to war after their loved ones have been murdered, and both Herculean men tower over their effete British antagonists on the battlefield. The first sketch, "Black Sampson," chronicles the heroism of a fugitive slave from the South who takes revenge on the British after they murder his Northern white employer and rape the man's daughter. Like other artisan republican heroes who embody the virtues of the working poor in the city-mystery genre, Sampson is a simple man; he has been taken in by the Maylands and works on their farm. "The hero whose savage virtue is yet recorded in every blade of grass, that waves above the field of Brandywine, was a poor man. A very humble man who had toiled from dawn until dusk, with the axe or spade. A rude man withal, who made his home in a miserable hut, yet still a Hero!"[36] Dutiful to the Maylands, who have protected him from being returned to slavery in the South, Sampson, a fugitive slave, joins the rebel fight against the British at the 1777 Battle of Brandywine.

Described as possessing a form notable for "its breadth of chest, its sinewy arms, its towering height, [and] Herculean outline of iron strength," Sampson is infused with the accents of working-class masculinity seen in Devil-Bug, Glow-Worm, and Musquito, and Duganne's luckless black laborer. Armed with a sharpened scythe, an extension of the honest labor he performs in the fields, and accompanied by his trusty white dog named Devil, a suggestive allusion to Lippard's infamous door-keeper of Monk-Hall, Black Sampson wreaks havoc on the British forces, who display the aristocratic airs of the wealthy white villains of city-mysteries. Lippard describes one of Black Sampson's kills: "How a third gentleman, while in the act of listening to my Lord Cornwallis, (who always went out to murder in clean ruffles and a wig, perfumed with *Marechale* powder,) was startled by the apparition of a giant negro, a whirling scythe, a white dog crimsoned with blood, and how when he saw this apparition a moment only, he never saw or felt anything more." By contrasting black Sampson with his companion dog that was as "white as the driven snow," Lippard draws attention to the singular image of multiracial vengeance they wreak on the battlefield against anti-republican forces. Moreover, in employing an abstract representation of whiteness as something blank, unintelligible, and terrifying just as in Poe's 1838 *The Narrative of Arthur Gordon Pym of Nantucket* and Herman Melville's 1851 *Moby-Dick*, Lippard collapses the racist Manichaean allegory that extols whiteness over blackness. Black Sampson and his white dog, Devil, the "fiend-animal," are a multiracial pair feared and dreaded by the British soldiers.[37]

In *Playing in the Dark: Whiteness and the Literary Imagination,* her influential study of canonical white American authors, Toni Morrison examines the way early Romantic texts construct a white American identity through exploiting an imagined contrast with blackness. "Africanism is the vehicle by which the American self knows itself as not enslaved, but free; not repulsive, but desirable; not helpless, but licensed and powerful; not history-less, but historical; not damned, but innocent; not a blind accident of evolution, but a progressive fulfillment of destiny."[38]

Lippard and company's "twice-told" tales of black and white artisan heroes indicate there were exceptions to the rule. When white working-class *popular* novelists sought to figure the dreams and anxieties of the multiracial working classes, they could produce moments of cross-racial identification that transcended racial lines and directed mutual frustration at the privileged classes. The fact that Lippard felt compelled in "Black Sampson" to include a disclaimer that he is not a "factionist" who "would lay unholy hands upon the American Union" that "may shelter black slavery in the south, and white slavery in the north," is a testament to the sketch's sympathetic representation of blackness.[39]

Following the twelve-page sketch of the charismatic Black Sampson, Lippard chronicles the heroism of a white blacksmith in a four-page sketch, "The Mechanic Hero of Brandywine." Sharing the physical prowess of Black Sampson, the unnamed Mechanic is a humble family man who goes to battle only after British soldiers harm his loved ones. The Mechanic is reminiscent of the Jeffersonian yeoman farmer who works to provide for his family, not to accumulate riches. "Here, at the time of the Revolution, there dwelt a stout blacksmith, his young wife and her babe . . . What feared he for the peril of the times, so long as his strong arm, ringing that hammer on the anvil, might gain bread for his wife and child?" After his wife and child are murdered while he is reporting to General George Washington on the British army's movements near his cottage, he is inspired, like Sampson, to take up arms. The righteous Mechanic—armed not with a scythe like Sampson, but with a hammer, a key symbol of the early labor movement—is infused with patriotic heroism. "Go there to Brandywine, and where the carnage gathers thickest, where the fight is most bloody, there you may see a stout form striding on, lifting a huge hammer into light. Where that hammer falls, it kills—where that hammer strikes, it crushes!" Like Sampson's slaying of the "gentleman" soldier, the Mechanic Hero does not spare a decorated officer. "Look! Another officer, with a gallant face and form—another officer, glittering in tinsel, clasps that blacksmith by the knees, and begs mercy."[40] The Mechanic Hero resonates with Black Sampson as he valiantly uses his Herculean strength to wreak vengeance on anti-republican forces, and, taken together, the two sketches form a class-accented diptych that transcends racial lines. This 1847 "twice-told tale" of the multiracial working classes performs even more progressive cultural work as it manifests in two city-mysteries of 1849, Lippard's *The Killers* and George Thompson's *City Crimes.*

The Killers: "Black Andy" and Elijah Watson's Cross-Racial Class Vengeance

Although Matt Cohen and Edlie L. Wong argue in their introduction to *The Killers* that the novel "marks a shift in Lippard's working-class politics, as it charts the growing significance of racial discourse to Lippard's class protest," the fact is, as we have seen, blackness had played a crucial role in the author's class protest in *The Quaker City* and *The Legends of the American Revolution.*[41] Nevertheless, they are correct that in retelling the Philadelphia race riot of 1849, Lippard develops a cross-racial economic critique through the characters of grogshop owner "Black Andy," as he is named in the text, and white apprentice Elijah Watson. Through the twice-told tales of Irish Catholic rioters' race-inspired attack on Black Andy's establishment and white Elijah Watson's victimization in the workplace, along with the wealthy villains' implication in generations of slave-trading, *The Killers* develops a dual critique of "wage slavery" and chattel slavery that does away with the apology to Southern readers that undercuts Lippard's representation of Black Sampson in *The Legends of the American Revolution.*

The Killers, which Lippard began serializing in his story paper the *Quaker City Weekly* on December 1, 1849, is based on the race riot on Philadelphia's election night two months earlier, when working-class Irish gangs attacked the California House, a black-owned bar in a predominantly African American neighborhood. Lippard reimagines the riot as the culmination of a conspiracy based in the economic exploitation of the multiracial working classes and illegal slave-trading off the coasts of Africa and Brazil. Two of the antagonists are college students: Cromwell Hicks, who plots to foment the riot in order to create a distraction and rob his stepfather, Jacob Hicks; and Don Jorge Marin, the vengeful Cuban son of the elder Hicks's slave-trading partner who has been arrested and executed in Brazil. Consistent with artisan republican class critique, Lippard establishes Cromwell's upper-class pretensions: recently expelled from Yale College, he lounges with Marin in a hotel room, "dressed in a flashy wrapper," sporting a "precocious beard," and resting his "patent leather" shoes on a table. In contrast to shop-owner Black Andy and hard-working apprentice Elijah Watson, Hicks and Marin are young anti-republican loafers who would rather make a quick buck than perform honest labor: "Young, vigorous and with tolerable talents, they were ashamed to work, and had no disposition to earn its wages by one effort of honest toil. Educated in the bar-room, the gambling hell and the brothel, they now saw the world before them."[42]

A more imposing villain is Cromwell Hicks's stepfather, Jacob, whose ambition and mastery of the new urban marketplace anticipates Hawthorne's insatiably greedy and morally corrupt Judge Jaffrey Pyncheon in his 1851 *The House of the Seven Gables*. Merchant, banker, and illegal slave-trader, Jacob Hicks "was that embodiment of inimitable energy, and grasping meanness, which in modern days is called a 'business man.'" In detailing the Hicks family's wealth, Lippard initiates a recurring theme linking "wage" and chattel slavery as mutual systems of exploitation that need to be eradicated. "His [father's] wealth—such was the popular rumor—had been acquired in the slave trade at a time when the slave trade was as legal, moral and religious, as stock gambling at the present day."[43] In an editorial in the *Quaker City Weekly* earlier that year, Lippard responds to and challenges a pro-slavery Southern letter-writer: "Can we attack Wages Slavery and be silent about Chattel Slavery? Are we to hold our peace about the enslavement of white men, because the discussion of that topic involves a review of the nature and results of Black Slavery?"[44] For Lippard, a labor advocate who opposed all forms of exploitation, generations of slave-trading sounds the depths of the Hicks family's immorality in *The Killers;* and, like Hawthorne's dramatization of class conflict in *The House of the Seven Gables,* "the wrong-doing of one generation lives into the successive ones."[45]

There is a lot at stake in Lippard's representations of the multiracial working class in the characters of Elijah Watson and Black Andy. To signal the squalid living conditions of the multiracial poor, Lippard indulges in sensational depictions of degradation that resonate with the moralizing writing of temperance reformers. The Watsons live in the poor district of Runnel's Court, where "whites and blacks, old and young, rumsellers and their customers were packed together there, amid noxious smells, rags and filth, as thick and foul as insects in a decaying carcass." However, in describing the neighborhood of Moyamensing, which had a large portion of working-class black residents and was a target during the race riot, Lippard tempers the sensationalism: "It cannot be denied that hard-working and honest people, reside in the Barbarian District. Nor can it be denied that it is the miserable refuge of the largest portion of the Outcast population of Philadelphia county."[46] Calling up his most famous "Outcast," the black working-class hero Devil-Bug, in this passage, Lippard elicits sympathy from his working-class readers for the victims of the marketplace who are left behind in the march of industrial "progress."

Lippard's description of white working-class Elijah Watson as a "wage slave" prefigures Herman Melville's 1853 "Bartleby, the Scrivener" in the young man's cadaverous appearance and poor treatment in the workplace. Elijah, the biological son of Jacob Hicks, is wasting away in solitary confinement in the Eastern State Penitentiary for passing a counterfeit bill on his father's bank, and his misfortune and desperation are written on his body. "It was the face of a boy of eighteen, hardened by hardship; the cheeks pale and sunken, the dark hair shaved closely around the forehead, and the eyes—leaden and lusterless—sunken deeply beneath the brows. There was a history in that face." Once Elijah serves his sentence, the young man is exploited in the workplace; he works as a compositor for a cutthroat publisher of, ironically enough, religious tracts. "The Proprietor cannot afford to pay full wages; he employs one half boys, and makes up the rest by cutting down the wages of the girls in the bindery." Elijah's fellow compositors bully him, saying, "I never liked his looks," or "Nor I—he has a downcast look!" and "His eyes are too deep set!"[47] After one of the workers reveals Elijah's recent stint in the penitentiary—Lippard's reminder that self-reinvention and upward mobility are a challenge for America's poor—he silently and solemnly leaves the employment without collecting his pay, a forlorn "wage slave" who cannot escape his past.

Meanwhile, Black Andy, nicknamed the "Bulgine," a slang term for a locomotive and a racially ambivalent term from minstrel songs, is a symbol of proud black masculinity.[48] African American cultural historian Dorothy Sterling notes that in the North, "most black men and women were forced to work as servants, bootblacks, waiters, porters," and the black community took great pride in those who were able to become small business owners.[49] In a letter dated August 23, 1862, to the black newspaper the *Pacific Appeal* in San Francisco, J. R. Starkey writes, "How differently would colored people be looked upon could our oppressors pass along the principal thoroughfares and read over the doorway of several first-class business houses the firm name of *Blackman & Co?* . . . If this were so, colored men generally would not be looked upon as a nation of steamboat waiters."[50] In this context, it is significant that Lippard features in *The Killers* a successful black business owner who single-handedly frustrates the plots of the aristocratic white villains, and offers a powerful rebuttal to the specter of slave-trading that haunts the text.

Black Andy plays a central role in the novel's denouement, heroically defending his establishment against the rioters and saving the life of Elijah Watson's sister, Kate. Cromwell Hicks, disguised as a member of the Killers gang, directs the rioters to the grogshop in order to create a cover for robbing his stepfather, who has come to seduce Kate Watson. In an earlier scene loaded with class and racial implications, Cromwell Hicks visits the grogshop as a Killer and overhears his stepfather's deal with Black Andy to abduct and restrain Kate for $50. Lippard writes, "After [Jacob Hicks] had gone, the Bulgine approached the prostrate loafer, and kicked him with his splay foot. 'Get out o' dis. Dis ain't no place for you, dam white trash.'"[51] This is a rare instance in popular literature in which a free black man in the North invokes a class epithet for poor whites. Lhamon Jr. explains that white working-class Northerners identified with blacks "in order to score blows against others of their class—'white trach' [*sic*]—who are cruel to blacks. But *white trash* is not a northern urban term; it is a southern black name for poor whites, which intensifies its usefulness as a marker of northern urban black/white affinity."[52] Here, Lippard uses Black Andy as a mouthpiece to condemn working-class whites who, by nature of their misplaced hostility toward blacks instead of their upper-class oppressors, lack virtue.

As part of its cross-racial economic critique, *The Killers* connects capitalism and chattel slavery as exploitive systems in the North: the former one produces the "wage slavery" suffered by Elijah Watson and the multiracial poor of Runnel's Court, and the latter one fuels race prejudice and race riots. That the two systems are reciprocal is made evident with the discovery of the wealthy Jacob Hicks's financial papers, "which implicated some four or five respectable houses in the profitable transactions of the African Slave Trade." Countering the widespread exploitation of the dispossessed characters, the text enacts examples of cross-racial justice. When Cromwell Hicks and Don Jorge Marin trap and rob Jacob Hicks in a room above Black Andy's bar, Lippard writes, "Had the thousands of widows and orphans, who had been robbed by Hicks as the Banker, have seen him now they would have been amply revenged." Similarly, after slave-trader Don Jorge is killed by a booby-trapped box hidden inside Jacob Hicks's safe, Lippard writes, "He lay dead upon the floor; as dead indeed, as any Negro that he had ever pitched from the deck of his Slaver, in the midst of the broad Ocean."[53] Through these sardonic reflections that celebrate the comeuppance of callous capitalists and the corrupt dealers in human flesh, Lippard weaves a thread of cross-racial class protest to appeal to the working-class readers of *The Killers*.

The "twice-told tales" of cross-racial class protest in *The Killers* are told through Elijah Watson and Black Andy. When Elijah, Jacob Hicks, and Cromwell Hicks come face-to-face in Black Andy's hotel room, where Kate Watson has been drugged, Elijah snarls with the irony of Devil-Bug, "Go at one another—come! He's a swindlin' bank director, and you're a slave pirate—you'll just suit. I'm only a Convict. I'm not good enough company for you two." The stalwart Andy acts decisively and saves Kate Watson from a conflagration set by the rioters. Having killed the younger Hicks in self-defense and preparing to defend himself against Hicks's Cuban partner Don Jorge, Andy strikes a defiant pose in a racially charged scene that calls up the bravery of Black Sampson: "In his rage, [Black Andy] planted his foot upon the back of the dead man's head, and showing his broad black chest, awaited the approach of Don Jorge . . . Unarmed, defenseless, [Don Jorge] was at the mercy of the giant, whose brute strength was sufficient to grind him to powder."[54] The class accents of these figures in the book's accompanying illustration are unmistakable: a scowling and well-dressed Don Jorge is portrayed with his formal top hat stylishly tilted downward and his left hand effeminately turned upward, while Andy clenches his left hand into a fist, the sleeve of his plain shirt rolled up, reminiscent of the iconography of the antebellum labor movement (see figure 2).

Like Devil-Bug, Andy sacrifices himself for the sake of an innocent young woman. When the rioters set fire to his bar, Andy carries

Figure 2. The Negro, "Bulgine": "Prostrate on his face, the blood from the wound trickling over the boards of the floor, and over him triumphant and chuckling stood the Negro, 'Bulgine,' the knife which he shook dripping its red drops upon his black and brawny arm," from George Lippard, *The Bank Director's Son*. Published in Philadelphia by E. E. Barclay and A. R. Orton, 1851. Courtesy of the American Antiquarian Society.

senseless Kate Watson to the roof, where white and black rioters pause from fighting and call on him to save her. Cohen and Wong highlight this scene that transcends racial lines: "[Andy's] heroic effort to save the innocent Kate re-signifies the rumored interracial relationship that instigated the actual attack upon the California House and allows Lippard to imagine a transient instance of solidarity across the divisions of class and race."[55] Although Andy dies in the fire (and Kate miraculously survives), it is through the heroic black man's death—the great leveler of humanity—that Lippard provides a final critique of Northern race prejudice. Following the burning of the bar, the corpse of the black small business owner is indistinguishable from the corpse of the wealthy white bank director: "The second day after the riot, two bodies were found in the cellar of the burnt hovel, their charred features, covered by wet and smoldering embers. Which was the body of the Bulgine, and which the body of Mr. Jacob D. Z. Hicks, none of the spectators could tell."[56] A short but racially complex novel, *The Killers* allies black and white working-class men against ambitious and dissipated villains. Published one year before the passage of the Fugitive Slave Law, which would compel many American authors—including the white authors of sensational fiction—to become more outspoken against Southern slavery, Lippard's *The Killers* was ahead of its time in protesting "wage" and chattel slavery, and entertaining its audience with satisfying moments of class vengeance.

City Crimes: Nero and the Dead Man's Cross-Racial Class Vengeance

In the final third of George Thompson's 1849 sensational novel *City Crimes,* the narrator pauses uncharacteristically in a text that foregrounds thrilling incident over exposition to document the history of a grogshop located across the street from the Catherine Market in New York City. The narrator explains that "every Sunday morning [the market] was the theatre of a lively and amusing scene, wherein was performed the renowned pastime of 'niggers dancing for eels.' All the unsavory fish that had been accumulated during the week, was thus disposed of, being given to such darkies as won the most applause in the science of the 'heel and toe.' The sport used to attract hundreds of spectators." Though this passage contains racial epithets that modern readers might anticipate from a novel written by and for the white working classes prior to the Civil War, it sets up one of the novel's sensational depictions of cross-racial class vengeance against the white middle and upper classes. *City Crimes*'s lower-class grogshop, "crowded with about forty men and boys, of all ages, conditions, and complexions," is run by Liverpool Jack, a brash working-class Bowery B'hoy, as indicated by his "red flannel shirt and tarpaulin hat." In a subplot involving the final humiliation of the fallen Dr. Sinclair, the multiracial patrons mock the once-proud and respectable minister, forcing him to give a drunken sermon, "a wild, incoherent harangue, made up of eloquence, blasphemy, and obscenity," and pelt him with rotten eggs.[57] Although the narrator expresses sympathy for the friendless man who is buried the next day in Potter's Field, Sinclair's downward spiral is figured through the deflation of middle-class pretensions by a cross-racial alliance of the working classes—a recurring form of class protest in Thompson's novel consistent with Lippard's "twice-told tales."

Lhamon Jr. contends that the black charisma inscribed in the "dancing for eels" at Catherine Market in the early nineteenth century fascinated working-class whites who "wanted to overlay this black cachet on their own identities—even as their own identities." For Lhamon Jr., white youths' attraction to blackness played a crucial role in the working-class accents and racial ambivalence of blackface minstrelsy, a popular form that drew disdain from the white middle classes: "Blackface action is usually slashing back at the pretensions and politesse of authority more than at blackness."[58] Rather than conforming to a master narrative that conceives of America's white working classes as racist, politically reactionary, and failures at adapting to new forms of economic life, Thompson, like Lippard, makes a populist critique against the excesses of industrial capitalism through racial discourse and cross-racial sympathy. In *City Crimes,* which relies on the cross-racial vengeance of its charismatic black footman, Nero, and its class-accented villain, the Dead Man, for class protest, Thompson's homage to Catherine Market demonstrates how antebellum popular forms could transcend racial difference in shared resistance to the middle class.

Not a great deal is known about George Thompson's life—he was born in 1823 and possibly died in 1873—except that he was a prolific writer of sensational fiction and was associated for a period in the 1850s with the flash press, prurient New York City weekly papers that focused on bawdy humor and sexual themes. In their introduction to Thompson's *Venus in Boston and Other Tales of Nineteenth-Century City Life,* which includes his novel *City Crimes* that I focus on, editors David S. Reynolds and Kimberly R. Gladman call Thompson "the most shockingly sensational and openly erotic American writer of his day." They estimate Thompson wrote more than twenty-four novels between 1848 and 1854, and they provide a bibliography of more than sixty extant books written by Thompson, sometimes under the pseudonym "Greenhorn." Reynolds and Gladman credit Thompson's popular novels with at times "subvert[ing] middle-class mores" and exposing the oppression of the urban poor.[59] More recently, Patricia Cline Cohen, Timothy J. Gilfoyle, and Helen Lefkowitz Horowitz assert that "Thompson's fiction . . . employed erotic themes as vehicles for militant radical democrats to expose the perversity and corruption of American ruling class."[60] However, these assessments of Thompson as a radical democrat author akin to George Lippard have been challenged by the work of Christopher Looby and Karen J. Renner, who find in Thompson's sensational writing appeals to middle-class values of domesticity and sentimental womanhood.[61] While Looby attributes "casual racism" to Thompson's writing and is right that subversive elements of sensational fiction are often outweighed by more conservative impulses, there are striking moments of cross-racial sympathy in *City Crimes* that reveal city-mysteries' broad attempts to build solidarity among the multiracial working classes.[62]

True to its subtitle promising a "startling revelation of the secret crimes of great cities," Thompson's *City Crimes* follows wealthy white philanthropist Frank Sydney's efforts "to penetrate into the more obscure portions of [New York City], where Poverty, too often linked with Crime, finds a miserable dwelling-place." As part of his "noble" adventure, which includes a hypocritical side trip to a prostitute, Sydney falls in love with and marries Julia Fairfield, a wealthy white woman who lives in the "aristocratic section of the city," and he becomes obsessed with bringing the Dead Man, the infamous leader of the Five Points's criminal underworld, to justice.[63] Unlike the Dead Man, who revels in his public ignominy and is a hero to the multiracial lower classes of Five Points, the ambitious Julia Fairfield secretly carries on an adulterous affair with her black footman, Nero. Through "twice-told tales," the Dead Man and Nero are exploited, imprisoned, and chastised by the privileged classes—represented respectively by Sydney and Fairfield—and the two social outcasts form an alliance based on their shared class interests.

Nero is central to *City Crimes*'s racially sympathetic class protest. Instead of reflecting the condescending romantic racialism of much of the abolitionist writing of the period, or the overt racism of plantation novels, Nero is a dynamic free black laborer who is exploited by his employer, enjoys a measure of revenge against his white mistress, and reinvents himself in Boston by assuming "the respectable occupation of barber." Described as "both educated and intelligent," Nero, like Devil-Bug, makes a performance of servility, in this case to help cover up the affair with Fairfield. Thompson writes, "The complexion of this [black waiter] was intensely dark, yet his features were good and regular and his figure tall and well-formed. In his demeanor toward his mistress and her guest, he was respectful in the extreme, seldom raising his eyes from the carpet, and when addressed, speaking in the most servile and humble tone." That Nero's obsequiousness is not natural but part of a skillful performance is underscored when he and Fairfield converse and romance one another behind closed doors, and he writes eloquent love letters to her. On one hand, Thompson's use of miscegenation to locate the depths of the wealthy Fairfield's depravity is sensational and exploits Nero's blackness. As she taunts her husband, Frank Sydney, "I consume with desire—but not for enjoyment with such as you, but for delicious amours which are recherché and unique! Ah, I would give more for one hour with my superb African, than for a year's dalliance with one like you, so ordinary, so excessively commonplace!"[64] Yet in the context of the novel's broader working-class politics, the literate, resourceful, and upwardly mobile Nero serves not only as a signifier of "charismatic" blackness, but also as a virtuous foil to the perverse wealthy classes, figured exclusively as white, which he leaves behind at novel's end.

Discursively, the novel betrays as much anxiety about the class transgression as the racial transgression that characterizes Nero and Fairfield's romantic relationship. In this way, the novel reflects the mundane reality of cross-racial living arrangements among the urban working classes, something that critics consider notable in Harriet E. Wilson's 1859 matter-of-fact treatment of miscegenation in the Northern states in *Our Nig*. At the beginning of the first novel published by an African American woman, Wilson has the "kind-hearted" black cooper, Jim, fantasize about rescuing the fallen white Mag from poverty: "He thought of the pleasing contrast between her fair face and his own dark skin." Wilson further normalizes this cross-racial love affair when the two characters marry, and the narrator challenges white readers not to judge them harshly because, "Want is a more powerful philosopher and preacher."[65] For Wilson, the interracial marriage is not only beautiful but also a not uncommon fact of life in the North. For Thompson, the illicit affair between black Nero and white Fairfield may titillate readers, but the text calls just as much attention to the class exploitation at the heart of the relationship.

Each time the narrator or the ostensible protagonist Frank Sydney comments on the affair, *City Crimes* invokes Nero's race and class status. For instance, the narrator is surprised that "the daughter of an aristocrat" is "yielding herself to the arms of a negro *servant!*" Similarly, Fairfield is a "wretch whose soul is polluted and whose body is unchaste, by vile intimacy with a negro *menial!*" And in a third example, Sydney, already exposed as a hypocrite, soliloquizes his shock that Fairfield would "surrender her person to the lewd embraces of any man—much more a negro *menial*."[66] It is significant that in an era marked by widespread race prejudice and racial hostility toward blacks in the North, Thompson gives equal force to the affair's class transgression, and thereby develops cross-racial identification among the working-class characters. Terms of self-identification carried racial implications, as David Roediger explores in *The Wages of Whiteness* and argues that early-nineteenth-century white workers preferred terms like "help," "hand," and "helper" to the term "servant," which implied a "master" and carried degrading associations with chattel slaves.[67] In *City Crimes,* the term "menial," with its disparaging attitude toward domestic work, dominates the linguistic landscape of class, and yokes the economic grievances of black Nero and the white Dead Man. By referring only to Nero and the Dead Man as performing "menial" labor in a novel replete with footmen, servants, waiters, and butlers, Thompson subtly reinforces their shared exploitation and paves the way for their explosive scene of cross-racial class vengeance against the upper classes.

Lori Merish argues in *Archives of Labor* that "racial signifiers could figure class resentments, aspirations, and desires" in antebellum writing about white seamstresses.[68] In *City Crimes,* Thompson appropriates elements of the slave narrative to develop the misanthropic white criminal the Dead Man into a spokesperson for the disempowered working classes. Like Devil-Bug, the Dead Man relates that he was an orphan and never knew his parents; he was "whipped" and "oppressed" in the Alms House in which he was raised; and, after fleeing his "overseer" at age fourteen, he worked for various families "in a *menial* capacity."[69] The affinity between the Dead Man's history and the slave narrative continues after Frank Sydney orchestrates the criminal's return to Sing Sing prison: flogged, monitored by an "overseer," and forced to perform cabinetmaking for low wages, the Dead Man becomes a sympathetic and vengeful "wage slave." The Dead Man escapes prison by shipping himself to a furniture warehouse; there he hears the wealthy proprietor brag about exploiting prison labor and then refuse to help a desperately poor woman whose husband he fired—so he burns down the establishment. In case the reader should miss the Dead Man's class-inspired arson, as he prepares to light a match he soliloquizes, "Thy power I now invoke, thou little minister of vengeance; for I hate the aristocrat who expressed his regret at my escape, because, forsooth! my services were valuable to him!—and now, as the flames of fire consume his worldly possessions, so may the flames of eternal torment consume his soul hereafter!" Identifying with the Dead Man, a skilled craftsman, over the morally bankrupt business owner, the narrator warns, "Your abominable treatment of that poor man is about to meet with a terrible retribution."[70]

Literary critic Carl Ostrowski has analyzed *City Crimes*'s debt to the 1849 *Narrative of the Life of Henry Box Brown,* the sensational account of a slave who mailed himself in a crate from Richmond, Virginia, to Philadelphia, a 27-hour and 350-mile journey to freedom. Ostrowski sees Thompson's intertextual borrowing as exploitative appropriation, and concludes that "[Thompson's] white, working-class readers would not have been sympathetic with the plight of escaped slaves mailing themselves North where they were seen as competition in the labor market."[71] But examining this borrowing alongside the cross-racial alliances renders the novel's racial politics ambivalent. Having established the Dead Man as a class-inflected "wage slave" through his exploited labor and his affiliation with Henry Box Brown's daring escape to the North, Thompson develops an artisan republican critique through the sensational conflagration that carries the potential for cross-racial sympathy.

Like Lippard's gleefully misanthropic Devil-Bug, the Dead Man is the novel's primary vehicle of class protest. Similar to blackface minstrelsy's and city-mysteries' lampooning of middle-class pretensions, Thompson's racially inflected Dead Man builds cross-racial identifications between white and black workers by mocking the professional classes. While Devil-Bug hums plantation songs as he tortures middle-class hypocrites, the Dead Man recounts his life of crime behind a series of oxymoronic professional disguises: a quack doctor who does not cure his patients, a libidinous deacon who takes advantage of his female parishioners, and a bibbing temperance reformer. Unlike the duplicitous and anti-republican forces that exploit the poor in *City Crimes,* the Dead Man is an avowed misanthrope and an iteration of the subversive literature's radical democratic hero, who, David S.

Reynolds argues, "lashed out angrily against what was viewed as deepening social corruption." The Dead Man's working-class accents are laid bare when, after suffering the loss of his right hand during battle, he replaces it with "a piece of iron like a sledge-hammer."[72] In this way, the Dead Man becomes a grotesque update of the labor movement's iconography of the proud artisan: rather than wielding a hammer as a tool for performing skilled labor, the hammer has replaced the hand itself, a reminder of horrific factory accidents, and a symbol of increasing mechanization and of the decreasing agency of laborers in the industrial workplace.

With white workers threatened by free black labor and not always inclined to see black workers as allies, it is remarkable that *City Crimes* strives to imagine cross-racial solidarity through ambivalent appeals to "wage slavery" and sympathetic racial representations. It is no coincidence that in Thompson's novel, the chapters in which black characters or racially inflected white characters like the Dead Man appear all contain the most ardent artisan republican rhetoric. The class protest enacted by Nero, the Dead Man, and the multiracial clientele of the low groggery comes to a head in the humiliation of Julia Fairfield, "the high-born lady" and serial adulterer. In the weeks leading up to her bigamous marriage to wealthy old bachelor Mr. Hedge, Fairfield is visited by the Dead Man, who, knowing that she is still married to Sydney, blackmails her. In the racialized scene, Fairfield's upper-class status is signified by her whiteness, which the Dead Man tarnishes through forced labor: He "would have the wretched lady become his menial—he would have her perform for him the drudgery of a servant. He ordered her to bring him wine, and wait upon him; and enforced the command with a blow, which left a red mark upon her beautiful white shoulder."[73] By the Dead Man forcing Fairfield to perform "menial" domestic tasks like he and Nero were forced to do, Thompson represents the haughty woman's humiliation in racial terms, as her compromised whiteness lowers her to the state of the multiracial plebeian classes.

When the Dead Man calls Nero to witness the woman's degradation, Nero, who harbors a class grudge, is happy to oblige. After

Fairfield began her scheme to marry Mr. Hedge, she ended the affair with Nero and told him, "You can, if you choose, re-enter my service as footman, and your wages shall be the same as those of any other servant of your class; but remember—henceforth I am the mistress, and you the menial." Nero relishes watching Fairfield forced, "with her delicate hands," to scrape the mud off the Dead Man's shoes with "an elegant pearl handled pen-knife," wash them with "rose-water in a china ewer," and dry them with a "cambric handkerchief."[74] The cross-racial economic critique conveyed in this scene looks ahead to Matthew Maule's mesmeric "enslavement" of the delicate aristocrat Alice Pyncheon in Nathaniel Hawthorne's *The House of the Seven Gables* two years later. Much like literary critic David Anthony's reading of Alice being "tainted by the racialized markings of class difference" because she is forced to perform "Jim Crow" jigs and menial tasks for Maule and his bride on their wedding night, Fairfield's reduced status is figured through compromised whiteness.[75] But unlike the canonical Hawthorne, who, according to Anthony, fails to see the destabilizing ambivalence inscribed in the "tropes of race" that he draws from blackface minstrelsy, popular novelist Thompson seems well aware of that ambivalence, and, as part of his novel's class protest, transforms it into expressions of cross-racial sympathy.

In a final example of *City Crimes*'s cross-racial economic critique, the racially diverse patrons of Pat Mulligan's tenement, groggery, and dancehall help to destroy the establishment to avenge the Irishman's cruel treatment of his poor tenants. Oxymoronic "honest criminal" Ragged Pete recounts how on a cold night Mulligan evicted a mother and her child because they could not pay rent, and in the morning found them frozen to death and partially eaten by hogs. Ragged Pete's gang plots to start a destructive row inside Mulligan's groggery, and, upon their arrival, the narrator describes the multiracial patronage engaged in a call-and-response dance associated with black culture. A "sable genius" nicknamed "the General" frantically plays a violin, and the music "was responded to, 'on the floor,' by about twenty persons, who were indulging in the 'mazy dance.' The company included old prostitutes, young thieves, negro chimney-sweeps, and many others."[76]

In *Five Points,* a history of the notorious working-class neighborhood, Tyler Anbinder references accounts of whites and blacks mingling "in sweet confusion in the mazy dance," confirming that Thompson is carefully documenting another local custom of race-mixing similar to his account of "dancing for eels" at Catherine Market.[77] In this subplot, white and black patrons converge to punish Mulligan for his cruel business practices: "As they all hated the Irish bully, and smarted under the remembrance of numerous insults and wrongs sustained at his hands, they with one accord fell upon him, and beat him within an inch of his life."[78] Thompson softens the nativism toward the Irish by having Ragged Pete's crew plan the attack in the bar of Bloody Mike, an Irishman who endorses the plot, and thereby keeps the focus on class difference rather than exploiting ethnic strife.

Thompson's *City Crimes* provides another important case study of how city-mysteries, as a popular form of working-class expression, complicate our understanding of the white working classes in the antebellum period. The novel's progressive representation of upwardly mobile working-class black footman Nero, along with its reliance on formal elements of the slave narrative to represent the white working-class cabinetmaker the Dead Man, realizes the potential for cross-racial sympathy in sensational moments that are more common than they are exceptional within city-mystery fiction.

The Heroic Slave: "He had the head to conceive, and the hand to execute"

In his 1845 *Narrative of the Life of Frederick Douglass,* Douglass, having claimed his manhood by fighting off the cowardly and coarse slave-breaker Covey, returns to the docks of Fells Point in Baltimore and is hired out as a caulker by his owner, Hugh Auld. Indignant that he is denied the fruits of his own labor, Douglass makes a free labor appeal that would have resonated with the Northern readers of artisan republican city-mysteries. "I was now getting paid, as I have said, one dollar and fifty cents per day. I contracted for it; I earned it; it was paid to me; it was rightfully my own; yet, upon each returning Saturday night, I was compelled to deliver every cent of that money to Master Hugh." Although this appeal to free labor ideology endorses the capitalist system, Douglass's appeal to the rights to the fruits of his own labor would have resonated with the white producing classes, who felt themselves at the whims and vagaries of an increasingly unstable wage economy. When Douglass closes the chapter by imagining Auld's unrightful theft of his wages as like the power of a "grim-visaged pirate upon the high seas," a common character within sensational fiction, the slave narrative reinforces a class-inflected correspondence with popular fiction that positions exploited labor against managerial greed.[79]

The fact that Lippard's *The Quaker City* and Douglass's slave narrative caused a sensation in the Northern press and enjoyed healthy sales when they were published in 1845 points to the potential for crossover readership and underscores their successful deployment of artisan republican and antislavery discourses. Reynolds indicates that *The Quaker City* sold over 200,000 copies within six years, and Robert S. Levine states that Douglass's "*Narrative* was the most successful slave narrative published in the United States . . . in all likelihood selling around 20,000 copies between 1845 and the early 1850s in the United States and abroad."[80] Two of the strategies of antislavery protest that Douglass introduces in his slave narrative—artisan republican appeals to the fruits of one's labor and sturdy masculinity—are developed in his 1853 novella *The Heroic Slave* and resonate with white-authored sensational fiction of the 1840s and 1850s.

Recognized as the first piece of African American fiction, *The Heroic Slave* is a fictionalized account of the successful mutiny aboard the slave-ship the *Creole* in November 1841 as it sailed with its human cargo from Richmond to New Orleans. The slaves commandeered the ship and forced a crewman to sail it to the British colony of the Bahamas, where they were free. The novella's class-accented tropes from city-mystery fiction coincide with Douglass's increasing attention in the 1850s to ameliorating the working conditions of blacks in the North. Some white labor activists charged that abolitionists, especially William Lloyd Garrison, were indifferent to the plight of Northern "wage slaves." George M. Fredrickson writes that "in the first issue of the *Liberator,* [Garrison] denied the existence of the conflict between wealth and property, or between labor and capital, and demonstrated his faith in an industrial order held together by the benevolence of the rich and the cultivation of Protestant virtues by the poor."[81] Thus it is significant that in the early 1850s Douglass expressed growing concerns about laborers in the North, and *The Heroic Slave*'s economic critique of chattel slavery would have appealed to the multiracial producing classes in the urban northeast. As part of promoting his idea for an industrial college that would serve Northern whites and blacks, Douglass, like George Lippard in 1849, insisted on the necessity to combat "wage slavery" and chattel slavery simultaneously. In an 1854 article outlining his plans for the industrial college, Douglass writes, "If there is one proposition which commands our hearty and instant assent more than another, it is that 'the FREE colored man's elevation is essential to the SLAVE colored man's emancipation.'"[82] As Robert S. Levine argues, "Though [Douglass] argued for black elevation as if white racism were an unrelated issue—that individual will alone could help blacks to succeed—it was much more often the case that he presented black self-help programs in the North as part of an antiracist struggle intimately related to, if not a necessary condition of, the struggle against racism and slavery in the South."[83]

In *The Heroic Slave,* Douglass's protagonist, the lead mutineer Madison Washington, is an imposing combination of brawn and brains. A literary descendant of the black and white mechanic heroes of working-class fiction, Washington is hyper-masculine and commands respect. Like Lippard's Black Sampson, "[Washington's] torn sleeves disclosed arms like polished iron . . . His whole appearance betokened Herculean strength." But unlike Lippard's black Devil-Bug, who is "savage" and sardonic, Washington is sophisticated and sincere. "He was just the man you would choose when hardships were to be endured, or danger to be encountered,—intelligent and brave. He had the head to conceive, and the hand to execute."[84] This rounded description of Washington's character resonates with black abolitionist James McCune Smith's figuring of Douglass as a proud laborer. In his introduction to

Douglass's 1855 autobiography *My Bondage and My Freedom,* Smith writes of Douglass, "At his daily labor he went with a will; with keen, well set eye, brawny chest, lithe figure, and fair sweep of arm, he would have been king among caulkers, had that been his mission." Struggling in New Bedford amidst what Smith calls "the caste-slavery of the north," Douglass the artisan republican hero worked hard "sawing wood, rolling casks, or doing what labor he might, to support himself and young family."[85] Like the ambitious and hard-working Douglass, who would become a leader among men, and like Black Sampson, who would manhandle anti-republican forces on the Revolutionary battlefield, Madison Washington possesses the swagger and black charisma that attracted the white working classes: "In a word, he was one to be sought as a friend, but to be dreaded as an enemy."[86]

Critics have noted *The Heroic Slave*'s sentimental cross-racial friendship between Washington and the white Ohioan Mr. Listwell, who overhears the heroic slave soliloquizing in the forest and is instantly transformed into an abolitionist. The genuineness of their cross-racial friendship is confirmed when Listwell provides Washington, who is in a slave coffle bound for New Orleans, with three metal files, and thereby abets the slave mutiny. But the white Listwell is also the primary vehicle of the novella's economic critique of chattel slavery. Arrested by the sight of the slave coffle, Listwell reflects, "And all to fill the pockets of men too lazy to work for an honest living, and who gain their fortune by plundering the helpless, and trafficking in the souls and sinews of men."[87] Listwell's artisan republican reflections resonate with his earlier experiences while staying on the outskirts of Richmond in a decaying tavern that calls up the Gothic labyrinthine dangers of Lippard's Monk-Hall and the ghastly personification of Edgar Allan Poe's House of Usher.

Despite "an air of grandeur" and "pretension," the tavern, which serves as a hotel, has declined with the "ineffaceable marks" of "time and dissipation." Reminding the narrator morbidly of "a human skull, after the flesh has mingled with the earth," the tavern porch has loose floorboards that create "effective man-traps in their stead for nocturnal ramblers." Like Monk-Hall, the tavern is threatening and disorienting to outsiders and greenhorns, and regionally it has the aura of Southern decay personified by the poor whites that loaf about rather than perform honest labor. "[The loafers] know everybody, and almost everybody knows them. Of course, as their title implies, they have no regular employment. They are (to use an expressive phrase) *hangers on,* or still better, they are what sailors would denominate *holders-on to the slack, in everybody's mess, and in nobody's watch.*" The poor whites' indolence is evident in their "vulgarity and dark profanity," and in their dehumanized description as "a brutal set of creatures" that are "worse than swine."[88] The picture of decay and of degraded poor whites anticipates Douglass's free labor arguments in *My Bondage and My Freedom* two years later: that chattel slavery exhausts the land and depresses the labor power of the whites who do not own slaves.

While Washington's friendship with the abolitionist Listwell stands out for its cross-racial sympathy, the potential for an even more radical cross-racial relationship is suggested between Washington and Tom Grant, the white, class-accented first mate of the *Creole.* In the weeks following the slave mutiny, a group of sailors led by the racist Jack Williams discuss the events on the *Creole.* Grant is marked as working-class when Douglass describes him as a "compact, manly looking person," and "the sturdy mate." Awed by Washington, Grant confirms for his listeners the black mutineer's hyper-masculine strength, calling up the bravery of Lippard's Black Sampson on the Brandywine battlefield: "You murderous villain, said I, to the imp at the helm, and rushed upon him to deal him a blow, when he pushed me back with his strong, black arm, as though I had been a boy of twelve." Although Grant does not overcome his race prejudice, he compares the black revolutionary to his namesake George Washington, a beloved figure in the antebellum period: "It was not that his principles were wrong in the abstract; for they are the principles of 1776. But I could not bring myself to recognize their application to one whom I deemed my inferior." Douglass represents the working-class Grant as being aware of how race prejudice has conditioned him to deny Washington's heroism, and the fact that Grant concludes his speech—and the novella—by admiring "the triumphant leadership of the [slaves'] heroic chief and deliverer, MADISON WASHINGTON," chronicles growth in the first mate's racialist thinking.[89] Although he is not a radical abolitionist like Listwell, the class-accented Tom Grant exhibits for Douglass the potential for cross-racial class solidarity built on the ideologies of artisan republicanism and "sturdy masculinity" that dominate white-authored city-mysteries.

Conclusion

While white authors of urban sensationalism like Lippard, Duganne, and Thompson relied on "charismatic" blackness and the slave narrative form to mount a cross-racial critique of class inequality in the North during the 1840s, the passage of the Fugitive Slave Law in 1850 would have a profound effect on the city-mystery genre. Lippard, especially, expanded his social critique to include a more forceful attack on chattel slavery. The next chapter of this volume focuses on the growing correspondences of class-accented antislavery discourse in white-authored sensational fiction and black-authored literature of the early 1850s. Just as Frederick Douglass and other black abolitionists increasingly advocated violent resistance to slavecatchers, Lippard's later novels came to endorse vigilante justice by fugitive slaves and their white supporters. Moreover, William Wells Brown's *Clotel* and Lippard's *New York,* published about the same time on opposite sides of the Atlantic Ocean, employ the rumored affair between Thomas Jefferson and Sally Hemings to protest chattel slavery in the South and socioeconomic inequality in the North, and to imagine cross-racial love and friendship as an alternative to intra-class racial hostility. The Fugitive Slave Law produced a two-pronged response of justified violence and cross-racial amity within the racially diverse literature that is the subject of this volume.

CHAPTER TWO

The Class Accents of Antislavery Reform

On September 18, 1850, Congress passed the Fugitive Slave Law as part of the broader Compromise of 1850, which admitted California into the union as a free state and allowed popular sovereignty in the newly established territories of New Mexico and Utah. The Fugitive Slave Law required Northerners to assist Southern slaveowners and their slavecatchers in recovering runaway slaves under penalty of six months' imprisonment and a $1,000 fine. As historians have noted, the Fugitive Slave Law galvanized the Northern abolitionist movement and helped bring the sectional crisis to a violent head a decade later. Among the literary responses to the Fugitive Slave Law, no text was more popular than Harriet Beecher Stowe's *Uncle Tom's Cabin,* first serialized in the *National Era* during 1851 and 1852, and published as a complete novel in March 1852. It sold three hundred thousand copies in the first year alone and was the first American novel to sell more than one million copies, making it the best-selling American novel of the nineteenth century. As a response to the Fugitive Slave Law, *Uncle Tom's Cabin* began receiving enormous critical attention more than one hundred years after its publication, spurred by Jane Tompkins's recovery and analysis of the novel in her groundbreaking 1985 consideration of popular texts, *Sensational Designs.* Countering the modernist proclivity to dismiss popular novels *because* they were popular, Tompkins attributes the power of Stowe's novel to its strategic rhetorical appeals to its Northern audience. "*Uncle Tom's Cabin* retells the culture's central religious myth—the story of the crucifixion—in terms of the nation's greatest political conflict—slavery—and of its most cherished social beliefs—the sanctity of motherhood and the family."[1]

The growing correspondences between representative white-authored sensational fiction and black-authored literature of the 1850s constitute a shared response to the passage of the Fugitive Slave Law. While white authors of urban fiction relied on charismatic blackness and multiracial artisan heroes to mount a cross-racial critique of class inequality in the North during the 1840s, the passage of the Fugitive Slave Law in 1850 strengthened the antislavery politics of city-mysteries. George Lippard, specifically, expanded his racially ambivalent class critique to include an economic critique of chattel slavery with strategies that echoed the antislavery writing of Frederick Douglass and William Wells Brown. Just as Douglass and Brown were advocating violent resistance to slavecatchers under an unjust system, Lippard's two novels—*The Empire City* (1850) and its expanded version, *New York: Its Upper Ten and Lower Million* (1853)—endorse vigilante justice by fugitive slaves and their white allies against the agents of chattel slavery and their corrupt, wealthy co-conspirators. Douglass, Brown, and Lippard balanced their endorsement of antislavery violence with representations of cross-racial amity and empathy. Specifically, Brown's *Clotel; or, The President's Daughter,* the first African American novel, and Lippard's *New York* employ the affair between Thomas Jefferson and Sally Hemings to document the history of socioeconomic inequality in the republic, to challenge American exceptionalism and deconstruct racial difference, and to idealize the potential for genuine cross-racial love and friendship among the multiracial working classes. I hope my analysis helps to ameliorate the problem cited by literary critic Ann duCille, who, while investigating the apparent non-existence of the Jefferson-Hemings affair in American history and the absence of Brown's *Clotel* in African American literary history, writes, "*Clotel* has become increasingly marginal within academic circles and, arguably, has little or no standing outside introductory-level African-American literature courses."[2] Brown, Douglass, and Lippard also mount carefully reasoned economic arguments about how chattel slavery has contributed to the degradation of Northern and Southern poor whites, whom the authors imagine as potential allies in the fight to end chattel slavery. Finally, these varied responses to the Fugitive Slave Law converge powerfully in Lippard's deathbed antislavery novel, the serialized *Eleanor; or, Slave Catching in the Quaker City,* as the white Herculean mechanic Adam Smith heroically frustrates the efforts of slavecatchers on a harrowing chase along the Mason-Dixon line in southern Pennsylvania.

Justified Antislavery Violence: Cross-Racial Response to the Fugitive Slave Law

In the June 9, 1854, edition of his newspaper, Frederick Douglass ran a pithy editorial entitled "The True Remedy for the Fugitive Slave Bill." Douglass's answer: "*A good revolver, a steady hand, and a determination to shoot down any man attempting to kidnap.*" In the editorial, Douglass contends that violent resistance will help to end both kidnapping and chattel slavery, and like his own Madison Washington and Lippard's sketch of Black Sampson, concludes by invoking the freedom-loving Revolutionaries: "Oh! That we have a little more of the manly indifference to death, which characterized the Heroes of the American Revolution."[3] This call to arms in 1854 is consistent with Douglass's defense of justified antislavery violence that began in earnest in the fall of 1850. One month following the passage of the Fugitive Slave Law, Frederick Douglass gave a rousing speech, "Do Not Send Back the Fugitive," before thousands of abolitionists and frightened blacks in Boston's Faneuil Hall. In his hour-long urgent remarks denouncing the law, Douglass uses graphic imagery consistent with city-mysteries to depict how his "terror-stricken brethren" who are returned to slavery "will have to submit to excruciating torture." Describing monstrous slaveowners anxious "to gratify a deep-seated, malignant and deadly revenge" against their returned slaves, Douglass recounts incidents of blood-dripping whippings and mutilation. That Douglass's sensationalism, a popular mode within city-mysteries, fired the emotions of his audience is captured in the news coverage, as the *Liberator* parenthetically records the crowd's reaction in one word: "(Sensation)."[4]

Douglass describes the "pursuing bloodhounds" and their employers as spiteful, deceitful, sadistic, and cowardly, and warns that the Fugitive Slave Law will transport the everyday violence on Southern plantations to the North. Douglass closes the speech by detailing the consequences of supporting the law, and paints a Gothic portrait of Boston streets "flowing with innocent blood." After alluding to the sacrifice of Crispus Attucks in the streets "where the blood first spouted in defense of freedom," a strategy resonant with Lippard's appeals to Revolutionary War heroes, Douglass presents the stark choice facing the people of Boston: "the slave-hunter will be here to bear the chained slave back, or he will be murdered in your streets."[5] Douglass had begun to challenge William Lloyd Garrison's nonviolent approach to ending slavery two years earlier when he set up his own newspaper, the *North Star,* in Rochester. According to Robert S. Levine, "Though he founded the *North Star* at a time when he avowed a commitment to Garrisonian principles of moral suasion, Douglass moved fairly quickly toward advocating violence as a proper response to slavery."[6] In his 1850 Faneuil Hall speech, Douglass describes a personal account of how he prepared to use violence against kidnappers. Detailing how a "party of these man-hunters" came to his house in Rochester and departed without finding him, Douglass, whose freedom had been purchased in December 1846 by British supporters, remained at risk of retribution and kidnapping. Hiding in the garret and keeping watch over the trap door through which the slavecatchers would have to enter one at a time, Douglass states, "And if they had made their appearance, he should, he said, have endeavored to greet them with a hospitality befitting the place and occasion! (Cheers.) Many of his neighbors had adopted the opinion, that when men divest themselves of every feeling of humanity, and act as bloodhounds, they should be treated as such."[7] Douglass's rendering of this suspenseful scene echoes city-mysteries' thrilling plots and righteous indignation on behalf of the multiracial oppressed.

The seeds of Douglass's endorsement of antislavery violence are evident in his public addresses of the late 1840s. In "The Slaves' Right to Revolt," delivered before the New England Anti-Slavery Society convention on May 30, 1848, Douglass invokes Revolutionary War rhetoric and praises heroic slaves for their violent resistance. Appealing to his Northern audience to implore Southern slaveholders to end slavery, Douglass writes, "Would you but do this, oh, men of the North, I know there is a spirit among the slaves which would not much longer brook their degradation and bondage. There are many Madison Washingtons and Nathaniel Turners in the South, who would assert their right to liberty, if you would take your feet from their necks, and your sympathy and aid from their oppressors."[8] More ominously, a month earlier, in an address before 1,200 blacks at the Shiloh Presbyterian Church in New York City, Douglass protested the American Colonization Society by warning slaveowners they are "sleeping on slumbering volcanoes." Countering the Colonization Society's construction of black slaves as timid and inferior with a class-accented image of strength and labor, Douglass offers a dire warning to those who do not work to end slavery: "That spirit in man which abhors chains, and will not be restrained by them, will lead those sable arms that have long been engaged in cultivating, beautifying, and adorning the South, to spread death and destruction there. (Great applause.)" Finally, in a class-accented passage that resonates with the sanguinary protest against "wage slavery" in city-mystery fiction, Douglass warns, "Those who have given us blood to drink for wages, may expect their day will come one day."[9]

Like Douglass's invocation of black revolutionaries, William Wells Brown integrates into *Clotel* a chapter on Nat Turner and his rebellion that resonates with class-inflected city-mysteries. Brown's novel has been critiqued for appealing to white readers through colorism and a reliance on the "tragic mulatta" figure. In the mid-1970s, literary critic Addison Gayle wrote what has become an influential critique of Brown's *Clotel,* calling its multiracial characters "blacks in white face," and dismissing the novel for its perceived colorism and capitulation to white, middle-class values. While Gayle's reading is valid, *Clotel* pauses in the chapter "The Arrest" to lionize black Herculean insurrectionists, which constitutes a correspondence not only with Douglass's Madison Washington but also with the capable black leaders of Lippard's fiction of the 1850s. In August 1831, Turner, an enslaved preacher, led a revolt over two days during which armed slaves killed approximately fifty whites before being cornered and subdued in nearby woods. In *Clotel,* Brown's version of Nat Turner "was made aware by too many proofs, that the slave could expect no justice at the end of the slave owner"; as a result, Turner led the rebels that "for a time bade defiance to their oppressors." In narrating the Turner rebellion as an act of justified antislavery violence, Brown includes another imposing black revolutionary named Picquilo, who resonates with Lippard's Black Sampson for his choice of weapon and with Lippard's sagacious black leader Royal Bill of *The Empire City* and *New York.* Brown writes that Picquilo "was a large, tall, full-blooded negro, with a stern and savage countenance . . . his only weapon was a sword, made from the blade of a scythe, which he had stolen from a neighboring plantation." Critics have identified Reverend John R. Beard's 1853 description of Haitian revolutionary Lamour de Rance in *The Life of Toussaint L'Ouverture* as a source for Brown's Picquilo.[10] The descriptions of Picquilo battling oppressors with a scythe blade, all the while exuding a "fierce" air and a "sanguinary" look, also call up Lippard's heroic portrait of Black Sampson in *The Legends of the American Revolution.* Given Brown's well-known penchant for borrowing from other literary texts, such as Lydia Maria Child's short story "The Quadroons," for *Clotel,* it is conceivable that Lippard's beloved book about the Revolutionary War had an influence on Brown's sensational chapter "The Arrest."

As part of a broad cross-racial protest against the Fugitive Slave Law, Brown's sympathetic representations of Nat Turner and Picquilo and Douglass's endorsement of justified antislavery violence have significant correspondences in Lippard's city-mystery writing of the early 1850s. From the leadership of fugitive black slave Royal Bill, referred to as "Old Royal" throughout Lippard's two novels, who presides over the vigilante organization known as the Black Senate; to the whipping of slaveowners and slaying of slavecatchers; and to the sympathetic portrayal of fugitive slaves, Lippard's *The Empire City* and *New York* reveal a white working-class author of sensational fiction who insists on violent resistance to the Fugitive Slave Law. That Lippard was publicly opposed to the Fugitive Slave Law is evident in the *National Era*'s brief report of a July 15, 1852, meeting in Philadelphia to repeal it: "The meeting was addressed by A. H. Duganne, George Lippard, Charles Goepp, and John Shedden."[11] With the horrors of slavery becoming even more visible to Northern readers following the passage of the Fugitive Slave Law, Lippard voices his growing opposition to chattel slavery through sympathetic portrayals of fugitive slaves who, when cornered, will resist their oppressors with righteous violence. In this way, Lippard informs his working-class readers that the Fugitive Slave Law is part of a vast system that exploits the most vulnerable members of an increasingly class-stratified society.

At the same time politicians were debating the Fugitive Slave Law, Lippard began serializing *The Empire City; or, New York by Night and Day* in his weekly story paper the *Quaker City Weekly* on February 3, 1849, and was still running weekly installments of the novel in May 1850, just four months before the law's enactment in September. That the debate over the law shaped *The Empire City,* which was published as a complete novel in the late summer or early fall of 1850, is evident in the extensive subplots involving fugitive slave leader Old Royal, recently escaped from the Royalton plantation, and the two fugitive slave siblings, the multiracial Randolph and Esther Royalton, whose white half-brother Harry Royalton is pursuing them from South Carolina to New York with the assistance of his slavecatcher Bloodhound.[12] Set in and around New York City, Lippard's *The Empire City* enacts justified antislavery violence against the slaveowner and the slavecatcher at the hands of Old Royal, whose retributive justice argues that violence should be met with violence. Given that Lippard is known to have shaped the latter installments of his serial novels in response to readers' reactions and to news events, it is possible that the introduction of the sixty-year-old Old Royal halfway through the novel is part of a concerted effort to respond to the Fugitive Slave Law in *The Empire City.* That Lippard encourages his readers to sympathize with the honorable fugitive slaves against their anti-republican oppressors is a testament to his class-inflected opposition to the Fugitive Slave Law.

Part three of the novel opens with the survivors of a horrible train wreck taking shelter in a hilltop mansion, including Harry and Bloodhound, who were tracking Randolph and Esther on the train. Aware of the provocative nature of this antislavery subplot, Lippard pauses in the narrative to defend the new direction of his novel. He asks readers for latitude because he has never refrained from showing, "in all its galling shames, the white slavery of the North, which crushes free men in the iron bondage of the factory, or dooms them to the accursed future of landless and hopeless toil." Nevertheless, like his appeals in the *Quaker City Weekly* to protest "wage" and chattel slavery alike, Lippard insists, "We cannot be silent when white slavery curses [Northern] soil; shall we be dumb when black slavery sends its ministers over the boundary line, and forces its most terrible features at once and in distinct hideousness upon our eyes." Lippard, as a white labor reformer who criticized middle-class abolitionists, whom he believed were indifferent to the needs of the working poor, claims his right to denounce chattel slavery as one of many forms of oppression in America: "Dare we not speak a word on this dreaded subject without having the words—abolitionist, dog—thrown in our teeth? While we attack the despotism of the bank, the corruption of the church, shall we not say a word—only a word—of the horrors that surround the slave-mart?"[13] As we saw in chapter one and will see further in *The Empire City, New York,* and *Eleanor,* Lippard had more than "a word" to say against slavery, and he joined with black abolitionists in justifying antislavery violence.

In *The Empire City,* with Harry and Bloodhound stalking them inside the mansion, Randolph and Esther are surprised to find their old friend from the plantation. Like the acclaimed Henry Box Brown, and the fictive Dead Man from Thompson's *City Crimes,* Old Royal explains that he mailed himself in a box to Philadelphia, where a Quaker directed him to safety in the rural mansion, now revealed to be a stop on the Underground Railroad. Lippard endows Old Royal with the working-class accents of Black Sampson and Douglass's Madison Washington: "The speaker was a huge Negro, whose bony limbs were clad in a suit of rich blue cloth. Almost gigantic in stature, with broad shoulders, long arms, and thick clumsy hands, the inky blackness of his face, was contrasted with the white cravat, which encircled but did not hide his muscular throat." Lippard also links Old Royal, whose dark skin is compared to anthracite, with *The Empire City*'s white Herculean mechanic John Hoffman, who is introduced in chapter one with "matted hair, black as anthracite."[14] With his working-class credentials established through cross-racial hypermasculinity and his piety established through his possession of his prized Bible, Old Royal transforms into a righteous agent of retributive justice against the oppressors of men.

The vigilante justice that Old Royal seeks becomes personified in the mysterious Court of Ten Millions, a small, multiracial group of which he is a member. These men disguise themselves, then put on trial and punish the corrupt and powerful anti-republicans who put their own desires ahead of the public good. Lippard's representation of vigilante justice, necessitated by the lack of public justice to right the wrongs of "wage" and chattel slavery, reflects literary critic Jeannine Marie DeLombard's claim that abolitionists attracted supporters by appealing to the broad "growing distrust for the judiciary" during the antebellum period.[15] In his city-mysteries, Lippard regularly lampooned duplicitous attorneys, judges, and other officers of the court who conspired regularly against the poor for personal gain. In *The Empire City* and *New York,* Lippard's masked Court of Ten Millions acquires its large sums of money by extorting corrupt bankers and slaveowners. Once the slaveowner Harry is subdued and put on trial, the Court's leader explains its purpose to punish wrongs that transcend racial lines: "Among these crimes, the Court of Ten Millions recognizes one as preeminently infamous. It is the crime committed by the man who uses his wealth or the accident of his social position as the means of oppressing any one of his fellow creatures—even the poorest and the meanest." This cross-racial economic critique is developed through artisan republican rhetoric when the Court states that its immense wealth, extracted from "foul" slave traders, "perjured" judges, and "fraudulent" bankers, is used expressly "to redress and punish those crimes, which, in the outer world, have been committed *for the love of money;* in other words, by *the thirst of Labor's fruits, without Labor's work.*"[16] In her analysis of the fugitive slave Randolph in *The Empire City,* literary critic Shelley Streeby asserts, "By insisting on the active virtue of a slave, Lippard aligns the oppression of free workers with the oppression of slaves and suggests that both problems represent nondemocratic antagonisms that must be addressed by immediate action."[17]

The vigilante court hears the testimony of fugitive slave Randolph against his cruel brother: instead of obeying their father's dying wish that he would protect his half-siblings, Harry had sold them to settle gambling debts and out of jealousy ordered the overseer to administer thirty-nine lashes to Randolph. Now found guilty by the Court of Ten Millions, Harry learns that he will receive thirty-nine lashes in turn, to be delivered by none other than his recently escaped slave, Old Royal. In a highly wrought scene of black violence against a white slaveowner, Old Royal invokes the biblical figure Ehud from the Old Testament book of Judges and relishes administering the blows to his legal master: "Ehud, I hab a message from God to dee!" Old Royal, invoking Ehud, who was sent by God to free the Israelites from their oppressors, metes out thirty-nine lashes to his slaveowner. With his retributive justice sanctified by the Bible, Old Royal takes gleeful satisfaction in his revenge, calling up the subversive vengeance of black Devil-Bug in *The Quaker City.* Speaking to Esther, who swoons at the sight of the naked and bloodied Harry, Old Royal exclaims, "Lor, Essy! Look-a *dar!* . . . Dars EHUD dat gib de lash to Massa 'Dulph, an' sole Essy at a raffle. Dar he am! Yah—ha—ya—hah!" Old Royal's actions may exploit readers' fears of a race war stoked by Nat Turner's slave revolt nearly two decades earlier and the more recent slave mutinies like the *Amistad* in 1839 and the *Creole* in 1841. But Lippard also appeals to Northerners' concerns about the violence that the Fugitive Slave Law will import to Northern states, and he holds slaveowners responsible for that violence. Harry's death in *The Empire City*'s epilogue is presented as deserved: "Harry Royalton returned to the South, where his existence was terminated by a pistol bullet in a fracas which his insolence had provoked."[18]

Lippard expands and develops Old Royal's character in the three years between the publication of *The Empire City* in 1850 and *New York* in 1853, giving him a more prominent role in the latter in administering vigilante justice against capitalists and slaveowners. The degree of violence rises from the humiliating whipping of Harry Royalton in *The Empire City* to the stabbing death of Bloodhound in *New York,* and in both instances, Old Royal oversees the justified antislavery violence. Just as he enhances the class critique in *New York* by developing white mechanic hero Arthur Dermoyne alongside John Hoffman, Lippard strengthens his protest against the Fugitive Slave Law and chattel slavery by expanding Old Royal's role and introducing additional fugitive slave characters. Although Old Royal remains the only black member of the Court of Ten Millions like he was in *The Empire City,* Old Royal in *New York* also presides over the Black Senate, a vigilante organization of twenty or thirty African Americans that mirrors the Court of Ten Millions—another instance of cross-racial "twice-told tales"—and protects fugitive slaves as part of the Underground Railroad. In an opening that parallels *The Quaker City*'s chapter "The Outcasts of the Quaker City," in which Devil-Bug presides over a motley group of the multiracial poor in a burlesque of Congress, *New York*'s chapter "Below Five Points" convenes with an ironic comparison of the Black Senate to the U.S. Senate: "This is the Black Senate, which has met for business tonight, in this den, two stories under ground. Its deliberations, in point of decorum, may well compare with some other senates,—one in especial, where 'Liar!' is occasionally called, fisticuffs exchanged, knives and pistols drawn; and it embraces representatives from all parts of the Union."[19] The light-hearted tone turns serious, however, as the fugitive slaves recount their desperate strategies of resistance on the Southern plantation, and narrate their daring modes of escape to the North.

Like Frederick Douglass's argument two years later in *My Bondage and My Freedom* that slaves cannot be accused of stealing under an immoral system like slavery, Lippard has a fugitive slave defend taking one of the master's pigs: "One day, in de 'baccy field, dis nigga says to hisself, says he, 'Dat are pig b'longs to massa, so does dis nigga. Dis nigga kill dat pig un eat 'um—dat be stealin'? Lordy Moses—no!

It only be puttin' one ting dat b'longs to massa into anoder ting dat also b'longs to massa:—dat's philosophy."[20] The heavy dialect, which is consistent with the less subversive form of minstrelsy coopted by the middle class in the early 1850s, is offset by the slave's sound reasoning and literate Old Royal's orderly presiding over the group, with "book in one hand and paper and pencil before him."[21] Lippard's blend of dialect and minstrel humor to represent the defiant Black Senate reflects critic Paul Gilmore's insight that "becoming a mass cultural form neither completely drained minstrelsy of all of its antislavery content nor totally eradicated its evocation of cross-racial identification."[22]

Lippard encourages his readers to sympathize with the fugitive slaves when Harry Royalton and Bloodhound stumble into the Black Senate's headquarters, hidden below Five Points in a literal manifestation of the Underground Railroad. Many contemporary readers would have been aware of the violence awaiting the returned fugitive slave from accounts publicized in abolitionist newspapers like the *Liberator* and the dailies. William Wells Brown's *Clotel,* published in the same month as Lippard's *New York,* draws on a sensational report from the *Free Trader* newspaper out of Natchez, Mississippi, to highlight the risks that fugitive slaves take when they flee. In chapter three, "The Negro Chase," Brown details how slave-hunters pursued two runaway slaves with dogs, and when they are caught but resist, one man is tied to a tree and burned alive. The newspaper account, which Brown quotes from, details how the slave "sent forth cries of agony painful to the ear, begging some one to blow his brains out." When he manages to burst the chains that secured him to the tree, members of the "Lynch court" finally do shoot the man. Then "he was picked up by some two or three, and again thrown into the fire, and consumed, not a vestige remaining to show that such a being ever existed."[23] Brown's integration of such horrific incidents makes clear the high stakes facing slaves who risk their lives to reach freedom in the North, and provides context for Lippard's portrayal of the callous slavecatcher Bloodhound and the terrified fugitives.

After Randolph arrives at the Black Senate and takes away his half brother, Harry, in the vain hope of rekindling their fraternal bond,

Bloodhound is left alone with the Black Senate. Carl Ostrowski reads the ensuing slaying of Bloodhound under Old Royal's watch as an indication that Lippard could not imagine blacks governing themselves and meting out justice fairly. Ostrowski writes, "The novel invokes a racialist assumption that while a white vigilante court [of Ten Millions] might be governed by reason and moderation, a black one, motivated by vengeance, would move swiftly toward uncontrolled, retributive justice. Absent a white judge governing his actions, Old Royal can no longer be counted on to limit punishment conscientiously to thirty-nine lashes."[24] While the slavecatcher's killing is graphic, the fugitive slaves, terrified of returning to slavery, which Douglass and Brown caution will end in torture and death, recognize in Bloodhound their tormenter and a personification of the corrupt Fugitive Slave Law. The fugitives exclaim, "'He stole me fader!' 'He took me mother from Fildelfy and sold her down south.' 'He kidnapped my little boy.' 'Dam kidnapper! he stole my wife!'"[25] Given the danger of this Underground Railroad station becoming exposed and their fear of being returned to slavery, the fugitives fulfill Douglass's warning that "the slave-hunter will be here to bear the chained slave back, or he will be murdered in your streets."[26] That Lippard sympathized with the fugitive slaves, including their violence against Bloodhound, is made clear when Dr. Fulmer, the white judge of the Court of Ten Millions who functions as the novel's moral barometer, writes in a letter to Randolph, "I have learned all that occurred last night,—the attack made on you by your brother,—your magnanimous conduct,—the awful, although richly deserved death of Bloodhound, his atrocious tool."[27]

A suggestive cross-racial correspondence is evident in Lippard's description of the slavecatcher's death, as it resonates with published accounts of the *Creole* mutiny of November 7, 1841, which William Lloyd Garrison reprinted in the *Liberator* from the New Orleans *Advertiser.* While there is no hard evidence that Lippard read the *Liberator* or Douglass's *The Heroic Slave,* published approximately one year before *New York,* it is plausible that Lippard was familiar with reports of the *Creole* uprising, given his immersion in the print culture of his time and his growing antislavery sentiment. In *New York,*

Lippard sensationally describes Bloodhound's killing: "But every shriek only seemed to give new fire to the rage of the negroes; and gathering closer round the miserable man, they lifted their knives, dripping with his blood, and struck and struck again, until his cries were still. As he uttered the last cry, he sprang madly into light, for a moment, shook his bloody hands above his head, and then fell to rise no more."[28] In the *Liberator*'s reprinted report of the slaying of John Hewell, the slaveowner's hired agent aboard the *Creole,* the captain describes how the mutineers killed Hewell after he fired a musket and tried to stab them. "He advanced, and they fell upon him with clubs, handspikes, and knives. He was knocked down and stabbed in not less than twenty places; but he rose, got away from them, and staggered back to the cabin, exclaiming, 'I am dead—the negroes have killed me!'"[29] The dramatic resonances between these two killings—the frenzied stabbing by desperate slaves, the rising and falling of the fatally wounded white victim—highlight the power reversal between agents of the slave power and the desperate slave. Sensationalism, a cornerstone of city-mystery writing, and graphic representations of violence converge in these resonant passages to remind Northern readers how, in Harriet E. Wilson's words, "slavery's shadows fall even there."[30]

Cross-Racial Correspondence: Plotting the Hemings-Jefferson Affair

On September 1, 1802, disgruntled political journalist and pamphleteer James Callender, who was stinging from President Thomas Jefferson's decision not to name him postmaster of Richmond, first circulated in print the salacious rumor that Jefferson had fathered children with his black slave Sally Hemings. Callender writes in the *Richmond Recorder,* "It is well known that the man, *whom it delighteth the people to honor,* keeps, and for many years past has kept, as his concubine, one of his own slaves. Her name is SALLY . . . By this wench Sally, our president has had several children. There is not an individual in the neighborhood of Charlottesville who does not believe the story;

and not a few who know it."[31] Although the editorial did not catch fire and humiliate Jefferson as Callender had intended, the rumor of Jefferson's interracial relations with Hemings would continue to circulate in abolitionist newspapers during the antebellum period. For instance, the anonymously penned poem "Jefferson's Daughter," first published in *Tait's Edinburgh Magazine* in 1839, was reprinted in the *Liberator* twice in the 1840s and in Douglass's *North Star* in 1848. In the poem, the speaker laments, "The daughter of Jefferson sold for a slave! / The child of a freeman for dollars and francs!"[32] As part of his editorial rebuttal in *Frederick Douglass' Paper* in 1852 to a *New York Tribune* article supporting colonization, Douglass highlights the hypocrisy between Jefferson's racist claims about blacks' moral inferiority in his 1785 *Notes on the State of Virginia* and his affair with Hemings. "It is a well known fact that Mr. Jefferson attached so little importance to these grand speculations himself, as to have entirely disregarded them in his practice. It is notoriously true that *grand-children* of our Democratic, and philosophical President are now wearing the chains of slavery in the Southern States."[33] Twenty-first-century historians like Annette Gordon-Reed have investigated the compelling evidence of the affair, and, according to geneticist Eugene A. Foster as reported by Robert S. Levine, DNA testing of Hemings's descendants in 1998 "demonstrated all but conclusively that Thomas Jefferson was the father of Hemings's youngest son, Eston."[34] Most recently, in June 2018, the Thomas Jefferson Foundation released a formal statement, "Monticello Affirms Thomas Jefferson Fathered Children with Sally Hemings," and has created an exhibit titled "The Life of Sally Hemings" that treats the rumor as settled historical fact.[35]

While in my view the modern scientific inquiry confirms the affair, what is more important to my purposes is that contemporary Northern abolitionists treated it as fact, and black writers like William Wells Brown and white labor advocates like George Lippard integrated the Jefferson-Hemings relationship as a plot device in their major works. In yet another example of cross-racial correspondence between early African American literature and white sensational fiction, Brown's *Clotel* and Lippard's *New York,* published only weeks apart at the end of 1853 on different sides of the Atlantic Ocean, employ the rumored affair in order to develop their shared critiques of chattel slavery, the Fugitive Slave Law, and class stratification.[36] Although historians believe the Hemings slaves were freed after Jefferson's death in 1826, Brown and Lippard fictionalize the couple's descendants as fugitive slaves in order to allegorize an indictment of the nation for failing to live up to its founding ideals of liberty and equality. The stark irony that a beloved president had sired children with a young slave woman literalized for middle-class abolitionists like Brown and working-class antislavery advocates like Lippard the glaring contradiction between the nation's democratic ideals and the harsh realities of chattel and "wage" slavery.

William Wells Brown was born a slave on a Kentucky plantation in 1814, and, after escaping from his new owner Enoch Price of St. Louis and safely reaching Cleveland in 1834, he worked as a steamboatsman on part of the Underground Railroad sailing fugitives across Lake Erie to Canada. Once he moved his family to Buffalo, New York, in 1836, Brown became active in middle-class temperance societies and worked the lecture circuit for the Western New York Anti-Slavery Society and later the Massachusetts Anti-Slavery Society. During the five years Brown and his family spent in England, from 1849 to 1854, Brown gave hundreds of abolitionist lectures and published a travel book in 1852 called *Three Years in Europe* and then *Clotel* in 1853. In "A Memoir of the Author" that precedes the text of *Three Years in Europe*, English abolitionist William Farmer relates Brown's attempt to start an industrial school to improve the material conditions for African Americans relocated to Canada. "Although a residence in Canada is infinitely preferable to slavery in America, yet the climate of that country is uncongenial to the constitutions of the fugitive slaves, and their lack of education is an almost insuperable barrier to their social progress. The latter evil Mr. Brown attempted to remedy by the establishment of a Manual Labour School in Canada."[37] Like Frederick Douglass's plans to found an industrial college in Rochester, New York, in 1853 for black and white youth, Brown's good intentions were never rewarded with sufficient financial support, but they reveal his concern for the black working class and his respect for honest labor. Brown returned to America after his freedom was purchased by Ellen Richardson, the same woman who helped secure Douglass's freedom in 1846, and he continued his career as an author and lecturer until his death in 1884.

Brown wrote *Clotel* in the early 1850s while living in England. The novel, which draws on the Jefferson-Hemings relationship for its antislavery critique, opens with the Sally Hemings character, named Currer, and her two daughters, Clotel and Althesa, being sold into slavery following the death of Jefferson, who is referenced in the book's subtitle ("The President's Daughter") and acknowledged by name in chapter one: "Thus closed a negro sale, at which two daughters of Thomas Jefferson, the writer of the Declaration of Independence, and one of the presidents of the great republic, were disposed of to the highest bidder." The novel follows the tragic lives of the three women: Currer dies in slavery of yellow fever; Clotel, fleeing slavecatchers, commits suicide by jumping into the Potomac River rather than be captured; and after Althesa and her white husband, a slaveowner, die of yellow fever, their two children are sold into slavery and die young. The daughters' and granddaughters' illustrious heritage does little to protect them from the cruel vagaries of chattel slavery, as the narrator reminds readers: "Thus died Clotel, the daughter of Thomas Jefferson, a president of the United States; a man distinguished as the author of the Declaration of Independence, and one of the first statesmen of that country."[38] For Brown, the rumored cross-racial affair between Jefferson and Hemings might not have been an established historical fact, but it was a powerful symbol of American hypocrisy. The fact that both quotes link Jefferson to his Declaration of Independence, which Frederick Douglass interpreted as an antislavery document, underscores in *Clotel* the gulf between the nation's purported exceptionalism and the harsh realities of chattel slavery.

Brown's focus on the Jefferson-Hemings affair also informs his novel's dramatic allegory involving the country's founding. As part of a class-inflected celebration of honest labor, Brown describes the November 1620 arrival of the *Mayflower*: "Here in this ship are great and good men. Justice, mercy, humanity, respect for the rights of all;

each man honored, as he was useful to himself and others; labour respected, law-abiding men, constitution-making and respecting men." By way of contrast to the parent of Northern "labour-honouring" institutions like the *Mayflower*, the Dutch slave-ship carrying the first African slaves that arrives on the very same day (per a bit of authorial license) in Jamestown, Virginia, is "the mother of slavery, idleness, lynch-law, ignorance, unpaid labor, poverty, and dueling, despotism, the ceaseless swing of the whip, and the peculiar institutions of the South. These ships are the representation of good and evil in the New World, even to our day."[39] Although the passage invokes free labor ideology that could alienate the working classes, who had grievances against the industrial marketplace, Brown's emphasis on "poverty" and "idleness," the latter a common signifier for the corrupt wealthy class in city-mystery fiction, contains artisan republican accents with broad appeal.

Whereas Brown's use of the Jefferson-Hemings affair in *Clotel* is fairly straightforward and well established among critics in African American literature, Lippard's use of the illicit relationship has received far less scholarly attention. Though Eric Lott states that in *New York*, Randolph's and Esther's grandfather could be "Thomas Jefferson, perhaps," and Shelley Streeby notes that "Lippard hints that Randolph . . . is a descendant of Thomas Jefferson," neither critic develops the line of inquiry or performs a comparative analysis of how the affair functions as a shared strategy of protest in *Clotel* and *New York*.[40] Like Brown, Lippard employs the rumored affair in *The Empire City* and especially in the expanded version of *New York* to protest the Fugitive Slave Law and chattel slavery, to challenge the myth of American exceptionalism through an allegory involving the *Mayflower*'s arrival, and to imagine the potential for cross-racial love and friendship embodied in the interracial relationship. Although Lippard's social critique in *New York* focuses on "wage" slavery far more than Brown's novel takes up Northern labor exploitation, the two authors' use of the Jefferson-Hemings affair converges in their shared indictment of the nation's shortcomings in 1853.

Evidence that Lippard was well aware of the rumored affair and its potential to mount social critique appears in his best-selling novel

The Quaker City, published eight years before *New York.* In "Key to The Quaker City; or, The Monks of Monk-Hall," a short piece he appended to the 1845 edition of the novel, Lippard provides further information about the main characters and their purported correlation to real-life figures. In reference to Devil-Bug, Lippard writes, "Who was Devil-Bug? Among 'the Revelation of the secret life of Philadelphia,' on which this work is founded, there is a singular document, which *states that Devil-Bug was the illegitimate child of a world-renowned statesman.*"[41] Lippard does not name Jefferson specifically, but the allusion is suggestive and has important implications for the novel's class and racial politics. Lippard's linking his class-accented hero to the Jefferson-Hemings affair not only reinforces Devil-Bug's blackness and tragic ostracism from society within the novel, but also provides evidence outside the novel of a white labor reformer helping to circulate and preserve the rumor in 1840s print culture.

As already shown in this chapter, Lippard protested the Fugitive Slave Law in *New York* through his portrayals of the sympathetic multiracial fugitive slave siblings Randolph and Esther Royalton; their dissipated and hateful slaveowner and brother Harry Royalton; and the coarse Bloodhound, whose slaying documents the violence associated with slavery that was increasingly imported to the North. But Lippard's representation of Randolph and Esther takes on greater thematic significance when he strongly hints that Thomas Jefferson is the tragic pair's deceased grandfather. Hiding in a mansion in New York City from Harry and Bloodhound and debating what they should do next, Randolph rejects Esther's suggestion that they flee the United States. Randolph cites their heritage as he shows Esther a miniature of their grandfather, whose features are visible in their slave-mother Herodia, and states, "Esther, we are the grandchildren of the man whose name is on the lips of the civilized world. Our mother was *his* child. *His* blood flows in our veins." Figured as Jefferson's daughter, Lippard's Herodia is like Brown's Clotel, and Randolph and Esther are like Clotel's daughter, Mary, who escapes slavery and experiences a bittersweet ending, married but exiled abroad. Randolph invokes the horrific violence of chattel slavery that befall Clotel and Mary when he continues, "Now let them cut and hack and maim us: let them lash us at the whipping-post, or sell us in the slave mart. Lash on! lash on! But remember, you are inflicting this torture upon no common slaves; for your whip at every blow is stained with the blood of——."[42] In depicting the Jefferson-Hemings affair, Lippard does not describe Herodia's mother, who would be the Hemings figure; however, like Brown in *Clotel,* he uses the illicit relationship to reinforce a broad critique of American society.

While less direct than Brown's stark contrast between the *Mayflower* and the Dutch slave-ship, Lippard roots *New York*'s inheritance plot, a common feature in city-mysteries, in the founding of the country. The Van Huyden estate, for which seven heirs contend throughout *New York,* has swelled to one hundred million dollars by the novel's setting in 1844. Lippard traces the Van Huyden family back to its arrival on Manhattan Island in 1620, and, given the well-known fact that the Dutch were largely responsible for early settlements in what would become New York state, it is possible that Lippard might be conflating the *Mayflower* in Massachusetts and the Dutch slave-ship in Virginia. "Between the pillars appear, upon the paneled walls, portraits of the Van Huyden family, in frames of oak, and walnut, and gilt, for seven generations; beginning with the grim face of THE ANCESTOR, who landed on Manhattan Island in the year 1620." This implied dual critique of "wage" and chattel slavery gains credence when Lippard's mouthpiece in the novel, the Herculean white mechanic and cobbler Arthur Dermoyne, announces his great hope for America: "May be the day will come when, gifted with wealth, I can enter the workshops of Philadelphia, and say to the workmen, 'Come, brothers. Here is CAPITAL. Let us go to the west. Let us find a spot of God's earth unpolluted by white or black slavery . . . And there,—oh, my God!—there will we, without priest, or monopolist, or slaveholder, establish in the midst of a band of brothers, the worship of that Christ who was himself a workman, even as he is now, the workman's God."[43] By alluding in *New York* to major historical events like the landing of the *Mayflower* and, obliquely, the arrival of the Dutch slave-ship, and by referencing national heroes like Thomas Jefferson as well as the rumored affair with Sally Hemings, Lippard makes his critique of growing class divisions in the North and chattel slavery in the South all the more exigent.

As we will see in the next section, William Wells Brown and Frederick Douglass balanced their militant endorsement of antislavery violence with portraits of cross-racial love and friendship as well as strategies for cross-racial solidarity with poor whites in the fight to end chattel slavery. Similarly, through his use of the Jefferson-Hemings affair, Lippard in *New York* suggests an ambitious if unrealized path to ending racial strife in America: miscegenation. Race-mixing, one of the most controversial elements of antebellum race relations among pro-slavery advocates and abolitionists alike, appears to be Lippard's panacea to stave off Jefferson's fears of a race war. In defending a proposal to colonize freed slaves, Jefferson writes, "Deep rooted prejudices entertained by the whites; ten thousand recollections, by the blacks, of the injuries they have sustained; new provocations; the real distinctions which nature has made; and many other circumstances, will divide us into parties, and produce convulsions which will probably never end but in the extermination of the one or the other race."[44] In what amounts to a response to Jefferson's prophecy nearly seven decades earlier, Lippard has Jefferson pass down to Herodia's firstborn son a secret solution, what Randolph tells Esther is, "an awful trust—of a work which, well fulfilled, will secure the happiness of all the races who people the American continent." The solution, never named outright, is referenced a second time when Randolph finds a letter from Jefferson directing that important information reach his grandson: "That packet contains matters which, carried into action by such a son, would do much, yes, everything, to establish the happiness of all the races on this continent."[45] What action is Lippard intimating? Is it the public revelation that Jefferson is the father of the slave girl Herodia, Randolph's mother, and thus an implicit endorsement of race-mixing? Given Lippard's bold integration of the Jefferson-Hemings affair and his sympathetic portrayal of race-mixing through the experiences of Randolph and Esther, it is plausible that in *New York* Lippard is asking his white and black working-class readers of the North to imagine a world in which love trumps racial difference.

Robert S. Levine notes that by representing a series of cross-racial relationships, *Clotel* "suggests that interracial love is possible, and that individuals have the potential to see their way past culturally inscribed racial boundaries and hierarchies. Nevertheless, Brown realistically emphasizes how such individuals are eventually destroyed by these hierarchies."[46] Similarly, in *New York,* Lippard qualifies the potential for interracial love through a dark and tragic outcome for Randolph and his white love interest, Eleanor Lynn. In *The Empire City,* the earlier version of *New York,* Lippard provides the couple with a blissful ending, as they marry and move to Italy with Esther and Eleanor's father, Bernard. In a striking passage describing a white bigot overcoming his race prejudice, Lippard writes, "Bernard Lynn,—the aristocrat,—the man of wealth, places his hand upon the head of the White Slave, and calls him—*son!* This he does, knowing the taint in his blood,—of the chains which a brother has power to fasten on his limbs; but, sweeping from his heart all the prejudices of birth and education, he sees before him, not a creature branded by descent from a race which some have classed with brutes,—but simply Randolph Royalton."[47] But such optimism is not to be found at the end of *New York.* Randolph, the fugitive slave, is terrified that the Lynns will discover his mixed-race background, allegorized as a "phantom shape" that dogs him like Bloodhound hunts him through the city.[48] When Harry reveals the secret to Eleanor's father, Bernard Lynn does not overcome his prejudice as he does in *The Empire City* but cancels the wedding in a rage; in turn, Randolph, psychologically unstable, drugs and rapes the young woman. Like the most corrupt aristocratic libertines of Lippard's city-mystery fiction, the desperate and haunted fugitive slave Randolph, once humiliated and rejected by racist whites, turns to sexual violence. Lippard's daring commentary about race in *New York* is clear: While Northerners are justified in resisting the Fugitive Slave Law with violence and should work to end chattel slavery in the South and "wage slavery" in the North, overcoming whites' deep-seated race prejudice would require a far more complex, long-term, and, at least for the present, elusive solution.

Courting the White Working Class, Potential Antislavery Allies

As the previous two sections have shown, white-authored sensational fiction and early African American literature advocated justified antislavery violence to resist the Fugitive Slave Law and employed the cross-racial relationship between Jefferson and Hemings to mount a class-accented critique of chattel slavery in the South and "wage" slavery in the North. Although they emphasized one form of oppression over the other to their constituent readers, white and black authors increasingly in the 1850s insisted that poor whites—whether in the North or the South—had a crucial role in helping to end all forms of oppression plaguing the nation. The 1850s writing of George Lippard, William Wells Brown, Herman Melville, and Frederick Douglass develops social critique through exposing prevailing representations of the white poor as ignorant and backwards, appealing foremost to the material needs of the poor rather than spiritual needs, and representing whites as capable of overcoming their race prejudice. Taken together, these authors' class-accented strategies refute the image of poor whites as "white trash" and reimagine them as potential allies in the fight to end chattel slavery.

As part of their dual critiques of "wage" and chattel slavery, an array of white and black authors in the 1850s protested mainstream portrayals of the working classes that sentimentalized and condescended to the poor. A broad cross-racial correspondence emerged among white and black authors committed to condemning labor exploitation in the North and the South, from George Lippard and Harriet E. Wilson to Herman Melville and William Wells Brown. In *New York,* Lippard draws attention to the way the theater and literature tend to mock the working poor. The white mechanic hero and cobbler Arthur Dermoyne tells the corrupt minister Herman Barnhurst, "As for the shoemaker . . . what of him? He is a serf, a slave, a Pariah. On the stage no joke is so piquant as the one which is leveled at the 'tailor,' or the 'cobbler;' in literature, the attempt of an unknown to elevate himself, is matter for a brutal laugh."[49] Six years later, in her novel *Our Nig,* Wilson confronts middle-class moralists who are quick to judge the weak and less fortunate members of society. Detailing the ostracism and poverty suffered by the fallen white woman Mag Smith, Wilson writes, "Who can tell what numbers, advancing just far enough to hear a cold welcome and join in the reserved converse of professed reformers, disappointed, disheartened, have chosen to dwell in unclean places, rather than encounter these 'holier-than-thou' of the great brotherhood of man!"[50] Critics have speculated that Wilson's unrelenting critique of Northern race prejudice is one factor that caused the novel to go quickly out of print in 1859, despite its having been published in the abolitionist hotbed of Boston, and critics P. Gabrielle Foreman and Reginald H. Pitts have noted Wilson's "sardonic tone that seethes just beneath the narrative's surface."[51] Exploring the convergence of anti-capitalist discourse and proslavery propaganda in *Our Nig,* literary critic David Dowling concludes, "Wilson's harrowing life story does prove that proslavery's depictions of northern working conditions . . . were not exaggerated, as Wilson exposes how oppressive many of those 'liberators' really were who so closely resembled the dominating and exploitative northern capitalists."[52] Wilson's frustration with middle-class condescension toward the poor is palpable when she writes, "Such was Mag's experience; and disdaining to ask favor or friendship from a sneering world, she resolved to shut herself up in a hovel."[53] The protest against class representation in *New York* and *Our Nig* constitutes a cross-racial correspondence that also resonates with the writing of Melville and Brown.

Critiques of representations of the poor who are specifically rural and white correspond in Melville's class-inflected diptych short story "Poor Man's Pudding and Rich Man's Crumbs" and Brown's antislavery novel *Clotel.* Melville's story appeared in the June 1854 issue of *Harper's New Monthly Magazine,* a periodical that literary critic Sheila Post-Lauria characterizes as "aiming to please all segments of the middle class" with its "family-oriented, entertaining, and moralistic fiction." That Melville published the story in *Harper's* is surprising, given the sharp irony directed at the middle-class narrator and his friend, a privileged and obtuse family man aptly named Blandmour. On a visit to Blandmour's country house, the narrator goes for a stroll and visits the lower-class Coulter family to test out his host's paternalistic belief that "through kind Nature, the poor, out of their very poverty, extract comfort." According to Blandmour, for instance, when the poor lack eggs for a recipe, they simply substitute with a "cup of cold rain water, which acts as leaven"; hence, a "Poor Man's Egg." However, when the Coulters invite the narrator to stay for dinner and serve him a plain meal that he refers to as "Poor Man's Pudding," they are insulted and become silent, leading to the reflective narrator's insight about the ways the middle classes conspire to assuage their class guilt.[54]

The narrator's reflections at the end of "Poor Man's Pudding," the first half of the diptych, call attention to the paradox of abject poverty in a mighty nation in the same way that abolitionists noted the irony of chattel slavery in a proud republic. "The native American poor never lose their delicacy or pride; hence, though unreduced to the physical degradation of the European pauper, they yet suffer more in mind than the poor of any other people in the world."[55] Careful to compare the American white poor's degradation to the English working classes rather than to chattel slaves, as pro-slavery advocates and some city-mystery writers were doing, Melville's narrator implicates American exceptionalist ideology in the poor's suffering in a way that calls up the stark contrast between democratic ideals and the institution of slavery.[56] According to the narrator, American exceptionalism causes more suffering "by furnishing [the poor] with the keenest appreciation of the smarting distinction between their ideal of universal equality and their grind-stone experience of the practical misery and infamy of poverty."[57] Published one year before Melville's antislavery critique in *Benito Cereno,* "Poor Man's Pudding and Rich Man's Crumbs" provides a sympathetic portrayal of the white working class and an indictment of the middle and upper classes without using the "white slavery" rhetoric that could compromise the antislavery protest of city-mystery fiction and rile abolitionists.

Melville's critique of class paternalism is instructive for appreciating *Clotel*'s similarly sympathetic portrayal of poor rural whites in the South as part of Brown's economic critique of chattel slavery and his cross-racial appeal to potential lower-class allies. While I agree with Katie Frye's assertion that *Clotel*'s "representation of whiteness rebukes racism by showing the destructivity, fragility, and instability of white ideology," Brown's appeals to cross-racial sympathy with poor Southern whites also reveal the middle-class underpinnings of that dominant ideology.[58] In the chapter "The Poor Whites, South," the missionary Hontz Snyder, a descendant of "the oldest Dutch families" in New York, which links him with Brown's critique of the first Dutch slave-ship, explains to Carlton, a fellow visitor to the Peck plantation, how he makes weekly visits to poor whites in the area. Like the narrator's visit to the Coulter family in Melville's "Poor Man's Pudding and Rich Man's Crumbs," Snyder is stunned by the physical degradation he encounters at the poor whites' unkempt abode: "It was a low loghut, and yet it was the best house in that locality. The woman and nine children were there, and the geese, ducks, chickens, pigs, and children were all running about the floor." Just as Mrs. Coulter resists the middle-class narrator's attempts to sentimentalize her family with "Poor Man's" euphemisms, the woman Snyder visits is resentful and appears to mock him. A professional missionary come to proselytize to the poor, Snyder greets the woman with, "I am hunting up the lost sheep of the house of Israel," to which she responds literally, "Well, you have a hard time to find 'em here. My husband lost an old ram last week, and he ain't found him yet, and he's hunted every day." Snyder's judgmental view of the poor whites as degraded and backwards is reinforced in his observation to Carlton, "It was some time before any of the children would come near me; one remained under the bed (which, by the way, was in the same room), all the while I was there." Synder's unnecessary parenthetical aside reveals his elitist view as much as it does the cramped state of the family's quarters or the children's fear of strangers. Although the text satirizes Snyder's haughty treatment of both the black slaves, who resist his attempts to interpret the Bible as sanctioning slavery, and the poor whites, he nevertheless is the one who argues that slave labor is the cause of the whites' degradation: "'You see,' replied Snyder, 'no white man is respectable in these slave states who works for a living. No community can be prosperous, where honest labor is not honored.'"[59] Like Melville's white, middle-class narrator, Snyder seems to have gained insight from his walking tour and helps Brown to express a free labor argument with an artisan republican appeal to honest labor.

As part of their shared cross-racial economic critique of "wage" and chattel slavery, Lippard, Douglass, Wilson, and Brown insist that the poor's material needs are as important as their spiritual needs. In contrast to the sentimental treatment of poverty in reform texts as well as the moral suasion and Christian typology of abolitionist texts of the period, these authors subordinate spiritual matters to material conditions. In Lippard's *The Empire City,* white mechanic Arthur Dermoyne is called an "infidel" by the corrupt minister Barnhurst, who tells his friend, an equally corrupt politician and banker, "Why, the fellow had the impertinence, no longer than a week ago, at the house of an intimate friend, to tell me that the Savior came to lift the masses from *temporal* as well as *spiritual* degradation."[60] As part of a pattern of insisting on relieving the poor's material needs, Lippard had lionized Quaker and social reformer Lucretia Mott a year earlier in his serial *Memoirs of a Preacher; or, The Mysteries of the Pulpit* in the thinly disguised character named Martha Lott. Consistent with his focus on ameliorating the suffering of the multiracial poor in Philadelphia, Lippard describes the Quaker's reputation as a pragmatic reformer when she visits a sick woman on her deathbed: "She was an Infidel—maybe an Atheist—her daily walks of life, it is true, defied, even sanctified scandal, but her belief, O! the belief of Martha Lott was terrible. It was even whispered she had said, that it was much better to feed the bodies of the poor, before you attempted to save their souls."[61] As a testament to his growing antislavery position, in a novel like *Memoirs of a Preacher* that exposes the duplicity and immorality of silver-tongued evangelical preachers, Lippard extols the virtues of a plain-speaking Quaker woman who was active in the abolitionist movement and ministered to the poor.

The contrast Lippard draws between humble Quakers and fiery evangelicals has a subtle correspondence in Douglass's novella *The Heroic Slave.* The "noble fugitive" Madison Washington, hiding in a tree in the woods, seeks assistance from an older slave he sees below.

Washington is willing to risk revealing himself to the old man after watching him pray quietly to himself. Desperately hungry for food, Washington asks the old man to purchase and return with crackers and cheese. Washington's reasoning is consistent with city-mysteries' suspicion of ostentatious display in the new urban environment: "He had already gained my confidence; as how could it be otherwise? I knew enough of religion to know that the man who prays in secret is far more likely to be sincere than he who loves to pray standing in the street, or in the great congregation."[62] Lippard and Douglass clearly align Quakerism and modest Christianity against evangelicalism and outward display, reinforcing their texts' cross-racial protest and focus on the material needs of the poor. Similarly, Wilson's *Our Nig,* a text preoccupied with class difference and labor exploitation, attributes the choices of Frado and her mother, Mag, foremost to economic necessity. Henry Louis Gates Jr. was the first critic to point out that in Wilson's novel, "Frado never truly undergoes a religious transformation, merely the *appearance* of one; as the text emphasizes, 'a devout and Christian exterior invited confidence from the villagers.'"[63] Skepticism that religious enthusiasm—often viewed as a self-serving performance—can succor the poor is a far-ranging cross-racial correspondence among white-authored sensational fiction and African American literature of the 1850s.

With their focus on the material needs of the oppressed, both Lippard's *New York* and Brown's *Clotel* invoke a Christ figure who identifies with the downtrodden. In *New York,* the white mechanic Dermoyne, who is committed to finding a place for laborers that is free of "wage" and chattel slavery, invokes a Christ figure that sympathizes with the poor. Dermoyne chastises professional clergyman Barnhurst for laughing at his being a cobbler, "as though the master you profess to serve, was not himself, one day, a workman at the carpenter's bench." Lippard's Christ of the Poor does not tolerate the abuses wrought by industrial capitalism and chattel slavery, as Dermoyne wants to create a utopia for the "worship of that Christ who was himself, a workman, even as he is now, the workman's God."[64] In *Clotel,* Georgiana Peck, who eventually marries a Northerner and frees her slaves, invokes the

Christ of the Poor in a heated debate with her father. Countering his claim that the Bible sanctions slavery, Georgiana argues, "And as for Christ, his whole life was a living testimony against slavery and all that it inculcates. When he designed to do us good, he took upon himself the form of a servant. He took his station at the bottom of society. He voluntarily identified himself with the poor and the despised."[65] Although Georgiana does not convince her father to renounce slavery, only to stop claiming that the Bible sanctions it, the young woman's appeal to a humble Christ figure who cares for "the poor" and "the despised" corresponds with Lippard's invocation of the carpenter Christ who would appeal to the multiracial working classes.

No other African American writer draws more effectively on city-mysteries to appeal to the working poor than Frederick Douglass. As an author who focused increasingly on the economic conditions of the multiracial poor in the North during the 1850s, Douglass uses Gothic imagery, artisan republicanism, and class-accented sensationalism to mount an economic critique of chattel slavery in his 1855 autobiography *My Bondage and My Freedom,* a major revision and expansion of his slave narrative published ten years earlier. These rhetorical strategies, which he combines with free labor ideology and hopeful anecdotes of whites overcoming their race prejudice, help Douglass to imagine and appeal to the white working classes as potential allies in the fight to end chattel slavery.

Douglass's class-inflected descriptions of setting in *My Bondage and My Freedom* are particularly detailed, deliberate, and thematically purposeful, demonstrating his arrival as an accomplished man of letters. Drawing on city-mysteries' Gothic descriptions of urban decay and class stratification, Douglass represents his birthplace, Talbot County on the eastern shore of Maryland, as a veritable wasteland, where free and honest labor is supplanted by chattel slavery. Known as Tuckahoe "to all Marylanders, black and white," the area "is seldom mentioned but with contempt and derision, on account of the barrenness of its soil, and the ignorance, indolence, and poverty of its people. Decay and ruin are everywhere visible." Douglass's frank depiction of the degraded white poor who live there is tempered in the subsequent paragraph when he imagines the hopeless economic conditions from their point of view. Douglass writes that he was born "in this dull, flat, and unthrifty district, or neighborhood, surrounded by a white population of the lowest order, indolent and drunken to a proverb, and among slaves, who seemed to ask, '*Oh! what's the use?*' every time they lifted a hoe." Douglass's depiction of the white poor is noteworthy for its sympathy, and he contrasts their condition with the inordinate wealth of the slave plantation through artisan republican rhetoric. In a scene resonant with the elaborate spread of food encountered by Ichabod Crane in Washington Irving's "The Legend of Sleepy Hollow," Douglass describes his master Colonel Lloyd's house adorned with European trappings and marked by unwholesome decadence. "The highly favored inmates of this mansion are literally arrayed 'in purple and fine linen,' and fare sumptuously every day! The table groans under the heavy and blood-bought luxuries gathered with pains-taking care, at home and abroad . . . Wines and brandies from France; teas of various flavor, from China; and rich, aromatic coffee from Java, all conspired to swell the tide of high life, where pride and indolence rolled and lounged in magnificence and satiety."[66] In a correspondence with city-mysteries' class critique of the aristocratic "upper ten" and sympathy for the "lower million," Douglass contrasts anti-republican slaveowners with their chattel slaves and impoverished non-slaveowning whites. While it is true the free labor critique of chattel slavery may overlook the effects of industrial capitalism in the North, Douglass's artisan republican critique gestures toward solidarity with the white working classes.

My Bondage and My Freedom draws explicitly on city-mysteries when Douglass, at age nine, is sent to live in the city of Baltimore with the Auld family, who are related to Colonel Lloyd through marriage. Like a newcomer to the labyrinthine city, Douglass reports how in Baltimore, "my country eyes and ears were confused and bewildered here." Initially alienated from the other boys, who would chase and tease him, Douglass, in the style of Benjamin Franklin, learns to navigate the urban space and to inspire sympathy from poor whites. Douglass ingeniously learns to read by soliciting help from white urchins, who, "for a single biscuit . . .

would give me a lesson more valuable to me than bread." However, it is not accurate to assume that Douglass does this through trickery and deception of poor whites who would not have otherwise assisted him; as he tells it, "Of all consciences, let me have those to deal with which have not been bewildered by the cares of life. I do not remember ever to have met with a *boy,* while I was in slavery, who defended the slave system; but I have often had boys to console me, with the hope that something would yet occur, by which I might be made free." Several years later, Douglass meets the older correlatives of these sympathetic poor whites as he works among Irish dockworkers on Baltimore's Fells Point. When Douglass tells the Irishmen that he is a slave, he describes their reaction: "They both had much to say about the matter, and expressed the deepest sympathy with me, and the most decided hatred of slavery. They went so far as to tell me that I ought to run away, and go to the north; that I should find friends there, and that I would be as free as anybody."[67] This experience contrasts markedly with the savage beating he endures years later on the Baltimore docks, but the fuller treatment he gives to the sympathy extended by these Irish workers in *My Bondage and My Freedom* as compared to the slave narrative shows the autobiography's stronger appeal to the white working class.

Douglass borrows further from city-mysteries as he describes his anxious and fateful experience with slave-breaker Covey in St. Michael's Village, another degraded area that "wore a dull, slovenly, enterprise-forsaken aspect." The term "bewildering," which does not appear in Douglass's 1845 slave narrative, appears four times in *My Bondage and My Freedom.* While Baltimore is initially "bewildering" to the greenhorn and life's trials "bewilder" the individual, Douglass describes his first experience as a field hand: "In my new employment I found myself even more awkward than a green country boy may be supposed to be, upon his first entrance into the bewildering scenes of city life." Douglass draws on the representational strategies of city-mystery writers, who appealed to their working-class readers' fears and anxiety toward an urban environment they perceived as mysterious, unpredictable, and dangerous. Furthermore, like many city-mystery villains who are not what they appear, the wiry and wolfish Covey is a duplicitous and crafty overseer. Rather than watch the slaves in an "open, manly and direct manner," Douglass describes how Covey would feign leaving the plantation, only to circle back and hide among bushes to observe the slaves. Covey "had the faculty of making us feel that he was always present. By a series of adroitly managed surprises, which he practiced, I was prepared to expect him at any moment." Like the most corrupt oxymoronic criminals populating city-mysteries, "No thief was ever more artful in his devices than this man Covey." As a result of Covey's deceit and brutality, Douglass describes himself as, "completely wrecked, changed and bewildered"—like the oppressed characters, whether fugitive slaves or the multiracial working poor, of white-authored city-mysteries.[68]

Douglass lays the foundation for an alliance with Southern poor whites in the same chapter that he details the brutal beating he received from racist white apprentices who refused to work with a black caulker in the Baltimore shipyards. In the chapter "Apprenticeship Life" Douglass attributes the white workers' hostility to broader workplace competition they were facing from slaves, "who work without wages." Douglass argues that "*the conflict of slavery with the interests of the white mechanics and laborers of the south*" will, in fact, "become an important element in the overthrow of the slave system." According to Douglass, the slaveowners, "with a craftiness peculiar to themselves," prevent poor whites from sympathizing with black slaves by "making the said white man almost as much a slave as the black slave himself . . . Both are plundered, and by the same plunderers."[69] Douglass's conviction that poor whites would need to play a role in overthrowing chattel slavery is echoed not only in city-mysteries' alliances among the multiracial working classes, but also in George Lippard's calls in the *Quaker City Weekly* to join the efforts to eradicate "wage" and chattel slavery.

Douglass further demonstrates his strategies for forming an alliance with working-class whites by closing *My Bondage and My Freedom* with two anecdotes in which whites overcome their race prejudice. Countering Thomas Jefferson's fears of a race war and at the same time reinforcing city-mysteries' representations of cross-racial friendships, Douglass rejects the assumption "that there is a natural, an inherent, and an invincible repugnance in the breast of the white race toward dark-colored people." Traveling on a crowded train from Boston to Albany, Douglass notices that no white person wants to sit in the open seat next to him. However, once Massachusetts governor George N. Briggs recognizes Douglass and sits next to him, "the despised seat now became honorable. His excellency had removed all the prejudice against sitting by the side of a negro; and upon his leaving it, as he did, on reaching Pittsfield, there were at least one dozen applicants for the place. The governor had, without changing my skin a single shade, made the place respectable which before was despicable." Similarly, while traveling on the Boston and New Bedford railroad, Douglass is denied an unoccupied seat by an indignant white man and is then approached by attorney and future Massachusetts governor John Henry Clifford. Douglass once worked as a servant in Clifford's home, and he describes the man in his text as holding a "pro-slavery position." Once their warm exchange is over, Douglass observes, "I found myself surrounded with friends," and he receives an apology, albeit "one of the lamest ever offered," from the rude passenger. Granted, Douglass is treated differently by the passengers only after the intervention of highly respected white men, but these hopeful incidents reflect his growing concern over blacks' working conditions in the North. Just one paragraph later, Douglass concludes his autobiography by declaring that "one of the best means of emancipating the slaves of the south is to improve and elevate the character of the free colored people of the north."[70] Given its appeals to the white working classes and its literary strategies resonant of city-mysteries, *My Bondage and My Freedom* reveals Douglass as a fierce antislavery advocate who gave increasing attention to broad working conditions in the North.

George Lippard's *Eleanor; or, Slave Catching in the Quaker City*

On January 5, 1854, the abolitionist newspaper the *National Era* announced that a "New Story by George Lippard" entitled *Eleanor* would appear in February in the *Philadelphia Sunday Mercury*. Although the

National Era was reluctant to recommend and praise lurid city-mysteries, as evidenced by their lukewarm review of Augustine Duganne's novel *The Knights of the Seal,* the editors endorsed the new story and compared it to Lippard's 1845 bestseller. Insisting on *Eleanor*'s accurate portrayal of slave-catching and ironizing Philadelphia's nickname with italics, they wrote, "The story is founded on *facts* connected with the operations of the Fugitive Slave Law in the city of *Brotherly Love,* and in point of interest is fully equal to Mr. Lippard's celebrated work, 'The Quaker City.'"[71] The novella, which spans sixteen chapters over seven installments between January 29, 1854, and March 12, 1854, in the Philadelphia weekly story paper, constitutes Lippard's most sustained and spirited attack against the Fugitive Slave Law and a final dual critique against "wage" and chattel slavery (see figure 3).

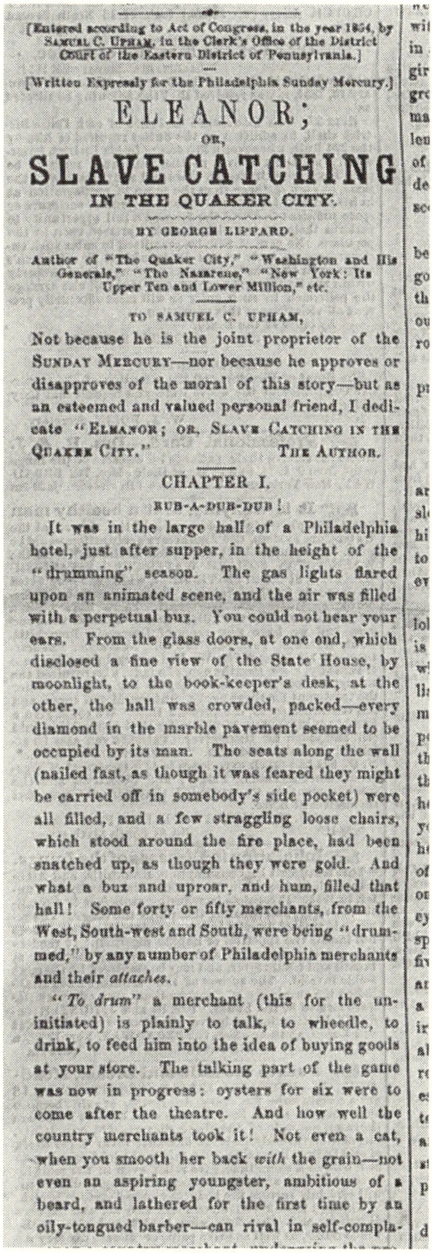

[Entered according to Act of Congress, in the year 1854, by Samuel C. Upham, in the Clerk's Office of the District Court of the Eastern District of Pennsylvania.]

[Written Expressly for the Philadelphia Sunday Mercury.]

ELEANOR;

OR,

SLAVE CATCHING

IN THE QUAKER CITY.

BY GEORGE LIPPARD.

Author of "The Quaker City," "Washington and His Generals," "The Nazarene," "New York: Its Upper Ten and Lower Million," etc.

TO SAMUEL C. UPHAM,

Not because he is the joint proprietor of the Sunday Mercury—nor because he approves or disapproves of the moral of this story—but as an esteemed and valued personal friend, I dedicate "Eleanor; or, Slave Catching in the Quaker City." The Author.

CHAPTER I.

RUB-A-DUB-DUB!

It was in the large hall of a Philadelphia hotel, just after supper, in the height of the "drumming" season. The gas lights flared upon an animated scene, and the air was filled with a perpetual buz. You could not hear your ears. From the glass doors, at one end, which disclosed a fine view of the State House, by moonlight, to the book-keeper's desk, at the other, the hall was crowded, packed—every diamond in the marble pavement seemed to be occupied by its man. The seats along the wall (nailed fast, as though it was feared they might be carried off in somebody's side pocket) were all filled, and a few straggling loose chairs, which stood around the fire place, had been snatched up, as though they were gold. And what a buz and uproar, and hum, filled that hall! Some forty or fifty merchants, from the West, South-west and South, were being "drummed," by any number of Philadelphia merchants and their *attaches*.

"*To drum*" a merchant (this for the uninitiated) is plainly to talk, to wheedle, to drink, to feed him into the idea of buying goods at your store. The talking part of the game was now in progress: oysters for six were to come after the theatre. And how well the country merchants took it! Not even a cat, when you smooth her back *with* the grain—not even an aspiring youngster, ambitious of a beard, and lathered for the first time by an oily-tongued barber—can rival in self-compla-

Figure 3. George Lippard, *Eleanor; or, Slave Catching in the Quaker City,* appearing in the *Philadelphia Sunday Mercury,* January 29, 1854, page one. Courtesy of the American Antiquarian Society.

Eleanor chronicles the harrowing tale of a young, multiracial fugitive slave woman living in Philadelphia, who is abducted by the coarse slave-catcher "Hell-bird," transported by carriage along the Lancaster turnpike and then by train to Baltimore for sale, pursued unsuccessfully by Herculean white mechanic hero Adam Smith on horseback, and ultimately rescued from a slave auction and adopted by an oxymoronic hero, the pistol-wielding "fighting Quaker" Elijah Carwin. Lippard's setting, the south-central Pennsylvania roadways along the Mason-Dixon line, was alive with abolitionist activity, as Frederick Douglass would testify one year later in *My Bondage and My Freedom:* Explaining his difficulty running away from his last owner, Hugh Auld, Douglass writes, "The railroad from Baltimore to Philadelphia was under regulations so stringent, that even *free* colored travelers were almost excluded"; moreover, "All the great turnpikes, leading northward, were beset with kidnappers."[72] Written from Lippard's deathbed as he was suffering from tuberculosis, *Eleanor* contains many of the working-class accents of city-mysteries, and in protesting the Fugitive Slave Law and developing an economic critique of chattel slavery, it shares significant correspondences with black-authored literature of the early 1850s.

The novella opens in the hall of a Philadelphia hotel, where merchants from the North and the South have gathered to "drum" one another, that is, Lippard informs the reader, "to wheedle, to drink, to feed him into the idea of buying goods at your store." Appalled at the capitalist excess on display throughout the room, Lippard's narrator reserves his greatest distaste and his most biting satire for the cozy alliance between the agents of "wage" and chattel slavery. "In another corner, are two lank men, with sharp faces, and little sparkling ferret eyes . . . There is such a look of low cunning and pure simple fiend-nature on each face. One is the overseer of a New England factory, managed on the 'screw system;' the other, a Southern negro trader. A sweet couple. It occurs to you, that a devil or two would complete this group; but it also occurs that there is no devil so low, or so reckless of his character, as to keep company with those who grind up human flesh until it comes out cotton."[73] This unsavory pairing echoes much city-mystery writing that routinely associates its aristocratic villains with labor exploitation in the North and slaveowning in the South.

In correspondence with African American literature of the early 1850s, Lippard represents chattel slavery as a system that corrupts and degrades everyone, including the whites who participate in it, such as Southern planter Blair Malcom, the white father of the fugitive slave Eleanor. Malcom visits sixty-five-year-old Quaker and wealthy farmer Elijah Carwin, who had agreed to watch over his son, Henry Malcom, who was attending medical school in Philadelphia. While informing Malcom that his son had fallen into gambling, forgery, and debt, and committed suicide only two months earlier, Carwin attributes the young man's dissipation to his upbringing on a New Orleans slave plantation. "'Had thee not,' [Carwin] said, in a low but firm voice, 'brought thy boy up in unlimited indulgence, accustomed to despotic control over every thing and every body around him, thee would not, now, mourn the forger and the suicide.'"[74] The moral degradation of whites who are involved in or exposed to chattel slavery resonates with observations made a decade earlier in Frederick Douglass's 1845 slave narrative. Writing about his slave-mistress in Baltimore, Sophia Auld, who had supported herself as a proud weaver before her marriage, Douglass describes her awful transformation as a result of participating in chattel slavery: "But, alas! this kind heart had but a short time to remain such. The fatal poison of irresponsible power was already in her hands, and soon commenced its infernal work. That cheerful eye, under the influence of slavery, soon became red with rage; that voice, made all of sweet accord, changed to one of harsh and horrid discord; and that angelic face gave place to that of a demon."[75] For white and black abolitionists, and for an antislavery labor reformer like Lippard, chattel slavery perverts and degrades the whites associated with it.

Elijah Carwin is Lippard's homage to Philadelphia writer Charles Brockden Brown, whose 1798 novel *Wieland* features a trickster and ventriloquist named Francis Carwin, who challenges the cultural assumptions of the privileged classes. Lippard felt strongly that Brown's Gothic writing was underappreciated; he published a short encomium to Brown in 1848 and dedicated the second edition of *The Quaker City* to him in 1849.[76] In *Eleanor,* Elijah Carwin voices the strongest arguments against the Fugitive Slave Law during a debate with Southern planter Malcom. Carwin opposes the law because it "blasphemes not only every line in the Bible, but every instinct of humanity." Relating a terrifying tale of the violence it imports to the North, Carwin speaks of arming his tenant farmers with pistols after they are attacked by a marauding band of slavecatchers—"human devils"—who believe they are harboring a fugitive slave.[77] Carwin's emphasis on how the Fugitive Slave Law makes visible firsthand the horrors of chattel slavery is consistent with Jeannine DeLombard's claim that abolitionists were appealing to eyewitness testimony in order to cultivate the increasing "legal spectatorship in the cheap press."[78] In response to Malcom's claim that Carwin must travel South and see slavery for himself before drawing any conclusions about the peculiar institution, the Quaker says, "We could not *all* of us go South, for the mere pleasure of counting the heads of your slaves . . . beside, the Fugitive Slave Law, supplies the whole North with knowledge on the subject of slavery. What sights it shows us!" Carwin goes on to recount fugitives being dragged through the streets and being shot at point-blank range in a river, a scene that echoes Douglass's description of overseer Austin Gore's killing of the resistant slave Demby on Colonel Lloyd's plantation. Lippard's description—"a black man, escaping from his pursuers, who hunt him through a quiet country town, takes refuge in a river, where the water is breast high, and is deliberately shot to death, by the human fiends who stand upon the river's bank"—owes something to Douglass's description nine years earlier—"to get rid of the scourging, [Demby] ran and plunged himself into a creek, and stood there at the depth of his shoulders, refusing to come out . . . Mr. Gore then, without consultation or deliberation with any one, not even giving Demby an additional call, raised his musket to his face, taking deadly aim at his standing victim, and in an instant poor Demby was no more."[79] Whether or not Lippard had read Douglass's popular slave narrative, both men appeal to readers' empathy through graphic depictions of violence against desperate slaves willing to risk their lives for freedom.

Lippard also endows Carwin with Revolutionary War spirit, echoing the class-accented heroes in his *Legends of the American Revolution* and Frederick Douglass's *The Heroic Slave*. When he races down the Lancaster turnpike in pursuit of the slavecatchers who have abducted Eleanor, Carwin follows in the footsteps of his father, who helped the colonists resist British tyranny. Carwin explains to Malcom, who assumes all Quakers are pacifists, that his father "was a friend, and of the regular order, but he took up arms, and was a captain to the Northern army, which, under the Quaker, Nathaniel Greene, freed the South from British domination."[80] When the two men pay Eleanor a visit only to learn she has been abducted, Carwin jumps into action and calls up the patriotic spirit of the Founding Fathers. "'I have [the pistols],' said Elijah, and his calm eyes lit up with an old Revolutionary fire."[81] This characterization enables Lippard to build a correlation between justified resistance against the British and justified antislavery violence against Southern slavecatchers. Even Malcom, a sugar plantation owner with two hundred slaves, channels one of Lippard's heroes, Thomas Paine, when they close in on his daughter and her kidnappers: "Now comes the time, my friend, that will try us. At the price of blood, we must rescue my daughter."[82] The two men's Revolutionary virtue is contrasted with the character of Baltimore small tobacconist Andrew Graw, the hypocritical brother of Eleanor's owner, James Graw. Although a shrewd debater who "always advocated the largest liberty for black and white, everywhere," Andrew, after his brother is killed and he becomes Eleanor's owner, happily sells the captured woman and goes on a bender. When he returns home to his family drunk and flush with bank notes, he sings, "In the Revolution / For liberty our fathers pulled their triggers, / In modern times / We all do save the U-n-i-o-n, and *catch niggers!*"[83] In Lippard's last novella, the hypocritical oppressor is not one of the usual suspects from earlier city mysteries—the corrupt politician, the lascivious minister—but the racist abolitionist who is not at all what he appears.

Although Carwin the wealthy Quaker expresses *Eleanor*'s most eloquent polemics against the Fugitive Slave Law and chattel slavery, Lippard appeals to his working-class readers through the Herculean Adam Smith, introduced as "the ideal of a hale, hearty, country blacksmith." Once he learns from Carwin and Malcom about Hell-bird's plot to take the kidnapped Eleanor to Maryland, Smith, who has been contracted to fix the broken axle on Hell-bird's carriage, joins the effort to rescue the young woman. In a chapter Lippard entitles "The 'Second' Massacre of Paoli," yet another subtle link between principled Revolutionary War and antislavery violence, Smith hammers away at the broken axle to help drown out the sounds of his two accomplices' attempt to remove Eleanor from the carriage: "Let Elijah and Blair but convey Eleanor to their carriage, and he would face alone, the entire horde of bloodhounds." When Hell-bird and his gang realize what is happening and shots ring out in the night, Lippard's humble blacksmith strikes a brave figure that resonates with his Mechanic Hero of Brandywine: "Adam stood erect, armed with the hammer, and showing out like a giant in the light of the fire." Even as he fights to rescue Eleanor, Smith utters racial epithets, as do the working-class gatekeepers they encounter along the Lancaster turnpike. Throwing hot coals into the kidnappers' faces and menacing them with his hammer, Smith exclaims, "Nigger catchers! men thieves! baby stealers! you come to Chester county, do you?"[84] Adam Smith is unique in Lippard's writing, as most of his white working-class characters do not use the racial epithet, and yet it is clear Smith is no friend to slavery. Like Douglass, Lippard figures the white working classes as potential allies to the antislavery cause. Carwin tells Malcom, "And those of your white people, who not owning a single negro, have begun to mill and farm, and make labor honorable, will they fight for a Slaveocracy, which holds no man respectable unless he owns negroes?"[85]

Although Lippard was vigilant in critiquing the effects of industrial capitalism on the multiracial working poor throughout his writing career, his critique of the Fugitive Slave Law and outspoken disapproval of chattel slavery challenges David Roediger's claim in *Colored White* that "no significant U.S. thinker or group managed to strike such a balance." In *Eleanor,* Lippard comes the closest to staking out what Roediger imagines as "an ideal middle position that effectively criticized wage labor while also acknowledging chattel slavery as the greater evil."[86] As a result of witnessing the violence produced by the Fugitive Slave Law, Carwin testifies to the unparalleled horrors of chattel slavery: "The Fugitive Slave Law woke me up, as it did hundreds of thousands of others, who had never mixed with Abolitionism. It taught us, that as terrible as is the White Slavery of English factories and mines; as fearful as is Wages Slavery, when it spoliates the poor of large cities, and great industrial districts; that Black Slavery is the very embodiment of all the evils of White Slavery, multiplied *ad infinitum;* the great Sum of all the villainies and tyrannies that ever existed beneath the sun."[87] The fact *Eleanor* builds a cross-*class* alliance between Carwin and Smith against the Fugitive Slave Law shows that the white labor advocate and best-selling novelist had come to the conviction that chattel slavery was as urgent and pressing an issue as the "wage" slavery he fought against throughout his life.

Conclusion

George Lippard, William Wells Brown, and Frederick Douglass—inspired by the passage of the Fugitive Slave Law—balance the necessity for antislavery violence with the hope for cross-racial friendship among the multiracial working classes, and develop their critique of Northern class stratification and Southern chattel slavery. In the next chapter, I demonstrate how anti-immigrant and anti-Catholic nativism, two powerful antebellum rhetorics, constitute another cross-racial correspondence among early African American writing and white-authored sensational fiction. Although the two strains of nativism function differently among the three writers and can articulate multiple class allegiances, anxiety toward newly arrived immigrants helped black and white authors alike to articulate class grievances and protest colonization, while hysteria toward Catholic immigrants in particular helped these same authors develop responses to industrial capitalism and chattel slavery.

CHAPTER THREE

The Cross-Racial Appeal of Nativism

"Make Room for the Dregs of Other Countries"

In late summer 1829, amidst violent race riots between working-class whites and blacks in Cincinnati, the short-lived monthly African American newspaper *The Rights of All,* edited in New York City by Presbyterian minister Samuel Cornish, asked, "Who does not wish to live in the goodly city of Cincinnati, we recommend all the outlaws of foreign countries to go there, and as an inducement we are authorized to inform them that the mob governs four evenings out of five, furthermore, the authorities have driven away all the virtuous and respectable people of color, to make room for the dregs of other countries. '*Hail Columbia, happy land.*'"[1] Cornish, who co-founded the first African American newspaper, *Freedom's Journal,* in 1827, was responding to an article in the *Cincinnati Sentinel* detailing recent mob action against African Americans sparked by the city's plans to enforce the Black Law of 1807.

Although Ohio's constitution of 1803 had banned slavery in the state, the Black Law required African Americans living in the city to have two sureties of $500 that vouched for their good behavior. Historian Nikki Taylor points out that the race riots were fomented, in part, by increased labor competition between working-class whites and blacks: between 1800 and 1829, Cincinnati's black population grew by at least 400 percent, fueled largely by free blacks and fugitive slaves from the South, while the white population grew by just 100 percent.

Taylor also attributes the Black Law riots to white middle-class professionals and upper-class merchants who feared the growing population of "impoverished African Americans residing in close proximity to their shops would hurt business." Concurrent with the growing numbers of African Americans, Cincinnati was experiencing a spike in immigration, particularly from Germany, during the second half of the 1820s. Antebellum German historian Emil Klauprecht explains that with the Ohio Canal navigable starting in 1827, immigrant boats began to arrive in 1828, and in "1830, the stream of German immigration began to pour into Cincinnati," helping to double the city's population by 1840.[2] In this volatile context of African American emigration from the South and German immigration from abroad, Cornish inaugurates in *The Rights of All,* contrary to the newspaper's all-inclusive title, an appeal to anti-immigrant nativism in order to defend blacks' right to be treated fairly and equally in the young republic, a line of argument that would endure in early African American literature and have a correspondence in the popular nativist press of the 1850s.

In the same September 18, 1829, issue of *The Rights of All,* Cornish ran an editorial by a "Pittsburgh Man of Color" who is even more emphatic about European immigrants being unfit for American life. "[Blacks] must be driven off even beyond the furthest boundary of the state to make room for . . . the scum and dregs of an European population, a population whose morals, manners, habits and pursuits I hazard nothing in saying, are much more at variance with the well being and prosperity of a state, than those of our free people of color."[3] The Pittsburgh letter-writer's indignation, combined with Cornish's construction of a mob comprised of the "outlaws of foreign countries," produces a portrait of immigrants as an unsavory lot who support the unjust Black Law and trample on the rights of native-born blacks. A less virulent instance of anti-immigrant nativism in the paper occurred a month earlier when Cornish protested the Black Law as well as colonization schemes that were more often based in race prejudice than in sympathy for the enslaved and oppressed. In "Barbarism in America," Cornish draws a sharp distinction between immigrants and the native-born when he responds rhetorically to a pro-colonization Ohio newspaper: "And why not send the Editor and the Authorities to their mother country, England, France, Ireland, Turkey, Algiers or Arabia, as may be, would there not be equal justice in it?" Cornish goes on to denounce any blacks who would support colonization to Africa as race traitors who "should in his efforts to remove the colored population from their *rightful soil, the land of their birth and nativity,* be considered as acting gratuitously unrighteous and cruel."[4] These polemical expressions of anti-immigrant nativism in the second-oldest African American newspaper appeal to the native-born status of African Americans who live and work in the country, and reappear in Cornish's next publishing venture, the *Weekly Advocate,* which was published from 1837 to 1842.

Negative representations of immigrants in the *Weekly Advocate,* subsequently titled the *Colored American,* provide a bridge between the anti-immigrant nativism in *The Rights of All* and the populist appeals to the native-born status of African Americans in the nativist press, as well as the 1850s writing of Frederick Douglass, William Wells Brown, George Lippard, and Frank J. Webb. With regular editorials encouraging black youth to become "mechanics and producers of the land," the *Colored American* employed the artisan republican rhetoric expressed in black- and white-authored appeals to the working classes.[5] Advocating in 1837 for black suffrage in the state of New York, Cornish makes an anti-immigrant appeal to his readers: "The rights and privileges of other citizens have been enlarged, while our own, and those of our brethren have been abridged. Foreigners and aliens to the government and laws—strangers to our institutions are permitted to flock to this land, and in a few years are endowed with all the privileges of citizens; but we, native born Americans, the children of the soil, are most of us shut out."[6] Cornish's frustration with immigrants' ability to vote in the state after just seven years is consistent with white nativist calls to extend the naturalization period to twenty-one years, the same number of years a native-born white citizen had to wait before voting.[7] Antebellum nativists did not typically call for ending or curbing immigration, but rather for limiting the voting power of immigrants, who provided cheap labor and were seen as a threat to democratic institutions. The way Cornish contrasts blacks as "children of the [American] soil" with immigrants as "strangers to our institutions" is echoed in his explanation for changing the name of the *Weekly Advocate* to *Colored American* after just two months in print. With strident populism, he writes, "In complexion, in blood and in nativity, we are decidedly more exclusively 'American' than our white brethren; hence the propriety of the name of our paper, COLORED AMERICAN, in spite of our enemies, who would rob us of our nationality and reproach us as exotics."[8] Cornish, who relates being denied restaurant service "by a foreigner" in New York City, and reports a sensational case whereby a black native-born youth was accepted to Yale Medical College only by pretending to be from East India, makes liberal use of anti-immigrant nativism to politick for equal rights for working-class blacks.[9]

Despite the fact the republic was founded by generations of immigrants, anti-immigrant animus has ebbed and flowed throughout American history, as evidenced by the rise of the Know Nothing Party in the 1850s, the Chinese Exclusion Act of 1882, the Johnson-Reed Immigration Act of 1924, the internment of Japanese Americans during World War II, and the widespread suspicion of foreigners during the Trump era of the twenty-first century. Historians estimate that at least five million Europeans immigrated to America during the antebellum period, and since they helped to supply cheap labor for the growing industries of the 1830s and 1840s, these newcomers became the targets of displaced craftsmen's grievances. According to historian Robert Ernst, native-born tradesmen, mechanics, and seamstresses complained, for instance, that the wave of Irish immigrants in the 1840s reduced the value of labor and eroded the apprenticeship system of labor.[10] In response to the increasing number of immigrants from Ireland, Germany, and England, nativist organizations sprang up in the 1840s in northeastern cities and started their own newspapers and magazines.

One such nativist organization, the Order of United Americans (OUA), attacked newly arrived immigrants and defended African Americans against colonization programs in its print organ, *Republic: A Monthly Magazine of American Literature, Politics and Art.* Edited by the OUA's co-founder Thomas R. Whitney, a nativist politician who was elected to Congress as a Know Nothing candidate in 1854, the *Republic* argued that blacks are more fit for American citizenship than newly arrived European immigrants. In a January 1852 anti-colonization piece entitled "The Colored People," Whitney writes, "America, the United States of North America, is the home of their birth, the land of their nativity, and they have no idea of being sent off to foreign lands." As an alternative to relocating African Americans abroad, Whitney makes a suggestion, half-ironically, that echoes Cornish's call in *The Rights of All,* to send corrupt Ohio authorities back to their home countries. "Probably those who talk about sending the American-born negroes to Africa, to die with the coast-fever, would be horrified at the idea of sending the Irish, German, and other foreign residents of this country, back to their own lands; but we can assure those discriminating philosophers that such a procedure would be the more rational and politic of the two, and equally humane." Although Whitney's editorial invokes the racist figure of "poor Sambo," the piece defends African Americans as "more intelligent, than the imported article of the lower class," and reminds readers of their military sacrifice, "the first blood shed in our revolution was that of a negro; and there are numerous instances on record of services rendered by his race, even by those in bondage, during the struggle for independence."[11] Whitney's populist defense of native-born blacks and appeal to their revolutionary spirit constitutes a cross-racial correspondence with the early black press, and, as part of their spirited rejection of colonization, the major writings of Douglass, Brown, Lippard, and Webb.

In order to appreciate the populist appeals in early African American literature and the sensational fiction of George Lippard, it is important to understand the colonization projects they were protesting. Founded in December 1816, the American Colonization Society advocated the emigration of free blacks and freed slaves to the colony of Liberia. Between 1821 and 1847, when Liberia became an independent state, thousands of African Americans emigrated to the fledgling colony being established on the far west coast of Africa. While the society had a wide array of supporters and detractors, abolitionist and pro-slavery alike, many of the leading black abolitionists, including

Douglass, vigorously spoke out against the colonization movement for assuming blacks could never succeed in America and for stoking whites' anxieties about race-mixing. One of the strongest literary expressions of colonization, to which Douglass, Brown, Lippard, and Webb are conceivably responding in their 1850s writing, is Sarah Josepha Hale's *Liberia; or, Mr. Peyton's Experiments,* a novel published in the summer of 1853 with the Harper Brothers of New York.

Inside *Liberia*'s Colonization Plot

At the end of Harriet Beecher Stowe's 1852 *Uncle Tom's Cabin,* in a conclusion Stowe would later state she regretted, the proud black artisan George Harris and his wife, Eliza, reunited and living in Canada, choose to move to and help colonize Liberia. Harris exclaims, "As a Christian patriot, as a teacher of Christianity, I go to *my country,*—my chosen, my glorious Africa!" In Stowe's novel, Harris understands that African Americans "have equal rights to mingle in the American republic as the Irishman, the German, the Swede," but he wants a nation of his own.[12] Susan Ryan observes that "George Harris arrives at his decision to emigrate from a position of strength rather than desperation, never relinquishing his right to remain in the United States or questioning his ability to survive in white society."[13] In contrast, Hale's *Liberia,* what Ryan calls "a piece of pro-colonization propaganda," argues that African Americans should emigrate to Liberia due to their inability to assimilate and succeed materially in America.[14] In order to promote its colonization agenda, *Liberia* develops racist arguments that freed African Americans are not industrious or business-savvy and are generally incapable of assimilating to white middle-class mores. Moreover, *Liberia* represents cross-racial hostilities as inevitable and perpetual, calling up Thomas Jefferson's fears of a race war and providing yet another argument for colonization. It is to these racist and fatalist claims of the colonization movement that Douglass, Brown, Lippard, and Webb respond with populist appeals that echo the anti-immigrant nativism of the early black and nativist presses.

When she published *Liberia,* Sarah Josepha Hale was serving as the literary editor of the monthly magazine *Godey's Lady's Book,* a prestigious position she held from 1837 to 1877.[15] *Godey's Lady's Book* was "the most popular periodical for women both North and South," and is best known for publishing literary works by Romantic authors like Edgar Allan Poe, Harriet Beecher Stowe, and Nathaniel Hawthorne.[16] The novel chronicles the experiments of Virginia plantation owner Charles Peyton, who, having been protected by his dutiful slaves amidst the threat of a slave revolt, keeps his promise to prepare a handful of his slaves for freedom. To that end, Peyton, presented sentimentally as one of the more liberal slaveowners, establishes a small band of slaves on a nearby farm. When this first experiment fails due to the newly freed slaves' indolence, he helps a black family relocate to Philadelphia. When this second experiment fails due to Northern race prejudice, the volatile marketplace, and the freed blacks' failure to manage their money, Peyton encourages them to help establish the colony of Liberia, the third and final experiment. The novel is anachronistic and takes liberties with the timeline for the sake of its thematic commitment to colonization: Peyton is present at the founding of the American Colonization Society in 1816 and his freed slaves sail on the inaugural voyage to establish Liberia in 1820, and yet the family living in Philadelphia is a victim of the 1849 Election Day riots that George Lippard depicts in *The Killers.* Ultimately, Hale's representations of Peyton's "noble" experiments to find a space for native-born freed black slaves in the rural South and the urban North depend on racist stereotypes, condescending skepticism toward racial uplift, and a fallacious belief in inevitable hostility between the white and black working classes—the very same white attitudes that Douglass hoped to counter with the formation of an industrial college, and that Brown, Lippard, and Webb resist through their novels' cross-racial populist appeals to the right of native-born blacks to stay and compete in America.

In *Liberia*'s second chapter, "Life on the Farm," Peyton makes an "attempt to free his servants and teach them self-reliance" by placing a group that includes ten strong men on a farm about three miles from his plantation. The first experiment begins auspiciously with the farm earning a profit in its first year, and Peyton rewards the slaves with their freedom. However, the second year does not go as well because, according to the text, the success of the first year and the comfortable safety net provided by Peyton made the freed slaves indolent. Peyton "marked, with bitter disappointment, the downward progress of what, in his sanguine visions, he had depicted to himself as the Utopia of the colored race." Eventually, the more enterprising black farmers ask for the farmland to be divided into individual plots, which leads to the overall degradation of the area and the failure of the experiment. Although Hale's novel sentimentally endorses Peyton's experiment to free his slaves and laments the idle farmers' inability to prosper, *Liberia* concludes that the former slaves are ill equipped to succeed in America. "With every earthly aspiration crushed out of his heart by the overpowering superiority of the white man in social and political advantage, it is no wonder he improves so slowly, or displays so little desire for intellectual cultivation."[17]

For the second experiment, in the chapter "Life in a City," Peyton frees and then sends a family—Ben and his wife, Clara, their two children, and Clara's younger brother, Americus—to set up a home in the North. Relocated to Philadelphia, Ben works as a coachman, Clara works as a seamstress, and Americus works as a waiter, but, despite their modest success, they are unable to assimilate to "respectable" society, to navigate the unpredictable marketplace, and to avoid racial violence. The hard-working family's attempts to rise in social status are treated with amusement and contempt by the very people, the Peytons, who have helped them move and should want the best for them. Two years into this second experiment, Charles Peyton and his wife, Virginia, are visiting Philadelphia and admiring from behind a well-dressed woman and her daughter who are taking an after-dinner stroll along fashionable Chestnut Street; Virginia even enthuses that she will take the woman as a model for the clothes she wants to purchase as gifts for her sister. But they are utterly "astonished" when Clara turns and they discover they have been admiring two of the objects of their social experiment. Virginia chastises Clara to Charles: "I thought Clara had more sense than to dress herself in that unsuitable way. I am sure Ben's wages can not support her long in that style. I must talk to her about it."[18] This narrative incident echoes historian Shane White's summary of an 1834 newspaper report in the penny paper the *New York Sun* in which a white dandy is shocked when the elegant woman he has been following down Broadway turns around and reveals that she is black. According to White, "For many whites a well-dressed black was an at least slightly comic figure, but such observations also carried an underlying sense of disquiet, a fretful complaint at the blurring of the former, relatively clear-cut racial boundaries."[19] Clara intuits the Peytons' haughtiness: "A consciousness that the surprise shown by her old master and mistress was not one of entire pleasure, prevented Clara from feeling perfectly at ease."[20] By having the black family subsequently fall on hard times, the text endorses the Peytons' condescending social judgment, and does not seem aware of the irony that the Northern race prejudice holding back the family in this instance has been imported from the South.

Liberia continues weaving its self-fulfilling prophecy that blacks cannot assimilate to white middle-class culture in the cruel comedy directed at the family's efforts toward intellectual self-improvement. When Ben and Clara entertain the Peytons at their modest home, and invite their erudite black friend Amanda Fitzwalter, the Peytons are troubled by their pursuit of music and their participation in the literary Philomathean Society, once again reinforcing the same race prejudice they—and colonizationists like Hale—believed made the Northern United States unsuitable for blacks. In response to hearing about the literary society's latest debate over the poetry of Byron and Shelley, "Mrs. Peyton hardly knew whether to laugh or be indignant at the absurdity of the whole affair, and Miss Fitzwalter's pompous manner. She was almost ready to believe the colored race were, as she had often heard, incapable of taking care of themselves, when she saw those to whom so much had been given—such careful, early training, so much religious instruction, and at last liberty—thus wasting their time and opportunities." Although Charles Peyton offers a lukewarm defense of their interest in Byron and Shelley, who "are not, to be sure, likely to be of any great use to them," the novel repeatedly mocks the black family's attempts at uplift, and is implicated in the same fatalist discourse of cross-racial enmity by which it attempts to justify its colonization project.[21]

Ben and Clara's family suffers for their intellectual pursuits and reluctance to save money, as the novel ominously warns the reader: "their life was not all sunshine." Not long after the Peytons return to their Virginia plantation, an antislavery fair is held in Philadelphia and stokes controversy, and at the same time "an old feud between the lowest class of laborers and the colored race had broken out afresh in the suburbs of the city."[22] Samuel Otter notes that *Liberia*'s "'anti-slavery fair' and targeting of interracial mixture evoke the opening of Pennsylvania Hall in 1838 and the attack on the California House in 1849, and the violence in the suburbs recalls the [racial] riots of 1834, 1842, and 1849."[23] In stark contrast to Lippard's representation of the 1849 Election Night riots as the culmination of *class* warfare between the white upper class and the multiracial working poor as figured in Black Andy and Elijah Watson, Hale represents cross-racial hostilities among the lower classes as the primary cause of the violence. In Hale's rendition of the rioting, a "gang of ruffians,"[24] a phrase that signals white and working class, breaks into a home and viciously blinds a black cobbler in front of his family; Americus is attacked while escorting a woman home from his white employer's house; and John, a black proprietor of an oyster-cellar, dies from head wounds sustained by a sling-shot fired by a member of the Killers gang. The culprits go unpunished, and for Hale, race violence in the North is inevitable and insurmountable, further justification for Peyton's third and final experiment, colonization in Liberia.

After the riots, the black family next becomes a victim of circumstance and of their own poor planning in Philadelphia. When Ben takes ill with rheumatism and loses his position as coachman, Clara, without savings to fall back on, struggles to keep the family afloat with seamstress work and charity from neighbors. Like a dark temperance tale, Ben becomes a drunkard, and their daughter takes to begging the streets in the bitter cold of winter. It is little wonder that given their extreme hardship and bad fortune, Ben and Clara are convinced by

Peyton—who gives them $300 toward travel expenses—to go to Liberia and help establish the colony, a project that consumes the second half of the novel. The couple is rejuvenated in Liberia, as Ben feels like a new man with "ambition once more aroused," and Clara and the children are once again happy.[25] *Liberia,* in contrast to the racially ambivalent class protest of white-authored sensational fiction, makes a scapegoat of the white working class as a racist monolith, and holds up middle-class values as the standards to which the black characters repeatedly fall short. For Hale and other proponents of colonization, the native-born status of blacks was not a claim to citizenship; their only rightful and promising claim to pursue life, liberty, and happiness was in faraway Africa.

The Convergence of Populism and Anti-Immigrant Nativism in Frederick Douglass's Writing

Frederick Douglass's opposition to colonization is apparent in his newspaper's literary notices of Sarah Josepha Hale's writing in the early 1850s. Although *Frederick Douglass' Paper* did not review *Liberia* when it appeared in 1853, his white literary editor and confidante, British abolitionist Julia Griffiths, ran a strong rebuke of the republication of Hale's 1827 novel *Northwood; A Tale of New England.* Retitled *Northwood; or, Life North and South: Showing the True Character of Both,* the 1852 version of Hale's novel does not meditate extensively on colonization the way *Liberia* does, and yet colonization is the main focus of Griffith's critique: "Mrs. Hale enjoins educating the slaves—but *why?* To help colonize Liberia. Then opens 'the glorious prospect' for the freed slave from America!! and then follows all the nonsense about his going forth '*as a priest, bearing the ark of God's covenant mercy to Ethiopia.*' The whole closes with suggestions to the reverend clergy to make collections in their churches on *Thanksgiving day* for educating and colonizing the people of color!!"[26] Griffiths's brusque dismissal of *Northwood*'s endorsement of colonization as "nonsense" and ironizing its idea of colonization as a "glorious prospect" likely explains why

Frederick Douglass' Paper never reviewed or even noticed the publication of Hale's *Liberia* the following year.

As part of his spirited rejection of colonization, Douglass regularly invoked African Americans' native-born status. Arguably his most powerful speech against colonization, "Slavery, the Slumbering Volcano" views the movement as a direct assault against free blacks and counters its fatalist claims of cross-racial enmity. "Under the garb of philanthropy and religion its efforts to degrade us have been as various as they have been grievous . . . Embodying all the malignity of the slaveholder, and all the negro-hating of the Northerner, it is our ever vigilant and bitter adversary." In the 1849 speech, Douglass admonishes colonizationists for "assum[ing] that the colored people, while they remain in this country, can never stand on an equal footing with the white population of the United States." With the skill of a seasoned rhetorician, Douglass concludes with an invocation of Revolutionary War heroes, "If it be left optional with a slave to go to Africa or not, we advise him not to go, but rather to remain here and add to the number of those who may yet imitate the example of our fathers of '76."[27] With patriotic allusions to the Franklinian process of self-making through the process of imitation as well as to the Founding Fathers, who transformed the colonies into a republic, Douglass insists on blacks' right to remain in America and make it their own.

Toward the end of his 1855 autobiography *My Bondage and My Freedom,* Douglass discusses his decision to return to America from his two-year sojourn in England. With his freedom purchased for one hundred and fifty pounds sterling by English abolitionists, Douglass records his conviction that he must return and serve as a spokesperson for his embattled black brethren in the North and the South. "I felt that I had a duty to perform—and that was, to labor and suffer with the oppressed in my native land." In his three invocations of America as his "native country" and "native land," Douglass echoes the introduction written for his book by black abolitionist James McCune Smith, which insists of *My Bondage and My Freedom* that "it is an American book, for Americans, in the fullest sense of the idea."[28] These populist appeals to African Americans' native-born status may not be a direct assault on newly arrived immigrants like we will see in Douglass's defense of his industrial college project, but they do align with white nativists' concerns that European newcomers might not be fit to exercise the responsibilities of American citizenship. Moreover, such populism circulated the country widely in the anti-colonization writing of Brown, Lippard, and Webb, authors whose writing can be viewed as a counter-response to the false narrative of cross-racial enmity in Hale's *Liberia.*

Although Douglass did not often invoke strident anti-immigrant nativism that was evident in the early black press and nativist newspapers, within his promotion of an industrial college for black and white youth in Rochester, New York, populist appeals to blacks' native-born status and anxiety about the impact of European immigration on job opportunities for Northern blacks converge. In a March 1853 letter to Stowe, which he reprinted in his newspaper later that year, Douglass solicits financial support for the industrial college through a populist appeal that counters the fatalist arguments of colonizationists against racial uplift. "The truth is, dear madam, we are *here,* and we are likely to remain. Individuals emigrate—nations never. We have grown up in this republic, and I see nothing in her character, or even in the character of the American people yet, which compels the belief that we must leave the United States."[29] Insisting on blacks' native-born right to live and work in America, Douglass strategically uses populism to promote an educational project for the multiracial working poor in the North.

To further press his case for the industrial college, Douglass expresses anti-immigrant nativist sentiment by focusing on the increasing need for native-born blacks to compete for jobs against desperate newcomers from abroad. In an urgent editorial titled "Learn Trades or Starve!," Douglass writes, "The old avocations, by which colored men obtained a livelihood, are rapidly, unceasingly and inevitably passing into other hands; every hour he sees the black man elbowed out of employment by some newly arrived emigrant, whose hunger and whose color are thought to give him a better title to the place."[30] In this instance, the white European immigrant has less claim to the nation than the African American who was born there, an argument that echoes nativists' defense of native-born whites. The following year, in an editorial in which he expresses his disappointment that Stowe did not support the project, Douglass calls on his readers to forge ahead and support the college because economic competition with white European immigrants will only intensify. Douglass writes, "The landing of poverty stricken thousands from the continent of Europe, at the wharves of New York, Philadelphia, and Baltimore—and the rapidity with which these thousands are displacing the colored man as a coachman, as a waiter, as a barber, as a whitewasher, as a boot-blacker, as a steward, as a stevedore, as a wood-sawyer, tells in language more impressive than we can command—the necessity for opening new channels of industry and new sources of support for our people."[31] While lacking the shrill tone and hyperbole of much anti-immigrant nativism circulating in the class-inflected nativist press, Douglass's writing, when it was aimed at improving the lives of the multiracial working classes, appealed judiciously to working-class nativist anxiety toward the "poverty stricken thousands" landing annually on America's shores.

Cross-Racial Populism in Anti-Colonization Novels of the 1850s

Like Douglass's polemical writing, Brown's *Clotel,* Lippard's *New York,* and Webb's *The Garies and Their Friends* resist colonizationist reasoning by arguing that African Americans are assimilable, that by right they deserve liberty and equality to pursue honest labor, and that cross-racial amity will trump enmity. Their populist appeals to African Americans' native-born status constitute an implicit expression of anti-immigrant nativism and another cross-racial correspondence between black- and white-authored novels in the 1850s.

William Wells Brown's *Clotel,* published in London just months after Hale's *Liberia* appeared in New York, mounts strong opposition to colonization through a class-inflected appeal to the native-born status of hard-working blacks. The novel's outspoken white abolitionist, Georgiana Peck, convinces her husband that rather than freeing and sending their slaves to Liberia, they should help them relocate to Ohio. Georgiana reasons, "Is not this their native land? What right have we, more than the negro, to the soil here, or to style ourselves native Americans? Indeed it is as much their homes as ours, and I have sometimes thought, it was more theirs. The negro has cleared the lands, built towns, and enriched the soil with his blood and tears; and in return, he is to be sent to a country of which he knows nothing." Brown's resistance to colonization echoes the class-inflected anti-immigrant nativism that appears in the early black press: through their exploited labor, native-born blacks are, in fact, more entitled to claim America as their own than the whites, native-born or immigrant, who have benefited from citizenship without performing such honest labors themselves. In a rebuke of Hale's representation of black indolence, Brown writes that the Carltons' slaves, once informed of their gradual emancipation, are inspired to work harder. "The bricklayers had been to work but a short time, before their industry was noticed by many . . . They were never tired of labouring, and seemed as though they could never effect enough."[32]

Later, Georgiana informs the slaves of the Ohio relocation plan, and, like Douglass, makes a populist attack against the racist underpinnings of colonization. "We have been urged to send you to Liberia, but we think it wrong to send you from your native land. We did not wish to encourage the Colonization Society, for it originated in hatred of the free colored people. Its pretenses are false, its doctrines odious, its means contemptible." Although in 1861 Brown would support black emigration to Haiti, he more often attacked colonization in speeches at black conventions and in his fiction. In an ironic passage that resonates with *The Rights of All*'s mocking proposal to send European Americans back to their homelands, Georgiana counters colonization writings that assert blacks should be sent as missionaries to Africa because they are "vicious": "If we send away the negroes because they are profligate and vicious, what sort of missionaries will they make? Why not send away the vicious among the whites for the same reason, and the same purpose?"[33] Brown's *Clotel* appeals to the native-born status of blacks to expose the racism of colonization schemes, and provides instances of cross-racial love and friendship to counter fatalist claims of cross-racial enmity.

Although George Lippard invests far more heavily in anti-Catholic nativism than anti-immigrant nativism in his writing, *New York* follows Douglass's and Brown's lead in combating colonization through populist appeals. When Randolph Royalton and his sister Esther, grandchildren of Thomas Jefferson, hide out in New York City from slavecatchers, Randolph rejects Esther's suggestion they flee to Europe. "'Europe!' he echoed. 'And must we go to Europe in order to be permitted to live? No, Esther, no! I am an American . . . While I live, I will not cease to assert my right to a place, ay, and no dishonorable place—on my native soil.'" Although Randolph and Esther disappear at the end of the novel, and, the narrator suggests, have left America for Europe—significantly, not Africa—Lippard's novel reinforces their right to live in America by virtue of the race-mixing that produced their illustrious heritage as descendants of the nation's Founding Father. Randolph declares, "I will not leave this country, in the first place, because I am of its soil . . . and because, first and last, it is no common right, which binds me to my native land."[34] In his novel marked by cross-racial sympathy among the working classes, figured through white cobbler Arthur Dermoyne and the formidable leader of the Black Senate "Old Royal"—with the greatest threat to the republic emanating from the Roman Catholic Church's headquarters overseas—Lippard counters colonizationist rhetoric through populist appeals and a mildly nativist alliance of native-born whites and blacks against an external threat.

African American author Frank J. Webb joins the populist appeals of Lippard and Brown in his 1857 novel *The Garies and Their Friends*. Webb counters Hale's colonization arguments in *Liberia* by combining anti-immigrant nativism toward the Irish with populist appeals for native-born blacks' assimilation into the greater American family. As literary critic Eric Gardner explains, a great deal is unknown about Webb's life due to biographers' tendency to confuse him with other men of the same name, but we can surmise that Webb was born in Philadelphia around 1828; he married in 1845 a multiracial woman named Mary who enjoyed success giving public readings of canonical texts in America and abroad; he published *The Garies and Their*

Friends, the second African American novel, in London at the end of 1857; and he died in Texas sometime in the 1890s.[35] Countering the previous critical consensus of *The Garies and Their Friends* as reinforcing white middle-class values of free enterprise, Samuel Otter argues that "Webb's narrator . . . does not capitulate to dominant values or recommend an elevation that is really a submission, in moves that many observers have seen as characteristic of Philadelphia's African American leaders or a wider devotion to 'respectability' in the nineteenth century."[36] My interest in *The Garies and Their Friends* lies in its sharing a cross-racial correspondence with the anti-immigrant nativism and populism in the writing of Douglass, Brown, and Lippard, which is in keeping with recent reassessments of the novel by Otter, Anna Engle, and Elizabeth Stockton.[37]

The title characters, the Garies, are a mixed-race couple (a slave-owner and his slave-wife) that moves to Philadelphia in order to marry legally and for their children to live freely and receive a quality education. As Otter notes, the climactic action of Webb's novel conflates a series of three race riots in Philadelphia between 1838 and the Election Night riots of 1849.[38] The Garies' primary antagonist is a classic villain of white-authored sensational fiction: their neighbor, Mr. Stevens, is a hateful and corrupt attorney who hatches a plan to destroy the Garies, and, as he happens to be a distant relative, to wrest the wealth from the unsuspecting family. Like the immigrant villains of the nativist city-mystery fiction of Augustine Duganne and Ned Buntline, Stevens has "Irish muscle" on the payroll: he blackmails a man named McCloskey, who killed a fellow Irishman during a drunken brawl, to foment a race riot so that it can serve as cover for murdering Mr. Garie. Historian Tyler Anbinder has documented that Irish immigrants fleeing the Potato Famine of the 1840s were a primary target of antebellum nativists: "2,000,000 decided to flee Ireland completely, and nearly three-quarters of that number came to America. The famine immigrants were the most impoverished, destitute, unskilled group ever to arrive in the United States."[39] And yet Webb tempers this anti-immigrant nativism by representing McCloskey as a victim of Stevens and by having the Irishman stop the mob from burning down the Garies' house after the patriarch is murdered. Despite the perception that native-born African Americans and Irish immigrants were always at odds over workplace competition, the working-class McCloskey responds to race-mixing with some ambivalence when Stevens orders him to kill Garie. "'Married to a nigger!' exclaimed McCloskey—'it's a quare taste the animal has—but you're not afther killing [Garie] for that; there's something more behind; it's not for having a black wife instead of a white one you'd be afther murthering him.'" The fact that the duplicitous attorney Stevens stokes the race riots by anonymously submitting incendiary letters to the local journals and papers, "particularly those that circulated amongst the lowest classes,"[40] places *The Garies and Their Friends*'s sensational working-class accents in dialogue with Lippard's *The Killers:* the Election Night riots are not sparked by cross-racial hostility among the working classes but manufactured by corrupt members of the white middle class.

In addition to the wealthy Garies, Webb's novel features the Ellises, a black working-class family led by a carpenter father, and, like Hale's *Liberia,* the novel follows the vicissitudes of life for free blacks in Philadelphia. Webb employs anti-immigrant nativism toward the Irish in a subplot involving the Ellises' young son Charlie, who is striving toward becoming a productive member of society. After Charlie Ellis breaks his arm running in the house and is bedridden, kindly white abolitionist Mrs. Bird offers to take him to the country to convalesce and attend a private school. Setting out on the train, the pair is accosted by the conductor, who insists they remove to the less comfortable "Jim Crow" car despite having paid full price. When Mrs. Bird resists, the conductor threatens them with force. "In the end, the conductor stopped the train, and called in one or two of the Irish brake-men to assist him if necessary, in enforcing the orders." Like McCloskey, who is in Stevens's power, Webb presents the "Irish muscle" as doing the bidding of their superiors. "'You had better let the boy go into the negro car, madam,' said one of the gentlemen, respectfully; 'it is perfectly useless to contend with these ruffians. I saw a coloured man ejected from here last week, and severely injured.'"[41] Webb complicates the conventional nativist portrayal of the Irish working class as violent and quick-tempered through the railroad conductor's racism and Stevens's conspiracy against Garie.

Webb further employs a populist appeal to the rights of native-born African Americans, and thus *The Garies and Their Friends* joins with Brown and Lippard in countering colonization. Unlike the Northern black family that finds peace and happiness only by settling in Africa in Hale's *Liberia,* Webb's Ellis family perseveres and finds a degree of contentment in America, despite the race riots that leave the Ellis patriarch maimed and unemployed. Webb's novel culminates in the marriage of Charlie Ellis and Emily Garie, who then partake in what is presented as a national tradition: "On the whole, it was an American supper, got up regardless of expense—and whoever has been to such an entertainment knows very well what an American supper is." The mild anti-immigrant nativism that insists on blacks' native-born right to live freely in America, not in Africa or in Europe, re-emerges in the novel's closing paragraph: "Charles and Emily took a voyage to Europe for the health of the latter, and returned after a two years' tour to settle permanently in his native city."[42] Webb makes clear that the Ellises belong in their "native" land, the American republic, and they will live there "permanently." They are not going anywhere.

Augustine Duganne and Ned Buntline: The Flexible Class Accents of Anti-Immigrant Nativism

Labor historians have shown that anti-immigrant nativism enabled white working-class identity construction during the 1840s, a decade of mass immigration from Europe. Sean Wilentz attributes nativism's rise to the economic depression that followed the Panic of 1837, and contends it provided a means for native-born laborers to articulate their class concerns. "While nativists offered no criticism of the ethics of liberal economic expansion—indeed, encouraged industriousness and sobriety—their cultural approach to political disorder revealed a genuine longing for a supposed golden age, before poverty, before immigration, before social conflict." Robert Ernst, detailing the emergence of "economic nativism" in New York City, writes that "the argument that immigrants were underselling the American worker in the labor market . . . was the most powerful appeal that could be made to men and women who were eking out a bare living during the ten years of hard times after the panic of 1837." Finally, Philadelphia historian Bruce Laurie posits that nativism "conveyed a strong sense of class identity," underscoring the potential role it could play in antebellum working-class protest.[43]

As we have seen, anti-immigrant nativism constitutes a cross-racial correspondence between early African American literature and white-authored sensational fiction, which, when combined with artisan republican appeals for native-born workers, could produce moments of cross-racial sympathy at the expensive of the immigrant. African American writers like Samuel Cornish, Frederick Douglass, Williams Wells Brown, and Frank J. Webb, along with white writers like Thomas R. Whitney and George Lippard, defend African Americans against colonization schemes and labor competition from abroad through anti-immigrant nativism, including populist appeals to blacks' native-born status. The potential for cross-racial sympathy among the multiracial working classes was realized when these writers combined anti-immigrant nativism and artisan republicanism. Significantly, Douglass's use of anti-immigrant nativism appears in his promotion of an industrial college for black and white youth of the working classes, and Lippard's figuring the grave threat to the republic as coming from abroad reinforces the cross-racial working-class alliances that dominate his novel *New York*. Yet among the popular city-mystery writers of the 1840s, none employed anti-immigrant nativism as liberally as Augustine Duganne and Ned Buntline, two working-class writers with strong ties to the nativist political movement and with starkly different views of chattel slavery. Both men portrayed newly arrived immigrants as criminals and easily duped henchmen in their sensational fictions. As we will see, in their representative texts of the 1840s, anti-immigrant nativist discourse, when tethered to artisan republicanism, could develop moments of cross-racial class protest against "wage" and chattel slavery; yet, when combined with unsympathetic and racist portrayals of blackness, could unwittingly serve the interests of the white middle classes.

Although Duganne is not particularly well known today, he published in multiple genres from the early 1840s until his death in 1884, and was a regular contributor of labor poetry to the abolitionist newspaper the *National Era*. Like his professional associates Lippard and Edgar Allan Poe, Duganne spent much of his writing career among the three cities that published the bulk of cheap fiction: Boston, Philadelphia, and New York. Born in Boston in 1823, Duganne released his first collection of poetry, *Massachusetts,* and his first city-mystery, *The Two Clerks,* in 1843. After moving to Philadelphia, where he befriended Lippard and got married, Duganne published several city-mysteries and also founded and edited a short-lived labor newspaper called *Iron Man* in 1849.[44] Around 1850 Duganne moved to New York City, where he was elected in 1855 to the state legislature as a nativist Know Nothing, and published his last major novel, *The Tenant-House,* in 1857. During the Civil War, Duganne served for two years as a colonel in the 176th New York Volunteers, and spent the final year of his commission as a Confederate prisoner in Texas.[45] Duganne's city-mysteries of the 1840s are useful for understanding the potential of anti-immigrant nativism to express cross-racial class protest.

Duganne's 1846 novel *The Daguerreotype Miniature; or, Life in the Empire City* relates the machinations of a Southern forger and purported slaveowner, Major Peyton Florence, to swindle an orphan, Arthur Warden, out of his inheritance, and to seduce a wealthy young woman named Rose Warrington. Warden, a working-class apprentice, survives a climactic knife-thrust to his breast because he is wearing a necklace containing a daguerreotype miniature of Warrington, whom he marries at the end. Although Major Florence is revealed to be "an adventurer, a gambler, a fortune-hunter" and flees to Mexico, Duganne establishes his villainy through artisan republican and antislavery discourses. "Major Peyton Florence was dressed, curled, scented, ruffled, jewelled—Major Peyton Florence had the reputation of a million—of slaves in any quantity—and cotton-fields innumerable—Major Peyton Florence was the observed—the courted—the caressed."[46] Duganne merges these artisan republican and antislavery discourses with anti-immigrant nativism when Florence hires two immigrants, referred to as "the Portuguese" and "the Scotchman," to rough up Dick Dolby, an "honest" Bowery B'hoy who is investigating forgers. According to Eric Lott, the Bowery B'hoy "exemplified the first U.S. working class subculture—the volunteer fireman bent on class travesty, the butcher wise in the ways of cultural bricolage."[47] When Major Florence hires the immigrants to rough up Dolby, they show no mercy and no fear: "On, on, through the streets, the lanes, and avenues; on, amid the loafers and small boys; on, over the gutters and crossings—dragged those terrible men the hopeless Richard Dolby. No pity moved their remorseless hearts—no kindly throb of sympathy awoke within their unrelenting bosoms . . . Did no fear of the Tombs restrain the copper-colored Portuguese or the pock-marked Scotchman? None!"[48] By aligning an albeit disguised wealthy slaveowner with immigrant henchmen against a young apprentice and a Bowery B'hoy, *The Daguerreotype Miniature* demonstrates how anti-immigrant nativism could gesture toward cross-racial class solidarity.

Two years later, Duganne's *Eustace Barcourt; or, The Illegitimate. A Story of Conflict Between Good and Evil* features a large gang of robbers—including Mike, an Irishman; Dick, a Catholic; and Mother Ann, a multiracial crone—that terrorizes the Jersey Shore. While the first half of the novel features the revenge plot of a poor and fallen woman spurned by a wealthy rake, the second half focuses on the gang's attempts to lure ships close to land and steal their cargo. Duganne combines anti-immigrant nativism toward Mike, a coarse Irishman with a thick "Milesian" accent and "the superstitious fear of his nation," anti-Catholic nativism toward Dick, and racialism toward Mother Ann, who kills Dick for the diamond-encrusted cross he wears around his neck. While this depraved trio of criminals forestalls cross-racial solidarity, Duganne later links Mike and the other gang members with chattel slavery: "The land-thieves of the west, the coiners of Montreal, the pirates of the West Indies, and the slave-stealers of the south, as well as the forgers and burglars of the Atlantic cities, are well aware of the immense trades union of which they are the components." Duganne also employs a simile evincing sympathy for the chattel slave to describe the vengeful spirit of Isabel, a seduced and abandoned woman. "But new thoughts came, like those which the slave feels, when after long years of misery and suffering, he bares his arm to the shoulder, and raises his knife over his fallen tyrant. Such thoughts as these—thoughts that come from wrong, nursed into revenge—thoughts that arise in a fair soul made foul by injury."[49] Duganne's figurative language not only coincides with the endorsement of justified antislavery violence in the writing of Douglass and Lippard of the late 1840s, but also looks ahead to Duganne's speeches against the Fugitive Slave Law in 1852 and his service for the Union Army during the Civil War.[50]

Duganne's artisan republican critique of chattel slavery in *Eustace Barcourt* paves the way for one of the more powerful examinations of racial hierarchy in city-mystery fiction. Although the youngest member of the pirate crew, the black cabin boy named Bill, is implicated in the theft of the passing ships' cargo, he resourcefully subdues a white traitor and openly questions the privileges of whiteness. When a gruff white sailor orders Bill around the ship with racial epithets, the boy reflects, "Brack rascal—de debbil! . . . Who mak' him white, I wonder!" It is hard not to hear the catchphrase of Lippard's sardonic Devil-Bug—"I wonders how that will work!"—echoing through Bill's insight that race is something made and malleable. Later, in a power reversal reminiscent of Devil-Bug's punishment of hypocrites and oxymoronic oppressors, Bill identifies and subdues white Yankee Simon, the gang's traitor. "Bill proceeded leisurely to pinion the Yankee, muttering to himself all the time. 'He t'hink he fool Bill—Bill fool de Yankee. Simon no match for dis nigger. Hi-yah!'" Although Bill quickly fades from the novel, Duganne's representation of the charismatic and cheeky cabin boy resonates with Devil-Bug, who relishes exposing duplicitous whites and challenging middle-class norms, including racial hierarchies. The black cabin boy gets the last word when he ties up and gags Simon: "You be quiet, white man."[51]

While Duganne's city-mysteries of the 1840s demonstrate the convergence of artisan republicanism and anti-immigrant nativism that echoed the early black press and could enable cross-racial sympathy, Ned Buntline's writing offers a case study of the ways anti-immigrant nativism, untethered from artisan republicanism and cross-racial sympathy, could undermine working-class solidarity and reinforce middle-class values. Considered a showman and a wag by historians and biographers, Ned Buntline was born Edward Zane Carroll Judson in New York in 1821 and died in 1886, and is best known for his postbellum Western dime novels and stage plays that mythologized the frontiersman William "Buffalo Bill" Cody. Like Duganne, Buntline was active in nativist politics and served in the Union Army during the Civil War. Dime novel historian Albert Johannsen credits Buntline with helping to found the nativist fraternal organization the United Sons of America in Philadelphia in the mid-1840s, and Buntline biographer Jay Monaghan reports that Buntline was a leader in the nativist Order of United Americans in the late 1840s.[52] Typical of Buntline's penchant for self-promotion, he asserted in the 1850s that he had coined the nativist Know Nothing Party's name, a claim that historian Tyler Anbinder has refuted.[53] However, Buntline's amusing boast in his weekly story paper that "Mysteries and Miseries" only became a common title within the American city-mystery genre after he published *The Mysteries and Miseries of New York* appears to be true.[54]

Buntline was well known in the literary world of antebellum New York. In 1838, he published sketches in the *Knickerbocker* magazine; he enjoyed popular success with his best-known city-mystery *The Mysteries and Miseries of New York* in 1848; he started a weekly story paper titled *Ned Buntline's Own* the same year; and in 1849, he found himself embroiled in the fallout from the notorious Astor Place Riot. The unrest, which ended after soldiers fired on and killed at least twenty civilians, erupted when working-class theater-goers protested that the British actor William Charles Macready was performing as the title character of *Macbeth* rather than their preferred native-born American actor Edwin Forrest.[55] Although Buntline was the only person convicted in connection with the rioting and spent one year in jail on Blackwell's Island, Peter Buckley notes that the provocateur was convicted ultimately for exacerbating the tension in his weekly story paper: "His crime issued from words, not actions."[56]

Despite the working-class inflections of the city-mystery genre exhibited by Duganne, Lippard, and George Thompson, and despite

Buntline's self-fashioning in *Ned Buntline's Own* as a friend to the native-born mechanics and artisans of New York City, the strategies of class protest in *The Mysteries and Miseries of New York* ironically reinforce middle-class values. Relying foremost on anti-immigrant nativism to demonize unskilled immigrants as the greatest threat to native-born workers and native-born merchants, Buntline's novel lacks the racially ambivalent artisan republican critique of "wage" and chattel slavery; in sum, Buntline's novel builds a xenophobic cross-class alliance against the newly arrived immigrant instead of cross-racial class solidarity.

The Mysteries and Miseries of New York, which was released in five parts between December 1847 and April 1848, uses a dangerous band of foreign criminals to tie together its voluminous plots and subplots. These socially ostracized characters are not the "likable criminals" and spokespersons for "radical democracy" that populate other city-mysteries, as they ultimately draw Buntline's sharpest social criticism. Known collectively as Jack Circle's Gang, the English, Irish, French, and Italian immigrants prey relentlessly on the native-born middle class throughout the novel. Englishman Jack Circle plots to rob wealthy philanthropist Mr. Precise, who hopes to build a rural home for the poor with his business profits; meanwhile, an Italian gypsy couple, the Genlises, abduct a white middle-class child, Willie Abingdon—as he patriotically watches a local militia march past his house—and hold him for ransom. The gang members were invariably criminals in their former countries, echoing *The Rights of All*'s anxiety about receiving "the dregs of other countries." Buntline writes, "Jack Circle seldom attended the bar himself, but either moved about among his customers, conversing with them, or absented himself in the back room, where none save himself and a chosen few could enter; for this was a kind of general assembling room for the English burglars and pickpockets, who, driven from their own land, pursued their 'profession' in New York."[57]

The Mysteries and Miseries of New York sensationalizes the dangers to the native-born middle class through racialized immigrant characters who are prone to criminality, incapable of assimilation, and a drain on public resources. Buntline exploits blackness in his description of Genlis, the so-called Gypsy King, who visits Jack Circle to hatch the kidnapping plot: "Two persons entered. [Genlis] was a tall, dark complexioned, shrewd looking fellow, in whose jet black eyes could be seen the fire of villainy and deep cunning. His arched eye-brows, aquiline nose, thin lips and curling black hair, all bespoke him a native of a foreign soil."[58] Buntline's deployment of what Toni Morrison calls "Africanism"—racially coded language used to denigrate African Americans and extol whiteness—exploits racial and ethnic difference. After the Genlises kidnap Willie, they extort money from the boy's desperate mother with the help of an Irish hack driver, a Native American Indian fortune-teller, and an African American dwarf. The fortune-teller prophesizes that the Gypsy King alone can provide the whereabouts of the lost boy, and the Irish hack driver takes the mother, blindfolded, to pay Genlis for information. When the mother confides to her husband about her mysterious visit to the Gypsy King, Mr. Abingdon erupts with a nativist rant against Irish immigrants: "Nearly all the hack-drivers in town are Irish, and a saucy, cheating, good for nothing set of scoundrels they are too. If you were to rake the dominions of his sulfuric majesty with a fine-toothed comb, you couldn't find a more unprincipled, rascally set!"[59]

The novel is replete with racist caricatures that reinforce a cross-class alliance between the white native-born upper and lower classes at the expense of working-class African Americans, yet one example will suffice. When a group of rowdy young white men descend on African American Pete Williams's bar in Five Points, an historical establishment popularized in Charles Dickens's *American Notes* in 1842, ringleader "Butcher Bill" picks a fight with black ex-convict Zack Reed. Butcher Bill "walked up to a herculean negro, a fellow who stood full six feet high, and was built very heavily . . . he had time to plant four or five terrible blows directly in the eyes and mouth of [Zack Reed] . . . The negro could stand no more, and he now cried enough."[60] Unlike the proud and Herculean class-accented black male characters that appear frequently in early African American literature and white-authored sensational fiction, Buntline's Zack Reed is a minor character in a digressive scene that dramatizes enmity between the white and black working classes.

The novel's anti-immigrant nativism is most pronounced in the polemical appendix. Over thirty pages, Buntline explains to readers that the danger of immigration is the primary lesson to take away from *The Mysteries and Miseries of New York,* and he includes numerous fan letters and reports related to crime in the city. In case the reader has somehow overlooked the connections he makes repeatedly between immigration and crime in the novel, Buntline writes, "All of the large gang of burglars, whom with their real names and characters, we have introduced in our work, are foreigners, and mostly Englishmen. The denizens of the horrible circle known as the 'Five Points' are principally Irish and negroes; some few Dutch, are also living there, but not one *American,* to a hundred foreigners, can be found there."[61] With immigrants serving as cultural shorthand for the vice that plagues northeastern cities, and a rural home for the poor providing the novel's paternalistic solution to class inequality, *The Mysteries and Miseries of New York* develops an alliance between native-born white workers and native-born white professionals that undermines cross-racial class solidarity.

Anti-Catholic Nativism Gets a Wide Circulation

Although anti-immigrant nativism could reinforce middle-class values and racial paternalism when untethered from artisan republican critique in antebellum literature, it nevertheless constitutes a cross-racial correspondence between early African American literature and sensational fiction when employed to protest colonization and develop class-accented critiques of "wage" and chattel slavery. The more common strain of nativism, directed at Catholic immigrants who were suspected of being more loyal to the Roman Catholic Church than the nation, resonated with the artisan republican argument that citizens should subordinate private wants to the good of the republic. The *Republic*'s nativist editor, Thomas R. Whitney, provides an answer to his own question, "Can a Roman Catholic Become a Citizen?": "A Romanist cannot renounce the Papal authority and yet remain a Roman Catholic; and if he cannot do that, how can he give allegiance to another government . . . In a word, how can he become an American citizen?"[62] Class-accented anti-Catholic nativism circulated widely in the early black and white popular presses, and, particularly after the rise of the Know Nothing Party in the early 1850s, appears in the writing of Frederick Douglass and George Lippard to help develop their dual critiques of "wage" and chattel slavery. In a recent analysis of the Protestant ethos informing *Uncle Tom's Cabin* in 1852, literary critic Elizabeth Fenton observes that because "Anglo-Protestant Americans were accustomed to viewing the Catholic Church as a threat to individual liberties, comparing chattel slavery to Catholicism did not require a great imaginative leap."[63] Fenton's analysis of these allied discourses focuses primarily on mainstream abolitionist texts, whereas her insights can also help to illuminate the racial sympathy that I argue is central to white-authored sensational fiction directed toward the multiracial working classes.

At the advent of the early black press in the late 1820s and the penny press in the early 1830s, hysteria toward the Catholic immigrant as a threat to the young republic had already gained a strong foothold in American letters and political discourse. Notwithstanding J. Hector St. John de Crèvecoeur's rosy expectation in his 1782 *Letters from an American Farmer* that in America "the various Christian sects introduced wear out and . . . religious indifference becomes prevalent," animus toward Catholics would have a long and stubborn history in America. Historian Ray Billington has chronicled the anti-Catholic animus that was encoded in the Puritans' initial settlement of the northeastern colonies and early schoolbooks like the *New England Primer.* "The settlers who came to America . . . carried with them to the new land the same hatred of Popery which characterized the England of that day." Although the *US Constitution* outlawed the legal disenfranchisement of Catholics at the end of the eighteenth century, anti-Catholic fears lived on in the popular imagination with the annual "Pope Day" parade, which culminated in the burning of the Pope's effigy. Robert S. Levine has documented that anti-Catholic conspiracy plots, which circulated widely during the French and Indian War of the 1750s, continued well into the nineteenth century. "To the vast majority of the new republic's first several generations it remained clear, as it was to the colonists, that Americans were *not* a Roman Catholic, 'savage,' satanic, aristocratic, or despotic people." Given the job competition created in part by scores of Catholic immigrants during the antebellum period, anti-Catholic nativism would prove a resilient class-accented rhetoric for black and white authors. For instance, Robert Ernst cites that while 35,000 Catholics lived in New York City in 1830, that number would climb to between 60,000 and 80,000 a decade later and would swell to 100,000 by 1850. Tyler Anbinder notes that during German emigration to America, "by the 1850s Catholic immigrants outnumbered Protestants."[64]

The first black newspaper, *Freedom's Journal,* announced in its inaugural issue that, "in respect to matters of religion . . . we would not be the advocates of any particular sect or party," yet in its pages anti-immigrant and anti-Catholic nativism converge to defend the rights of working-class blacks.[65] In addition to encouraging black mechanics to settle "in this Republican country" as they are "attached to its climate and soil" and lamenting missionaries' focus on oppressed Europeans at the expense of America's native-born poor, *Freedom's Journal* mocks the perceived superstition and idolatry of Catholicism.[66] In an 1829 article entitled "Trickery Exposed," the editors recount how Catholic priests in Lisbon dug up an effigy and, having "proclaimed it to be the effigy of an eminent saint," rigged it to nod or shake its head accordingly in response to visitors' questions. When the contraption did not work correctly and the priest grew impatient in front of his audience, "a boy popped his head from behind the curtain, and exclaimed 'it is not my fault, sir, the string has broken!'"[67] While the tone is playful, the "exposé" of "trickery" exploits prevailing anti-Catholic anxieties, and anticipates such sensational nativist tracts of the subsequent two decades like the 1836 *Awful Disclosures of Maria Monk, or, The Hidden Secrets of a Nun's Life in a Convent Exposed!* and William R. Taylor's 1845 *Popery Exposed!*

The *Weekly Advocate* and *Colored American* of the late 1830s and the class-accented Boston weekly story paper the *Star Spangled Banner* of the early 1850s mount a shared defense of the Sabbath, underscoring the potential for cross-racial sympathy through anti-immigrant and anti-Catholic nativism. According to Tyler Anbinder, "The fact that the newcomers drank and caroused on Sundays particularly offended American Protestants accustomed to a quiet observance of the Sabbath."[68] Consistent with nativist fears that immigrants committed a disproportionate amount of crime, the *Weekly Advocate* and *Colored American* link Catholics' disregard for the Sabbath to an increased crime rate. In a January 1837 editorial entitled "Keeping the Sabbath," Robert Sears, one of the *Weekly Advocate*'s white editors, argues, "The light of history shows that in nominal Christian communities in which the Sabbath has ceased to be regarded as a day of holy rest, as is the case in all Catholic communities, crimes are as abundant, and moral principle is as much unknown, as in heathen lands."[69] A few months later, an editorial entitled "Sunday Hair Dressers" (signed "S. A.") praises a report from the *Pittsburgh Anti-Slavery Newspaper* that black barbers have begun observing the Sabbath and closing their shops on Sunday: "We have no doubt, but if all were to do likewise, an orderly public would sustain them."[70] These two examples demonstrate the early black press's use of anti-Catholic nativism to insist that the native-born black working class is virtuous and deserving of equality.

Published in the Boston weekly story paper the *Star Spangled Banner* fifteen years later, "Working on the Sabbath" is a testament to the longevity of popular print representations of African Americans defending the Sabbath. The humorous sketch features a free black employee, Caesar, educating a family of white farmers, presumably Catholic immigrants, about the importance of honoring the Sabbath. The sketch begins, "We have seen a capital anecdote lately, about a family of such people [who work on the Sabbath], who were pretty severely rebuked by a colored man in their employ." When Caesar is called to bale the hay, he refuses on moral grounds: "I cannot work any more on the Sabbath; it is not right." The precocious son argues with Caesar, asking, "But you would not pull your cow or sheep out of the pit on the Sabbath, Caesar?" To which Caesar wittily responds to close the sketch, "No, not if I had been trying all the week to shove them in; I would let them lie there."[71] As discussed in the next chapter, the *Star Spangled Banner* is noteworthy for serializing sensational fiction that features black working-class protagonists, as well as racially liminal artisan republican white heroes. "Working on the Sabbath," in which a sympathetic black worker scolds a white employer for abusing the Protestant day of rest, corresponds with the anti-Catholic nativism in the early black press and gestures toward cross-racial sympathy among the native-born multiracial working classes.

Anti-Catholic Nativism in Douglass and Lippard

Anti-Catholic discourse persisted in tracts, sermons, and popular novels during the 1830s and 1840s, and, as a result of increased immigration and economic unrest, experienced a resurgence in the late 1840s and early 1850s with the rise of such nativist political parties as the Order of the Star Spangled Banner and the Know Nothing Party. Elizabeth Fenton reminds us of "the age-old assumption that Catholicism is anathema to democracy," and claims that antislavery literature like *Uncle Tom's Cabin* "depend[ed] upon anti-Catholicism."[72] Frederick Douglass's writing for the most part eschewed anti-Catholic rhetoric: His 1845 slave narrative credits Irish political leader Richard Brinsley Sheridan's "mighty speeches on and in behalf of Catholic emancipation" with inspiring him to "abhor and detest [his] enslavers," and he remained a strong supporter of Irishman Daniel O'Connell, a leading figure in the fight for Catholic emancipation from discriminatory English laws.[73] Robert S. Levine reports that Douglass's speeches in Ireland during 1845 and 1846 "conveyed his sense of common cause between U.S. slaves and the Irish working poor," and that he would spend time visiting victims of the Potato Famine.[74] Nevertheless, the growing affinity between abolitionism and anti-Catholic nativism during the 1850s helps to account for Douglass's and Lippard's ambivalent use of the divisive rhetoric. As Protestant ministers in the 1850s increasingly "condemned 'rum, Romanism, and slavery' as the three evils cursing the nation," black and white writers employed anti-Catholicism in another cross-racial correspondence.[75]

When recounting in his 1855 *My Bondage and My Freedom* the slaves' failed plot to run away from Mr. Freeland, Douglass writes, "We were all, except Sandy, quite free from slaveholding priestcraft."[76] Douglass represents the designing slaves as a "band of brothers," and struggles to account for the strong possibility that one of their own, Sandy Jenkins, betrayed them. Douglass's pairing of the figurative term "priestcraft," which captures nativist suspicion of Catholic priests as scheming and deceitful, with "slaveholding" measures his disappointment in Sandy's deception and his outrage over slaveowners' manipulation of the Bible to defend chattel slavery. With the plotting slaves deceiving their slaveowner, Sandy deceiving the plotters, and slaveowners deceiving themselves and others about the horrors and injustices of slavery, Douglass relies on the fear of Catholic conspiracy that inheres in the term "priestcraft" to appeal to his readers. The fact Douglass's treatment of the runaway plot in the 1845 slave narrative does not employ "priestcraft" underscores nativism's widening appeal in the 1850s.

Similar anti-Catholic figurations to help denounce slavery appear in the literary notices of *Frederick Douglass' Paper.* In the September 3, 1852, issue, Douglass's literary editor, Julia Griffiths, calls Mary Eastman's novel *Aunt Phillis's Cabin* a "Jesuitical, mischievous book" for its defense of slavery and disingenuous response to *Uncle Tom's Cabin.* Two months later on November 5, 1852, Griffiths labels Sarah Josepha Hale's republished novel *Northwood* as "Jesuitical and mischievous in the extreme" for defending slavery with the Bible. Literary critic Jenny Franchot explains that there was special animus toward the Jesuit order of Roman Catholic priests in the nineteenth century. "Political phobias in particular were shaped by the centuries-long tradition of suspicion toward the Jesuits, confessors to generations of European royalty and hence the supposed masterminds behind domestic and international politics."[77] Douglass's writing and literary notices do not express explicit fears of Catholic conspiracy or denigrate Catholic immigrants the way the nativist press did, but the use of anti-Catholic metaphors demonstrates the divisive rhetoric's growing popularity and association with antislavery politics.

As a leading labor advocate in the late 1840s and early 1850s, Lippard cautioned against anti-Catholicism's potential to splinter working-class solidarity, particularly in his home city of Philadelphia, a hotbed of nativist agitation during the 1840s. Historian Bruce Laurie notes that in 1830s Philadelphia, most laborers were native-born, but after the two waves of European immigrants, at least two-thirds of whom were poor Irish, during the 1840s, "the proportion of foreign-born Philadelphians [increased] from 10 to nearly 40 percent of the male labor force."[78] A firsthand witness to the violent Kensington nativist riots of 1844 that pitted native-born artisans and their native-born employers against immigrant artisans and their immigrant employers, Lippard was unwilling to scapegoat Catholic immigrants.[79] Literary critic Shelley Streeby asserts in her study of popular literature about the Mexican-American War, "In contrast to Buntline and Duganne, whose nativist beliefs made them fearful of adding large numbers of Catholics and 'foreigners' to the nation, Lippard often denounced organized nativism."[80] Lippard's reluctance to employ anti-Catholicism is evident not only in his promotion of the anti-sectarian secret society the Brotherhood of the Union but also in anti-nativist editorials in the *Quaker City Weekly*.

In the 1849 "A Thought for the Bigots of All Colours," one of many defenses of Catholics in his weekly story paper, Lippard writes, "The name of Catholic with them is a synonym of devil; to hate the Catholic is their religion; Persecution is their God. It is against this blind rage, my friends, that I, a Pennsylvanian, a Protestant, appeal."[81] A month later in an encomium to a century-old graveyard located in his hometown of Germantown, Pennsylvania, Lippard praises the peaceful spot's freedom from sectarianism and calls up de Crèvecoeur's melting-pot of religious difference. "This soil is sacred from creeds. Here rests the Indian and the white man; here sleep in one sod, the Catholic, Presbyterian, Quaker, Methodist, Lutheran, Menonist, Deist, Infidel. Here, creeds forgotten, all are men and women again, and not one but is a simple child of God."[82] Rather than distinguishing people according to their religious beliefs or their race, Lippard saw only large-scale economic difference between the haves and have-nots.

Despite these appeals to religious tolerance, as anti-Catholicism became increasingly associated with the antislavery movement, Lippard in 1853 made strategic use of nativism in *New York* to build a cross-racial alliance among native-born black and white "wage" slaves and to protest the Fugitive Slave Act and chattel slavery. In her transatlantic study of nativist literature, literary critic Susan Griffin argues that "the cultural shorthand of anti-Catholic stereotypes and narrative structures provide nineteenth-century writers with a means of depicting and discussing the changes and problems of the day." Griffin adds, "While the nativist novelists differ in their class allegiances, each depicts the brotherhood of true Americans as uniting men of all ranks and stresses the fraternity's artisan membership," which were some of the very working-class readers that sensational white authors like Lippard were targeting.[83] Lippard's decision to publish *New York* in Cincinnati, a hotbed of nativist activity, with H. M. Rulison, a prolific publisher of nativist texts such as Anthony Gavin's *The Great Red Dragon; or, the Master-Key to Popery* and Isaac Kelso's *Danger in the Dark: A Tale of Intrigue and Priestcraft,* is indicative of the novel's liberal use of anti-Catholicism.

In *New York,* an exposé of corruption, hypocrisy, and conspiracy among the wealthy classes, Lippard employed anti-Catholic nativism to develop artisan republican class protest. Since at least the 1830s, nativist texts had constructed the Roman Catholic Church as antirepublican and conspiratorial. In his 1835 popular treatise *Foreign Conspiracy Against the Liberties of the United States,* nativist agitator and telegraph inventor Samuel Morse writes, "Popery is a Political system, despotic in its organization, anti-democratic and anti-republican, and cannot therefore co-exist with American republicanism."[84] In *New York,* multiracial groups of working-class vigilantes thwart the schemes of Northern "merchant princes," Southern slaveowners, and agents of the Roman Catholic Church. In each case, the grandeur and decadence associated in the public mind with Catholicism distinguishes the villains from the artisan republican heroes. For instance, the Temple, *New York*'s equivalent to *The Quaker City*'s Monk-Hall, is a "lofty mansion" of ill repute where merchants, politicians, and clergymen dress in Catholic costume to seduce unsuspecting virgins. With rakes disguised as popes and cardinals and their seduced victims disguised as dancing girls, the mistress and host of the Temple, the Midnight Queen, describes the festivities to her newly arrived guests: "Masked and veiled, shut out from the world by impenetrable walls, they are commencing one of the orgies, which awoke the echoes of the Vatican, in the days of Pope Borgia."[85] Rodrigo Borgia, who served as Pope Alexander VI from 1492 to 1503, the period of European discovery of America, was reviled among nineteenth-century nativists for his perceived immorality and sexual license; Susan Griffin calls him "the touchstone for Catholic corruption."[86] Observing the disguised revelers, a guest muses, "Are we indeed in New York, in the nineteenth century,—or is it Rome, in the days of the Borgias?"[87]

In addition to the anti-Catholic imagery, which Samuel Otter generously refers to as Lippard's "ambient anti-Catholicism," *New York* develops a Morse-like subplot in which Catholic conspirators plot to overthrow and subjugate the American government.[88] A mysterious Prelate of the Roman Catholic Church articulates how they will undermine the American republic by controlling the educational system and the elective process. During the antebellum period, nativists politicked to require public schools to use exclusively the King James version of the Bible, and complained that immigrants enjoyed undue influence at the polls by forming voting blocs for the Democratic Party. In this context, the Prelate articulates an anti-republican plot that would stoke nativists' greatest fears: "It is our true policy, then, to absorb and rule over the Republic of the North. To make our Church the secret spring of its Government; to gradually and without exciting suspicion, mould every one of its institutions to our own purposes; to control the education of its people, and bend the elective franchise to our will . . . The hour will come, when the flimsy scaffolding of Republicanism will fall, and as it falls, our Church will stand revealed, her foundation in the heart of the American Republic." Although Lippard cautions that nativists unwittingly strengthen the Catholic Church's influence in American politics by demonizing Catholic voters and he distinguishes between warring factions within the Roman Catholic Church, the subplot ends in Vatican City on the ominous note that a cataclysmic religious war is brewing in America. The Legate, a wealthy American who is working against the corrupt elements inside the Vatican, announces, "The Pope and the church in the hands of crowned and mitred miscreants, who having crushed the last spark of Liberty in the Old World, will not be long ere they open their trenches before her last altar in the New World! Away to the New World then; if the battle must come, let us, let the friends of humanity, strike the first blow!"[89] By presenting the coming religious war as a fight over republican principles, Lippard posits that the "absolutist" faction within the Roman Catholic Church seeks nothing less than to enslave the American people, as figured sympathetically through the working-class white mechanic hero Arthur Dermoyne and fugitive slave Old Royal, thus reinforcing a dual critique of "wage" and chattel slavery.

With Catholic imagery figuring the depravity of the villains and the Roman Catholic Church plotting against the republic, anti-Catholicism converges with antislavery sentiment in *New York* in a suggestive scene between Randolph Royalton, the fugitive slave who is passing as white and hiding out with his sister, Esther, and Bernard Lynn, the former Carolina planter who has returned from Europe, where Randolph once rescued his daughter Eleanor from a seducer during a short stay in Florence. Randolph poses as a Southern slaveowner and invites the Lynns to dinner in hopes of pursuing a relationship with Eleanor. In the candlelit dining room, Randolph is surrounded by luxurious china, the ostentatious trappings of both the slaveowner and the powerful Roman Catholic. "The service of plate which loaded the table was of massive gold. Everything breathed luxury and wealth." Overcome by the splendor, Lynn whispers to his host, "You planters know how to live! . . . By George, friend Randolph, you are something of a republican, but it is after the Roman school!"[90] Lynn may be referencing the perceived decadence of Rome prior to its fall in this ironic quip, but given the novel's repeated association between Catholicism and "wage" and chattel slavery, it is hard not to hear a veiled reference to the "Roman" Catholic Church. Lynn's compliment provides a subtle example of how Lippard links the ultimate non-producer, the Southern slaveowner, with the aristocratic grandeur of Rome and the Roman Catholic Church. Like Frederick Douglass's writing of the 1850s, Lippard's *New York* strategically employs anti-Catholic nativism when it could augment the more pressing critique of chattel slavery.

Augustine Duganne, the Know Nothing Novelist

On September 16, 1857, the *New York Tribune* reported on the nativist American Party's state convention in Syracuse, New York, and cited Know Nothing politician Augustine Duganne declaring to the audience, "Americans shall rule America."[91] Duganne released his last full-length novel, *The Tenant-House; or, Embers from Poverty's Hearthstone,* in New York City in 1857 with Robert DeWitt, a prolific publisher of sensational fiction. With Lippard having died of tuberculosis in February 1854, and Buntline having relocated to a remote cabin in the Adirondack Mountains, where he turned to writing historical fiction and "clean outdoor romance" for weekly story papers, *The Tenant-House* functions as the last gasp of the city-mystery genre that blended representation of the labyrinthine city with Gothic horrors while emphasizing class conflict.[92] Yet unlike Duganne's 1840s city-mysteries' working-class protest figured through artisan republicanism, progressive images of blackness, and nativism, *The Tenant-House* reinforces such middle-class values as modest moral reform and racial paternalism as it demonizes anti-Catholic immigrants as depraved criminals and the greatest threat to the nation. In this way, *The Tenant-House* replicates Ned Buntline's anti-immigrant nativism and racism in *The Mysteries and Miseries of New York* and realizes Lippard's caution that nativism could splinter working-class solidarity and ultimately serve the interests of the status quo.

Duganne's nativist proclivities culminated in his election as a Know Nothing to represent the sixth district of New York City in the state assembly of 1856.[93] The Know Nothings, formally known as the

American Party, won numerous elections in the mid-1850s, including gubernatorial races in Maine and Pennsylvania, and ran Millard Fillmore for president in 1856.[94] Arguably the first instance of a third party in American politics, the Know Nothings made anti-Catholicism mainstream in the 1850s. Like W. T. Lhamon Jr.'s claim that the middle class began to coopt blackface minstrelsy in the 1850s, the working-class protest and cross-racial sympathy common to sensational fiction of the 1840s and early 1850s gave way in *The Tenant-House* to xenophobic and racist alliances between native-born whites of the working and middle classes.[95] Tyler Anbinder's analysis of surviving membership rolls of Know Nothing lodges reveals that the nativist party of the 1850s did not draw disproportionately from the working class. "When occupational data concerning Know Nothing lodge members is compared with random samplings of those eligible for membership in the Order, one actually finds that the Know Nothings attracted an approximately average proportion of both artisans and professionals."[96] *The Tenant-House* reflects the growing middle-class accents of anti-Catholic nativism in the 1850s: When authors like Duganne and Buntline privileged the rhetoric of nativism and divorced it from artisan republicanism and racial sympathy, their sensational fiction replaces a critique of "wage" and chattel slavery with moral reform and racial paternalism, in turn confirming the important role that progressive representations of blackness played in developing the working-class protest of earlier city-mysteries.

The Tenant-House follows two primary plot lines in New York City: a Christian philanthropist's efforts to improve the lives and beautify the homes of degraded white and black tenement dwellers, and a wealthy Jewish landlord's efforts to rescue his kidnapped daughter from a nefarious band of Italian Catholic immigrants. Granby, an older and wealthy Protestant bachelor, provides a template for rational middle-class reform. Having been made aware of homeless white children struggling in the city through his chance encounter with a homeless newsboy, Granby shares with his black servant Samson a paternalistic solution to poverty: "It is here, in the midst of these habitations, that reforming influences should be set at work; here, in the tenant-house, ought to be planted a school, wherein to gather, as in a sheepfold, the poor lambs who are outcast from the flock of society. Yes, Samson! the miserable and squalid offspring of these poor people might thus be made infant missionaries, to carry to their depraved homes an influence and power of good, whereby whole families should be reformed and elevated."[97] Granby's goal of transforming the urchins into well-behaved and God-fearing children who will convince their parents to stop drinking alcohol and work harder is consistent with the moralistic reforms Duganne advocated during his stint as a New York assemblyman. According to the 1903 history *The Tenement House Problem,* Duganne's five-person committee that investigated the living conditions in New York's tenant-houses over a seven-day period in 1856 recommended improved ventilation and cleanliness, no renting of cellar apartments, passable stairways, the prevention of prostitution, and temperance.[98] While the recommendations include practical improvements for safety, the moral tone of the committee's report is embodied in *The Tenant-House*'s wise white reformer. Surrounded in his well-appointed home with middle-class trappings and a conspicuously placed Bible, Granby is the sober philanthropist whose relief for the working poor is largely cosmetic and wishful.

In the novel's second plot line, the character of Monna Maria, the matriarch of a large family of Italian Catholic organ-grinders, is designed to stoke nativist anxieties toward newly arrived immigrants. The family's cramped tenement serves as a "rendezvous and lodging-place for yellow-faced and black-hearted men, belonging to that 'army of Italy' who traverse, night and day, with heavy load, the streets of this metropolis."[99] The sinister aspect of the performing organ-grinders is borne out when Monna Maria orchestrates the kidnapping of the landlord's daughter Rachel Kolephat, renames her Ninetta, trains her to become a ballerina, and forces the terrified girl to turn over her meager earnings from dancing. Duganne indulges in racial essentialism in his portrayals of the Jewish landlord and "usurer" Mordecai Kolephat and his lonely tenant Mallory the Miser, but both men are redeemed in the text and spend their wealth, like Granby, on ameliorating the plight of the poor. Tyler Anbinder notes that "Know Nothings did not condemn Jews or Judaism," not only because of "the minute size of the antebellum Jewish-American population," but also because nativists "believed that Jews could make fine American citizens" on account of their "republican propensities, evident in the democratic administration of their congregations."[100] Consistent with the Know Nothings' ambivalence toward Jewish immigrants, *The Tenant-House* directs its most virulent nativism toward the Italian Catholic family.

While Protestant reformer Granby resides in a warm, middle-class home, Monna Maria lives the life of an ascetic. Her small apartment, which houses Ninetta and more than a dozen organ-grinders, is decorated only with the symbols of her Catholic faith. "Monna Maria's household articles were, therefore, very few; but conspicuous among them was a sort of altar, opposite the fire-place, formed of an oblong packing-box, covered with a white cloth, whereon were a crucifix and a glass bottle, containing water from the church, and over which hung several colored prints, representing the agony of Christ, and the Virgin Mary. Here, in solitude, Monna Maria, a bigot and ascetic, was used to practice her superstitious devotions—here, in fanatical endurance, she framed new penances to undergo, new chastisements wherewith to torture her miserable body." Dictatorial and imperial, Monna Maria invokes Catholic tenets to defend the kidnapping, and expects to be rewarded in heaven for raising the Jewish girl as a Roman Catholic. In *The Tenant-House,* Monna Maria represents the threat that the Catholic religion, not class stratification or chattel slavery, poses to the republic. When Monna Maria dies in a climactic fire she sets to kill Ninetta and prevent the girl's rescue, Duganne reflects, "Thus Monna Maria communed in the darkness, believing, in her superstition, that she did no wrong. O Human Heart! This poor Italian woman is not alone in her bigotry! Alas! How many of the refined, the educated, the gospel-taught are in our midst, who build up about their spirits a wall of fanaticism, like unto Monna Maria's."[101] With Monna Maria and her band's sensational crimes dominating the plot and the denouement, *The Tenant-House* demonizes Italian Catholic immigrants and builds a cross-class alliance between native-born, white, middle-class Protestant reformers and the white working-class urchins who are transformed—like Horatio Alger Jr.'s Ragged Dick a decade later—into "respectable" young men and women.

By investing heavily in anti-Catholicism and middle-class reform, *The Tenant-House* forestalls the cross-racial class solidarity of earlier city-mysteries, and figures black characters exclusively through romantic racialism and paternalism, calling up the most racist plantation literature of the period. In contrast to Lippard's Herculean black male heroes who reinforce the value of physical labor over abstracted forms of middle-class power and authority, Duganne's Herculean black servant, Samson, embodies the myth of contented servitude. Although Samson, with "muscular breast" and "labor-seamed hands," shares the class-inflected physical strength of Lippard's heroic black male characters, he is made virtuous through his dutiful service to Granby. Once Granby establishes a Sabbath school for tenement children, the white philanthropist and his black servant pray together for its success. "A weather-beaten, scarred, but honest and intelligent countenance was that of the negro, with a look of child-like confidence as he listened to the teachings of the 'Good Book' . . . Together, with God's holy Word before them, these earnest worshippers prayed in humility for the weary and way-worn of all His family. Master and servant—black and white—united in a heartfelt supplication for their common humanity." Granby's and Samson's shared religious faith obscures their economic relationship, which is rooted in chattel slavery. Granby tells Samson, "Did I not say, years ago, that I had found in my poor slave, as then you were, a friend who would never desert me? . . . We have been called 'Master' and 'Slave,' but your bondage to me, Samson, has been that of the heart."[102] Granby's compliment to his former slave fetishizes chattel slavery as a benign institution and is a far cry from slavery's horrors as detailed by Lippard's desperate fugitive slaves in *New York*.

In response to Granby's offer for "freedom and competence" twenty years earlier, Samson insists—in thick dialect—that he does not regret staying with Granby. "'Nebber! Nebber!' sobbed the negro. 'Samson hab a white heart in his black bosom, and close down dere is de face ob massa, jes' like a lookin'-glass, forebber and ebber. Bress de Lord, dat put sense in de nigger's head.'" Samson has a place, albeit a subordinate one, in Granby's Christian family circle, and yet their relationship built on patronage rather than contractual employment renders Samson the "contented slave" of Southern plantation fiction. Like Lippard's homage to Quaker abolitionist Lucretia Mott, Duganne's Samson serves to complement Granby's spiritual idealism by suggesting that the Sabbath school should also attend to the children's material needs: "An' if dere was such a ting as to gib 'em suthin' to eat, an' suthin' to take away home, for de ole folks to eat, whenebber dey was good children, an' larned de lesson—kind o' 'ward o' good behavior, like, massa—you know."[103] Granby thanks Samson and follows his advice, but the former slave lacks the heroism and the gravitas of Lippard's charismatic Black Sampson, Black Andy, and Old Royal. In Duganne's paternalist hands in the 1850s, Samson is shorn of his locks.

With the slaveholding aristocratic villains of earlier city-mysteries replaced by fanatical Catholic immigrants, and lacking an artisan republican critique of class inequality and a progressive engagement with blackness, *The Tenant-House* displaces working-class protest in favor of a middle-class celebration of Protestant reform and capitalist logic. It is telling that the *Southern Literary Messenger,* which would be associated increasingly with pro-slavery sentiment during the 1850s, would commend *The Tenant-House* in 1859 for "its reference to the sufferings of the poor of New York City. The book details horrors very far surpassing the inventions of Mrs. Stowe concerning Southern Slavery."[104] In analyzing Duganne's popular novels opposing the Mexican-American War, Shelley Streeby notes, Duganne's "anti-imperialism derived from nativist beliefs about the importance of keeping foreigners and Catholics out of the republic, as well as from pacifist, radical republican, and antislavery convictions."[105] Moreover, Duganne would take up arms for the North and come to view the Civil War as a moral crusade against slavery, writing in 1866 that "Slavery had taken the sword; it was to 'perish by the sword,'" yet his last city-mystery in 1857 relies foremost on nativism and lacks the dynamic cross-racial class critique that I have shown once dominated the popular genre.[106]

Conclusion

The combination of anti-Catholic bigotry, middle-class paternalism, and romantic racialism of *The Mysteries and Miseries of New York* and *The Tenant-House* underscores the crucial role that "charismatic" blackness plays in the working-class politics of earlier city-mysteries by Lippard, Duganne, and Thompson. It is no coincidence that the sympathetic representations of virtuous, assertive, and proud black artisans regularly accord with the strongest expressions of artisan republicanism in the city-mysteries published between 1844 and 1854. Furthermore, as I have shown, anti-immigrant nativism, when deployed in opposition to colonization schemes, constitutes a cross-racial correspondence between early African American literature and white-authored sensational fiction. The next chapter uses a case study method to explore the class-accented correspondences that exist between a popular weekly story paper and the early black press. Serialized fiction, literary reviews, editorials, and news articles tell a similar story of a shared desire for cross-racial sympathy among the multiracial readers of antebellum popular print culture.

CHAPTER FOUR

Class-Accented Sensationalism in the Black and Popular Presses

After visiting Harriet Beecher Stowe at her Andover, Massachusetts, home in the early part of 1853, Frederick Douglass eagerly complied with her request that he write a letter detailing his ambitious plans for an industrial college open to black and white youth in the North that she could take with her to England that spring and use to solicit funds. Stowe and Douglass had become allies in the fight to end chattel slavery: while penning *Uncle Tom's Cabin* for its serialization in the *National Era,* Stowe had written to Douglass requesting information about his experiences in slavery, and amidst the controversies that erupted after the novel's release as a complete text in 1852, Douglass defended it in his newspaper against all detractors, whether offended Southerners who questioned its verisimilitude or Northern black activists who were suspicious of its colonization ending.

As Douglass relates their meeting in his autobiography *The Life and Times of Frederick Douglass,* first published in 1881, Stowe wanted to assist free blacks in a material way. Douglass recounts their meeting: "'I have invited you here,' she said, 'because I wish to confer with you as to what can be done for the free colored people of the country. I am going to England and expect to have a considerable sum of money placed in my hands, and I intend to use it in some way for the permanent improvement of the free colored people, and especially for that class which has become free by their own exertions.'"[1] Although Stowe's financial support proved insufficient—she raised on her sojourn abroad just $535, which she turned over to Douglass for his personal use—and she lost interest in Douglass's educational project that would never come to fruition, the energy he devoted to the project and the space he provided the proposal in his weekly newspaper between 1853 and 1855 reveal his growing concern for the plight of black and white workers alike. Like George Lippard's announcement that the Brotherhood of the Union would be open to people of all races and religions, Douglass's school would admit pupils "without reference to sex or complexion."[2] The shared attention to ameliorating the multiracial working class's material conditions appears in *Frederick Douglass' Paper* and Boston's class-accented weekly story paper the *Star Spangled Banner,* and their cross-racial strategies of class protest constitute another correspondence between white- and black-authored writing circulating in antebellum popular print culture.

Frederick Douglass' Paper's promotion of an industrial college for Northern blacks and whites, along with its favorable reviews of white-authored sensational fiction like Emerson Bennett's 1855 *Ellen Norbury* and antislavery fiction like Mary Hayden Green Pike's 1854 *Ida May*, employs the same strategies of class protest found in white-authored serialized fiction of the period: artisan republican pride in the skilled crafts, sensational depictions of multiracial misery in urban settings, and cross-racial alliances among the dispossessed. Todd Vogel, one of the first literary critics to consider labor issues in the early black press, argues that black newspapers adapted republicanism to critique racist hiring practices in the Northern marketplace and to promote black uplift. "In these free black newspapers, authors used narratives of elevation—stories about getting ahead in society through work—to create an alternative social understanding about jobs and citizenship that overturned the antebellum system of privilege given to those considered 'white.'"[3] While I do not disagree with the claim, Vogel's analysis overstates the relationship between white and black workers as predominantly hostile, and thereby obscures the early black press's appeals to working-class solidarity that could at times transcend racial lines.

Running concurrently with *Frederick Douglass' Paper,* Justin Jones's *Star Spangled Banner,* which ran from 1846 to 1857, regularly serialized white-authored sensational fiction featuring black and racially liminal heroes, and the two newspapers' cross-racial correspondences become even more pronounced when that fiction is contextualized within the *Star Spangled Banner*'s racially sympathetic news reports and advertisements for antislavery displays at P. T. Barnum's American Museum. Because it is impossible to generalize about the bewildering juxtaposition of racial representations that circulate throughout antebellum print culture, this chapter's case study method provides an effective means of highlighting in a prominent black newspaper and a popular weekly story paper the same patterns of cross-racial economic critique that I have shown exist in African American literature and white-authored sensational fiction of the 1840s and 1850s. In doing so, this comparative analysis challenges the respective master narratives that position middle-class uplift at the center of the study of the early black press, and that locate racism and reactionary politics at the heart of white-authored working-class literary forms.

"Learn Trades or Starve!"

In the March 4, 1853, edition of *Frederick Douglass' Paper,* just four days before he would write his letter of support for Stowe, Douglass published an urgent editorial—underscored by an exclamation point—about the necessity of free blacks becoming skilled craftsmen. That Douglass himself wrote this editorial is suggested by the similar sentence structures that appear four days later on March 8, 1853, in his letter to Stowe. Like white labor activists and city-mystery writers invoking artisan republicanism as a counter-ideology to liberal capitalism, Douglass extols the virtue of the honest labor of the producing classes who work skillfully with their hands. As part of his opposition to black employment solely in the service industry, Douglass asserts in "Learn Trades or Starve!": "We must show that we can *do* as well as *be;* and to this end we must learn trades. When we can build as well as live in houses; when we can *make* as well as *wear* shoes; when we can produce as well as consume wheat, corn and rye—then we shall become valuable to society."[4] The parallel constructions juxtapose the artisan republicanism of skilled carpenters, cobblers, and farmers with the middle and upper classes that are preoccupied with fashion ["wear shoes"] and consumption ["consume wheat, corn and rye"], resonating with city-mysteries' idealization of the skilled and humble craftsman. Douglass uses the same parallelism in his March 1853 letter to Stowe, which he published in *Frederick Douglass' Paper* in December 1853, when he writes, "We must not only be able to *black* boots, but to *make* them."[5]

Douglass's promotion of the industrial college is a reaction to the widespread racism facing blacks seeking apprenticeships with skilled white artisans. Four years before Frank J. Webb would dramatize such prejudice as hindering young apprentice Charlie Ellis in *The Garies and Their Friends,* Douglass, who details in his slave narrative the workplace violence he endured on the docks of Baltimore, writes to Stowe, "Prejudice against the free colored people in the United States has shown itself nowhere so invincible as among mechanics . . . At this moment I can more easily get my son into a lawyer's office to study law than I can into a blacksmith's shop to blow the bellows and to wield the sledgehammer."[6] In "Learn Trades or Starve!," Douglass, instead of privileging classical education for free blacks, believes study of the mechanic arts is the surest means to "the elevation of the masses" in what is rightfully their native land. While the classically educated black man "finds few inducements to remain in this country" and "is isolated in the land of his birth," according to Douglass, free blacks and their white allies in the North should encourage black youth to learn "useful and lucrative trades." Frustrated with race prejudice among the middle and upper classes that possessed the means to train black youth, Douglass implores white abolitionists to take on black apprentices. "We appeal to the abolitionists, what BOSS anti-slavery mechanic will take a black boy into his wheelwright's shop, his blacksmith's shop, his joiner's shop, his cabinet shop . . . Where are the anti-slavery milliners and seamstresses that will take colored girls and teach them trades, by which they can obtain an honorable living?"[7] Douglass's appeals to raise money for the industrial college would run weekly in his newspaper for two years through March 23, 1855, and corresponded with white labor advocates' celebration of the honest labor of the producing classes.

While Douglass's increased focus during the 1850s on the working conditions of Northern free blacks aligns him with white labor advocates who believed most abolitionists neglected class concerns, Douglass viewed his Northern industrial college project as playing a critical role in protesting Southern slavery. For Douglass, black men training and becoming skilled craftsmen countered the claims of Southern slaveowners and their apologists, who contended blacks could not be successful on their own. "If there is one proposition which commands our hearty and instant assent more than another," editorializes Douglass, "it is that 'the FREE colored men's elevation is essential to the SLAVE colored man's emancipation.'"[8] He would elaborate this point in his letter to Stowe: "The most telling, the most killing refutation of slavery, is the presentation of an industrious, enterprising, upright, thrifty, and intelligent free black population. Such a population, I believe, would rise in the northern states, under the fostering care of such a college as proposed."[9] Northern free labor ideology and abolitionism also converge in black proponents' support of the industrial college project. In the introduction to the second edition of *Autographs for Freedom* in 1854, which was an anthology of antislavery literature published in Rochester, New York, to raise funds for abolitionist activities, black college professor Charles Lewis Reason condemns Southern and Northern types of slavery. In a passage that resonates with Lippard's insistence in the *Quaker City Weekly* on protesting "wage" and chattel slavery, Reason writes, "Abolitionists ought to consider it a legitimate part of their great work, to aid in such an enterprise—to abolish not only chattel servitude, but that other kind of slavery, which, for generation after generation, dooms an oppressed people to a condition of dependence and pauperism."[10] Although Douglass and Reason, and Lippard and other city-mystery writers, emphasized chattel and "wage" slavery respectively, the fact remains that the most prominent spokespeople in the abolitionist and labor movements were committed to ending all forms of oppression and exploitation.

Douglass argued pragmatically that the black masses would benefit economically through learning the crafts more so than receiving an exclusively classical education, but this does not mean he did not see the value of such an education. In fact, Douglass imagined an industrial college that offered a balanced curriculum of practical training and classical education. As part of his "Plan of the American Industrial School" that he ran weekly in his newspaper from 1854 to 1855, Douglass listed two regulations: "a. For every branch of Literature taught, there shall be one branch of handicraft also taught in the School. b. Each pupil shall occupy one half his time when at School, in work at some handicraft, or on the farm."[11] The fact the study of "Literature" would comprise half the youths' time is in keeping with Douglass's awareness of the value of literacy in his own experience surviving and escaping slavery. The industrial school's dual focus on craftsmanship and literature corresponded with his newspaper's reviews of both sensational and antislavery literature. The "Literary Notices" section of *Frederick Douglass' Paper* provided favorable reviews of sensational novels, including Emerson Bennett's urban mystery *Ellen Norbury* that sympathizes with the "slaves at the North—white and black,"[12] and Mary Hayden Green Pike's *Ida May,* a popular antislavery novel marked by graphic depictions of violence, the enslavement of a Northern middle-class white girl by a cast of white and black tormenters, and cross-racial alliances that resonate with the white-authored sensational fiction serialized in the *Star Spangled Banner.*

Popular Novel Reading and the Early Black Press

The antebellum period was marked by slowly changing attitudes toward fiction reading: it could enrich the mind and strengthen one's morals, or, as some critics warned, could stoke and pervert the imagination of impressionable youths. An instructive example, the publication of *The Quaker City* in 1845, spawned a flurry of positive and negative reviews in the local press, and, in the words of David S. Reynolds, "divided Philadelphia into two camps, with poor workers taking Lippard's side."[13] John S. DuSolle, the editor of Philadelphia newspaper the *Spirit of the Times,* called the novel "a disgusting mass of filth."[14] Lippard was compelled to defend his best-selling novel against charges of lurid sensationalism and obscenity, and in the preface to the novel's second edition in 1849, addresses the firestorm: "Shall I tell how [the novel] has been praised—how abused—how it has on the one hand been cited as a Work of great merit, and on the other, how it has been denounced as the most immoral work of the age?"[15] In a view that corresponded with abolitionist newspapers' focus on the political content of antislavery fiction, Lippard saw his novel as a class allegory that would serve as "an effective instrument in the cause of human progress."[16] Despite the *National Era*'s recommendation in 1854 of Lippard's antislavery novella *Eleanor,* the popularity of his city-mysteries enabled Lippard's name to be used as cultural shorthand for lurid writing. In the July 18, 1850, review of Augustine Duganne's re-released 1845 novel *The Knights of the Seal,* the reviewer for the *National Era* laments, "This is, in some respects, a clever production, but written too much in the [Joseph Holt] Ingraham and Lippard style for our entire approbation."[17] The *National Era*'s reservations in 1850 about the city-mystery writing of Duganne, whose poetry they published regularly between 1847 and 1854, reflect the abolitionist press's uneasy relationship with sensational fiction; this relationship would grow friendlier in the literary reviews of *Frederick Douglass' Paper.*

Amidst the explosion of popular print culture featuring sensational crime reports and serialized fiction during the 1830s and 1840s, cultural critics, in keeping with a tradition in American letters dating back to the eighteenth century, raised the alarm about the perceived dangers of reading fiction, which included its perceived propensity to foster self-love, and in essence, to cultivate independent—or what the cultural elite might call "intractable" or "anarchic"—thinking. The penny papers, sustained by the increasingly literate white and black working classes in the urban northeast, appealed to their readers with shocking and thrilling crime reports and human interest stories as well as serialized fiction that critic Dan Schiller argued were class-accented with artisan republican rhetoric and expressed a nascent, and sometimes open, hostility toward the middle and upper classes.[18] The early black press's attitude toward fiction reading, and of popular fiction specifically, evolved dramatically between 1827 and the mid-1850s: the anxieties toward fiction expressed by the first African American newspaper, *Freedom's Journal,* would be replaced with praise for sensational urban novels in *Frederick Douglass' Paper.*

Literary critic Frankie Hutton argues that the early black press largely reinforced middle-class values in their broad appeal to racial uplift. "The middle class aspired almost constantly to respectability through education, temperance, industriousness, upright living patterns, and involvement in a variety of self-elevation organizations."[19] In keeping with the prevailing conventional view of novels as frivolous wastes of time and an impediment to rational, sober thinking, a *Freedom's Journal* editorial from 1827 asserting the civic importance of educating free blacks cautions, "In general, works of fiction mislead the mind not previously fortified; and so far from imparting solid advantage, they lead the reader to make calculations which are slender as the spider's web, deceptive as the ignis fatuus, retarding the mind from making substantial progress, and obstructing the prosperity of our race."[20] *Freedom's Journal*'s anxiety toward novel reading spans the paper's run. An editorial entitled "Good Advice to Young Men," reprinted from the *St. Johnsbury Herald* of Vermont near the end of *Freedom's Journal*'s run in 1829, sums up the black paper's view of fiction. Advising mechanics and apprentices to read their Bible in the winter evenings, the writer closes with a familiar caution: "One more word, young friends, if you want amusement for your evenings in a way that will be far *worse* than useless, you can have it by reading novels."[21] This anxious treatment of fiction reading in the late 1820s, just prior to the emergence of the penny press, is typical of the period, and illuminates the ambivalent treatment of sensational novels in the black press of the 1830s and 1840s and the promotion of such novels in *Frederick Douglass' Paper* in the 1850s.

Edited during its run from 1837 to 1841 in New York City by Reverend Samuel Cornish, the *Weekly Advocate,* later the *Colored American,* offers a nuanced perspective on sensational fiction, which was becoming more popular among the masses and thus a growing target of the cultural elite. Although the *Weekly Advocate* and the *Colored American* regularly covered high-profile murder cases through original reporting and, more commonly, reprints from around the country where the crimes had occurred, the newspaper reflected what Nina Baym sees as literary reviewers' propensity to judge novels according to a Victorian moral schema that marginalized the popular novel. "Between 1820 and 1860, reviews increasingly asked questions about the views of life contained in a novel and judged novels as superior when their views accorded with a vision of a morally governed universe."[22] In an 1837 editorial tellingly titled "Licentious Literature," the *Weekly Advocate* addresses the rise of the penny press and picks up where *Freedom's Journal*'s cultural anxieties toward sensationalism left off. In response to the opening question, "What is the general character of our penny papers, or 'respectable sixpennies'—our pamphlets, periodicals, poems, and tales of fiction," the writer concludes, "Many of our public papers are curses instead of blessings. Reader, what are their contents? Is not Vice called Virtue; and is not every exertion made—every artifice used to trap the unsuspecting and inexperienced part of mankind?"[23] Two years later, rather than dismissing cheap fiction altogether, an editorial titled "Means of Elevation: The Press" draws moral distinctions *among* popular novels. Although the writer regrets that the cheap press has been converted by some men "into a vehicle for the promulgation of immoral licentious books and periodicals," the writer concludes, "But I cannot agree with those persons who condemn, promiscuously, every tale of fiction, which may be produced—for I hold that a good moral may sometimes be conveyed by them, provided that they are properly written, and cleansed from all impurities."[24]

Despite the early black press's condemnation of popular fiction for sacrificing scruples in the interest of pecuniary gain, the *Colored*

American, like many other newspapers of the day, was not averse to running shocking news reports that would interest and entertain their readers. On January 12, 1839, the editors reprinted a report, highly narrative in form, from the *Buffalo Commercial Advertiser,* with the overtly sensational title, "A Thrilling Incident." In a nod to the proliferation and popularity of sensational fiction, the author promises a narrative that is as interesting as "the most highly wrought tale of fiction."[25] In chronicling a barely averted boiler explosion on a ship caught in a gale on Lake Erie, the writer takes pains to imagine the engineer's terror: "True, the awful horrors of an explosion were vividly before him—the mangled limbs, the scorched and lifeless bodies, the death shrieks and the groans of the hapless victims, were before his eye and on his ear." The cool-headed engineer, marked as subordinate to the ship's dictatorial captain, acts courageously and risks his life to save others, and in the report's conclusion, is extolled for his virtue. "This intrepid act was not a rash, vainglorious attempt to gain the applause of a multitude by a foolhardy exposure of life in some racing excursion; it was not the deed of a drunken and reckless man . . . but it was the self-possessed and determined courage of one whose firmness is worthy of all admiration."[26] Although the narrative gains credibility by distinguishing itself from fiction, ending with the reflection that "actual realities are indeed 'stranger than fiction,'" the sensational descriptions and the figure of the virtuous and humble engineer are hallmarks of the city-mystery genre that would eventually garner Frederick Douglass's praise for its working-class accents and cross-racial appeal.

As literary critic Elizabeth McHenry points out, Frederick Douglass sought in the *North Star* and *Frederick Douglass' Paper* to create "a forum for black writers," and to promote black writers as not only political but also imaginative, and that they should not be limited to the slave narrative form. McHenry writes, "Douglass sought to advance the unprecedented idea of the creative parity between black and white writers . . . Douglass's placement of the work of the most celebrated white European and American writers next to that of black writers insisted on the equality of their literary, cultural, and artistic pursuits." Editorials on fiction reading and the literary notices from the *North*

Star and *Frederick Douglass' Paper* between the years 1847 and 1855 display a softening of anxieties about the dangers of reading novels, and tentatively embrace class-accented sensational fiction that correlates with Douglass's own class politics and the growing attention he gave to the working conditions of free blacks in the North. Douglass biographer Benjamin Quarles credits Douglass's newspaper editorships with giving him "a keen awareness of the problems confronting the rank and file of Negroes whose modest abilities were insufficient to bestride even the lower hurdles of color prejudice."[27] Although white-authored city-mysteries drew faulty analogies between chattel slavery in the South and "wage slavery" in the North, Douglass's critique of Northern working conditions and his promotion of skilled trades resonates with sensational fiction's class protest and cross-racial sympathy.

References to fiction reading that appear in the *North Star*, published from 1847 to 1851, form a bridge from the *Colored American*, with the former running such anxious editorials as "Novel-Reading Monomaniacs," which in 1847 ridicules a Harvard graduate who proudly claimed to have read three thousand novels during his college years, and columns that assert in 1848 and 1849 respectively that women would live longer if they "renounce their novels and their indolence," and that young men would do well to abstain from novels and whiskey punch, as both are "injurious to the brain."[28] And yet, by 1852, following the serialization of *Uncle Tom's Cabin* and Douglass's spirited public defense of Stowe's novel, *Frederick Douglass' Paper* was running articles that normalized sensational fiction reading for the black working class and promoted cheap fiction in its literary notices. An editorial, "Heads of the Colored People—The Washerwoman," written expressly for the newspaper by correspondent James McCune Smith under his pseudonym "Communipaw," praises the proud, hard-working black washerwoman whose small, hot apartment has a table displaying John Bunyan's *Pilgrim's Progress* as well as "a nice 'greasy novel' just in from the circulating library."[29] The juxtaposition of the religious and popular texts serves to soften the divide between "high" and "low" cultural forms, and acknowledges sensational fiction reading among the black working class.

Reflecting Douglass's attention to working conditions in the North and his appeals to Southern whites during the 1850s, his newspaper's favorable reviews of sensational fiction helped to foster cross-racial alliances between white workers and abolitionists. While *Frederick Douglass' Paper* regularly recommended antislavery novels such as Royall Tyler's *The Algerine Captive* and Stowe's *Uncle Tom's Cabin,* it also promoted more overtly sensational fiction that was preoccupied with class stratification. For instance, on May 4, 1855, the newspaper endorsed Emerson Bennett's *Ellen Norbury; or, The Adventures of an Orphan* as part of a larger defense of novel reading. Bennett, who wrote primarily frontier romances, worked as an assistant editor for Ned Buntline's *Western Literary Journal and Monthly Review* in the 1840s, and would never be mistaken for an abolitionist, combines graphic descriptions of abject poverty found in sensational city-mysteries with the figure of the orphan girl found in sentimental fiction. Run over by a sleigh, locked in a cellar, sent wrongly to jail, and ultimately rescued from her antagonists, Ellen Norbury, with her bewildering movement through the streets of Philadelphia, enables Bennett to depict scenes of multiracial squalid living conditions in the so-called Infested District. *Frederick Douglass' Paper*'s literary editor, Julia Griffiths, who signed the review with her initials, defended the novel: "We commend the Preface, especially, to the attention of those good people, who make it a rule to decry all books that are entitled '*novels.*'"[30] Griffiths's positive review of the novel, which was released by Philadelphia's T. B. Peterson, a prolific publisher of cheap fiction, including Lippard's and Duganne's city-mysteries, uses popular keywords from city-mysteries and matches almost verbatim a sentence in Bennett's preface: "The object of Mr. Bennett . . . appears especially to be to call attention to the *miseries* and vices that exist in great cities."[31] Without considering whether or not the novel is sufficiently "moral," the review concludes with a frank acknowledgement of the rising popularity of cheap fiction: "The Book will be extensively read."[32]

While it is impossible to know how much beyond the preface of Bennett's novel Griffiths read before writing her review, *Ellen Norbury*'s eleven-page preface does not equivocate that its primary focus will be on Northern "wage slavery." After a sensational promise to provide the reader with "thrilling scenes and incidents of everyday occurrence amongst the poorest and most degraded class of a large city," Bennett states his novel's object: "I knew it was fashionable in certain quarters to talk very sympathetically about the slaves at the South; but I knew at the same time, that within fifteen minutes' walk of the headquarters of some of these charitable associations, hundreds of human beings, both white and black, were annually perishing of cold, starvation, and neglect—perishing for the want of the most common necessaries of life." Unlike Lippard's assertive black heroes, black characters appear in *Ellen Norbury* as criminals, small shop keepers, or, most often, members of the multiracial working poor who languish in pestilent tenements. For example, Bennett's description of the Infested District resonates with Ned Buntline's sensational depictions of the degraded poor: "White and black, male and female, young and old, are here, in some instances, crowded into a cold, damp, slimy, underground apartment, a dozen in a place not large enough to lodge one decently, and really not fit to be used as a dog-kennel."[33] Although Bennett's representation of blackness is largely exploitive throughout the novel and lives up to the critical charge made against white-authored sensational fiction, the fact *Ellen Norbury* draws attention to the suffering of the multiracial working classes at a time that Douglass's newspaper was strategizing how best to improve the working conditions of Northern free blacks would have helped to garner the book positive attention in Griffiths's literary notices.

Frederick Douglass' Paper's endorsement of *Ellen Norbury* is even more significant in light of the criticism Bennett's novel received one week later in William Lloyd Garrison's the *Liberator* on May 11, 1855. The unnamed reviewer begins by stating that the novel is "designed to excite heartfelt sympathy for the perishing classes in our large cities, by thrilling sketches of their situation." However, the *Liberator*'s reviewer takes umbrage with Bennett's preface for indicting missionary and abolitionist societies that do not help the Northern poor living in their midst. In rebuttal to Bennett's claim that it is "fashionable to talk very sympathetically about the poor slaves at the South," the reviewer states ironically, "To our knowledge, these most afflicted of the human family have never been brought within the arena of 'fashion,' to be recognized as worthy of a single glance of commiseration. On the contrary, it is still the 'fashion' to spit upon them, to resist every effort to emancipate them, to treat them as a leprous race." The *Liberator*'s review ends with muted optimism for the novel's success: "'Ellen Norbury,' we trust, will do something to awaken an interest in all classes who need to be succored and saved."[34] The two reviews in *Frederick Douglass' Paper* and the *Liberator* reflect, respectively, Douglass's increasing attention to the plight of the Northern multiracial poor, and white labor advocates' perception that abolitionists like Garrison were fixated on ending chattel slavery at the expense of ameliorating the effects of "wage slavery."

While his newspaper's reviews of *Ellen Norbury* reveal Douglass's concerns for the multiracial working poor in the North, his treatment of *Ida May*, an antislavery novel that caused a sensation and was suspected initially of having been written by Stowe, focuses attention on the impact of chattel slavery on the white poor in the South. From the haughty elitism of slave-owning whites who disdain free labor, the representation of rural whites as degraded "clay-eaters" and "crackers," the linguistic connections made between black slaves and poor whites, and the depiction of genuine cross-racial friendship, Mary Hayden Green Pike's 1854 novel *Ida May: A Story of Things Actual and Possible* reflects Douglass's appeals in the early 1850s that figured non-slaveowning whites as potential allies in the fight to abolish chattel slavery. Through its publication of favorable reviews and lengthy excerpts from *Ida May*, *Frederick Douglass' Paper* demonstrated that Douglass brought his editorship to bear on connecting and critiquing labor conditions in the North and the South for his readers.

The Reception of *Ida May*, "This Thrilling Southern Story"

Mid-way through *Ida May*, a dinner party is held at the Wynn house, the South Carolina plantation where "white slave" Ida May and her elderly slave companion, Venus, have been purchased and placed into service. As the men sip their wine after the meal, they notice ten-year-old Ida May, and, speculating on her past, discourse on the benefits of chattel slavery for poor whites. Contrary to free labor ideology, one gentleman remarks that Ida, "may be one of the poor whites, and in that case, she would be much better off to be a servant here than to live at home. It may be, too, that she was sold instead of being stolen." Using class epithets that the novel does not fully reject, the gentleman continues, "I have frequently seen white children who were thus thrown into the market. These miserable 'clay-eaters' often sell their children, and I suppose the Virginia 'crackers' do the same; and in my opinion, it is the best thing they can do for their children."[35] In her survey of the demonization of poor whites whose very existence exposes the lie of American exceptionalism, historian Nancy Isenberg explains that the term "white trash," coined as early as 1821, "gained widespread popularity in the 1850s" as working-class whites were treated as biologically degenerate.[36] When the novel's hero, the young Walter Varian, nephew of the imperialist and cold-hearted slaveowner Mr. Wynn, objects, the dinner guest vigorously defends the aristocratic way of life and rejects free labor. Poor whites "are lower even than our negroes, and if they were all to come under negro laws tomorrow, it would be far better for the next generation than it will be for them to remain as they are. It has always been so, and always will be. There *must* be two classes in every society." Invoking the same paternalism that slaveowners used to defend their peculiar institution, the gentleman concludes, "The learned, the cultivated, the wealthy, must be the *patricians*; and the laboring class must be the plebeians, and it makes little difference whether they are black or white."[37] In building this regional contrast between slave labor in the South and free labor in the North, Pike constructs an economic cross-racial alliance between chattel slaves and poor whites, both of whom are treated with contempt by the slaveowning class.

Though Varian insists on universal education for blacks and whites, frees and provides his slaves with a tract of land in Ohio, and marries the feisty abolitionist Ida May, Pike invests in the period's derogatory images of working-class whites, even as she encourages the reader to see them as collateral victims of chattel slavery. When Ida May and her father are accused of abolitionism for educating and preparing their slaves for freedom, a mob forms to drive them from town, and they must be whisked away. Pike describes the majority of the mob as composed of "clay-eaters," which she pauses to define: "Clad in the coarsest and the scantiest garments, subsisting principally on 'turpentine whiskey,' and appeasing their craving for more substantial food by filling their stomachs with a kind of aluminous earth which abounds everywhere, they are squalid and emaciated to a frightful degree; with yellowish, drab-colored complexions, eyes that are dull and cold as the eyes of a dead fish, and faces whose idiotic expression is only varied by a dull despair or a devilish malignity." Described as a degraded breed and with dehumanizing characteristics that still haunt perceptions of the white working poor in the twenty-first century, they are as "destitute of any idea of religion or morality as the swine that feed around their doors, and are looked down upon by the negroes with a contempt which they return by a hearty hatred." In Pike's view, which was not uncommon for the period, the white poor's poverty kept them in competition with black slaves and free blacks in the South, as well as alienated, isolated, and stuck at the bottom of the class hierarchy. Despite indulging in class stereotypes rooted in biology, Pike attributes the degradation of the poor whites to the slave system: "These wretched beings, crushed and degraded to the last extreme of poverty and ignorance by the operation of slavery, that cuts them off from all the labor to which their capacities are suited, are nevertheless among its warmest supporters."[38] Pike laments the plight of poor whites, and she asserts that chattel slavery is not in their economic interest and has rendered them fit for little more than farm labor.

Mary Hayden Green Pike was born into a Baptist family with abolitionist sympathies in Maine, and, according to literary critic Jessie Morgan-Owens, published three novels in the 1850s—*Ida May*, *Caste*, and *Agnes*—and would publish a poem memorializing radical abolitionist John Brown in 1859.[39] Although the cross-racial alliances that Pike draws in *Ida May* between black slaves and degraded working-class whites in its representation of Ida May's kidnappers are a far cry from the virtuous alliances between black and white artisan heroes that populate Lippard's and Thompson's city-mysteries, Pike's multiracial villains are equally dehumanized by chattel slavery. Ida's two kidnappers, who abduct the five-year-old girl as she is walking near her home in rural Pennsylvania with her white attendant, Bessy, are marked by their thick dialect and amorality. The white ruffian, Bill, espouses the same paternalism as the wealthy dinner guests at the Wynn plantation when he tells the frightened child, "We're goin' to *sell* ye to some nice man, that'll be kind enough to larn ye what yer ought to do, and take care o' yer; and yer can't think how much better off ye'll be than if yer was to be home, where ye'd have no good master, nor be nothin' but a poor devil of a free nigger when ye got growed up." Nick Kelly, Bill's co-conspirator, offers a blunt defense of his actions based on the economic opportunity produced by chattel slavery: "If I can make more money tradin' niggers than any other way, I'll do it, just the same as the wolf eats the lamb when he's hungry; it's a law of nature, and always will be, for the strong to prey upon the weak."[40] Bill and Nick Kelly are opportunists who abduct free black and white children in the North and sell them into slavery, and their trafficking with impunity back and forth between Pennsylvania and the border states serves as an anxious reminder of a border made porous by the Fugitive Slave Law of 1850.

The white kidnappers are abetted by black slave Chloe, a dynamic and memorable character whose job is to "break in" the abducted black and white children inside a cave near Hagerstown, Maryland, just south of the border with Pennsylvania. An unapologetic misanthrope who relishes whipping the children to avenge the selling off of her mother and her own seven children by cruel slaveowners, Chloe insists on a "radical democracy" of pain that contrasts with the kidnappers' paternalism. While Bill cautions Chloe to go easy on delicate Ida May, Chloe takes sadistic pleasure in whipping the girl senseless. "'I wants ye to cry—I like to hear ye—it's moosic,' said the hag, pausing with the rod uplifted, to enjoy [Ida's] agony of terror. 'Cry now—cry loud!' and, as she spoke, the rod descended on the bare, delicate shoulders. 'Cry, ye white wolf-cub! cry, ye white bear-whelp! scream, ye little rattlesnake!—I likes to hear ye—cry away—I'll make ye pay for the blood of my child, where the whips cut her!'" When Ida passes out and falls into a stupor, Chloe, with irony that calls to mind Devil-Bug's torture of the white middle-class Byrnewood Arlington, says, "I don't like ter have folks *die*—that's too good, de a'n't no pain in *dat*—I likes ter have 'em live, and moreudder, I wants dis little brat to live, so I can do it again." Like Devil-Bug, Chloe was made into a misanthrope, the grotesque creation of an unjust society. In response to Bill's observation that God did not answer her prayers that her newborns would die rather than face a life of enslavement, Chloe says, "Dere a'n't no Lord—dere a'n't nothin' but de debil, and he hab it all his own way in dis yer country."[41] Although Chloe disappears from the text soon after the kidnappers head south to sell the children, her challenge to American exceptionalism resonates through the remainder of the novel as the characters who become enlightened about the horrors of chattel slavery struggle against its defenders.

The cross-racial alliance between Chloe and the kidnappers, which is based on their mutual contempt for the world, is balanced by the cross-racial friendship between Ida May and the black slaves among whom she lives. When she is finally reunited with her father, Ida May declares, "This is Walter Varian . . . he redeemed me from slavery . . . this is Venus, my mauma, who saved my life, when suffering and hardship had nearly killed me, and has watched over me and waited upon me ever since. My two best friends! O, father, you must love them both!" Ida has the sympathy for the oppressed like Little Eva of *Uncle Tom's Cabin,* but as the survivor of chattel slavery, she also has the spunk of Capitola Black of E. D. E. N. Southworth's 1859 *The Hidden Hand* to stand up, defend, and free slaves. In addition to the amity between Ida and Venus, Ida sympathizes with Alfred, a slave on the Wynn plantation, who, like George Harris of *Uncle Tom's Cabin,* is a skilled craftsman anxious to flee to the North. When Mr. Wynn uncovers Alfred's runaway plot and locks him in the attic in preparation for a whipping in the morning, Ida confronts Wynn in the library and threatens him with the specter of slave revolt. Ida's jeremiad resonates with Lippard's ominous warning—"Wo Unto Sodom"—issued in *The Quaker City* to the monopolist and the slaveowner. "'The hour of *revenge* will come,' said Ida, trembling at her own words. 'Do you not fear that all this anguish, all these wrongs, will hasten an hour of retribution, when the fearful debt shall be paid which has been accumulating through so many generations? What shall hinder its coming soon, if men like Alfred are driven to desperation with persecution and torture?'"[42] In this radical moment, the angelic Ida May channels the fire and brimstone of her former captor Chloe and becomes an unlikely but capable spokesperson for the enslaved.

The publisher Phillips, Sampson, and Company of Boston first sold copies of *Ida May* on November 22, 1854, though there were numerous reports of delays during the second half of November. A publisher's ad printed on January 4, 1855, in *Frederick Douglass' Paper* claimed that twenty thousand copies had been sold in just twenty days. While publishers' claims are difficult to verify and often inflated, there is no doubt the novel caused a sensation in the abolitionist press, and not only because of speculation that Stowe was the author of *Ida May.*[43] During the 1850s, forty-two references to *Ida May* appeared in the *Liberator,* twenty-six references appeared in the *National Era,* and twenty references appeared in *Frederick Douglass' Paper.* Many of these references are within advertisements penned by the publisher, but each of the three abolitionist newspapers published original reviews of the novel. The *National Era* printed one review, the *Liberator* printed two, and *Frederick Douglass' Paper* printed five, three of which included excerpts from the novel. When we compare the various reviews, we see that Douglass's enthusiastic endorsement of *Ida May* strategically includes excerpts that privilege the voices of the black slave characters over the titular white heroine, and that downplay the novel's sensationalism by describing holiday customs on the plantation rather than the kidnappings and beatings. Although *Frederick Douglass' Paper* was embracing sensational novels like *Ellen Norbury* in its literary notices of the 1850s, in light of the relentless criticism in the Southern press that Stowe had exaggerated the horrors of chattel slavery in *Uncle Tom's Cabin,* Douglass's newspaper was careful to preempt the same charges against *Ida May.*

The first review of *Ida May* appeared in the *National Era*'s literary notices on November 16, 1854. In lieu of an excerpt from the novel, the review provides an accurate summary of the novel up to the point at which the enslaved Ida May discovers her former identity. The summary does not mention the misanthropic slave Chloe or the tragic suicide of the rebellious slave Alfred, the novel's most compelling and assertive black characters, though the review was the first to label *Ida May* "an anti-slavery novel, second in power only to *Uncle Tom's Cabin*." Having the well-respected abolitionist newspaper that serialized *Uncle Tom's Cabin* endorse the novel's political content would have strengthened its credibility and boosted its sales. The reviewer, however, is forthright about *Ida May*'s romantic elements: "It is more artificial than [*Uncle Tom's Cabin*]—deals more with extraordinary, but still possible, events—contains more unusual surprises and coincidences; still it keeps within the ordinary limits of verisimilitude."[44] Given the sensational nature of the kidnapping tale and the unlikely reunions that occur among the characters throughout *Ida May*, this review is more accurate than the *Liberator*'s and *Frederick Douglass' Paper*'s insistence on the novel's verisimilitude.

The next day, on November 17, 1854, the *Liberator* and *Frederick Douglass' Paper* published original reviews accompanied by different excerpts from the third chapter of *Ida May*. The *Liberator*'s review, which consists mostly of a concise summary of the main plot, offers one primary claim: "It is a work of remarkable power, without any exaggeration of tone or misrepresentation of any of the every day actualities of slavery at the South."[45] The excerpt, which takes up three full columns on the front page of the *Liberator*, includes the beginning of chapter three, detailing the kidnappers' trek into Maryland and ending with their arrival at the cave. This is precisely the place where *Frederick Douglass' Paper* takes up its excerpt of "this thrilling Southern Story" on November 17, 1854. The excerpt in Douglass's newspaper includes the physical description of Chloe, and, importantly, her tragic slave experience as a mother separated from her seven children. Before a defiant and vengeful Chloe speaks or whips Ida May, the excerpt in *Frederick Douglass' Paper* ends, leaving its readers with a sympathetic and realistic depiction of a woman broken and scarred by chattel slavery. With this excerpt, the literary notice likely written by Julia Griffiths proves its claim that "the scenes of Southern Life, given in *Ida May*, are sketched by a master hand. One feels their reality. There is nothing melodramatic, nor has the author 'set down aught in malice.'"[46] This is the approximate point at which the excerpt in the *Liberator* resumes, providing its readers with the rest of chapter three, which includes the most violent depiction of black rebellion in the novel—Chloe's brutal beating of Ida May and her defiant protest invoking the devil. While the *Liberator* relates the sensational whipping of Ida May, Julia Griffiths chooses innocuous passages for the subsequent excerpts printed in *Frederick Douglass' Paper.*

The next excerpt of *Ida May* selected by Griffiths is an especially safe choice, although it still contains pointed antislavery logos resonant with Douglass's 1845 slave narrative. In the December 8, 1854, issue, Griffiths introduces the excerpt as coming "from the *thrilling* novel, entitled 'IDA MAY,'" which contradicts the sentimental tone and banal subject of the passage.[47] Taken from chapter ten, eight years after Ida May has dramatically recovered her identity from a chattel slave to a free young woman, the passage describes a Christmas celebration on the Wynn plantation. More consistent with the patrician tone of Washington Irving's 1819 *The Sketch Book of Geoffrey Crayon,* which details the manners of English manor life, than a polemical antislavery text, the passage constructs a romantic portrait of plantation life: "It is Christmas Eve in the cabin. It is Christmas Eve in the hall. Everywhere lights are flashing, and merry voices ring out on their air." Channeling Irving's racist and cartoonish descriptions of lower-class blacks in "The Legend of Sleepy Hollow," Pike describes the Wynns and their white guests dancing "to the lively strains that proceeded from a fiddle held in the hands of 'Uncle Ned.' Everybody feels like dancing when Uncle Ned fiddles, and he knows it, and rejoices in his power, as he sits on the piazza, just outside the open window, nodding his head, and rolling his eyes, and opening his mouth so that every one of his white teeth glistens in the light that streams over him." The black fiddler, a common figure of entertainment in antebellum writing, is drawn from the 1840s folk song "Old Uncle Ned," according to Jessie Morgan-Owens. The cheerful passage ends with the appearance of Aunt Venus, Ida's former caretaker, who, over the past eight years as a slave, "seemed to have renewed her youth instead of growing old."[48] In the excerpt, amidst these romantic representations of life on the slave plantation for white and black alike, Pike describes the customs for the slaves during the week of Christmas.

Nine years earlier in his slave narrative, Douglass had described the holidays as "one of the grossest frauds committed upon the down-trodden slave." By encouraging their slaves to spend the week inebriated, slaveowners seek to "disgust their slaves with freedom, by plunging them into the lowest depths of dissipation." Similarly, Pike explains that some slaves spend the week visiting loved ones on neighboring plantations or fishing and hunting and improving their cabins, while other slaves spend it inebriated. Pike notes that "temperance is very strictly enforced at other times," underscoring the fact that intemperance is, in fact, permitted by the slaveowners, and she attributes the fact that "these enjoyments are so wholly animal gratification" to "degraded beings, chattelized through long generations."[49] Pike's critique of slavery is less direct than Douglass's, and yet it tempers the romanticism that otherwise dominates the passage.

Through the end of 1854 and the beginning of 1855, *Frederick Douglass' Paper* continued to print weekly coverage of *Ida May*, including numerous advertisements from the publisher and reprints of reviews from other newspapers. A brief in-house review on January 12, 1855, signed J. G., celebrates the novel as "a valuable addition to the Anti-Slavery Literature of the country," and a novel "bound to electrify the reading public."[50] A week later, the newspaper runs its third and final excerpt from the novel, this time from chapter twelve, which covers Alfred's failed escape plot and eventual suicide. *Frederick Douglass' Paper* breaks the excerpt into two parts, opening with Wynn confronting and subduing Alfred in the library. After eliding Ida May's spirited pleading for Alfred and threatening a slave revolt, the excerpt resumes with news of Alfred's suicide and his mother's speech to Wynn. Unlike Ida May's immediate threat of violence, Alfred's mother, Abby, focuses on justice in the afterlife, a less sensational but no less powerful threat. Abby warns Wynn, "Repent! for, behold, the day cometh that shall burn as an oven, and all the proud, yea, and all that do wickedly, shall be as stubble, and the day that cometh shall burn them up saith the Lord of Hosts." Moreover, Abby is invested with the supernatural force of an avenging angel: "There was a lurid light in her eyes, and with her pale, stern face, her tall figure elevated to its utmost height, and her hand raised with a prophetic earnestness, she looked like one inspired." Although Wynn is ultimately unmoved by Abby's jeremiad, "he had quailed before the influence," and it is significant that Griffiths chose to relate the grieving mother's passionate judgment on her slaveowner.[51] In its carefully selected excerpts and favorable reviews of the novel, *Frederick Douglass' Paper* effectively balances its claims for the sensational *Ida May*'s verisimilitude with its endorsement of the novel's passionate antislavery protest.

Cross-Racial Sympathy in the *Star Spangled Banner*

The *Star Spangled Banner,* edited by prolific dime novelist Justin Jones, ran weekly in Boston between 1846 and 1857, distinguishing it as one of the more successful and longer-lived story papers of the antebellum period. While an edition typically included short sketches and news items, an occasional poem, pithy witticisms, and advertisements, the weekly story paper foremost serialized fiction that appealed to its working-class audience through sensational plots, melodramatic contests between good and evil, and cross-racial sympathy. Like Lippard's *The Quaker City* and Thompson's *City Crimes,* serial fiction in the *Star Spangled Banner* pitted white, black, and racially ambiguous working-class heroes against dissipated libertines, wealthy aristocrats, and corrupt politicians, all of whom pursued personal desires at the expense of the greater republic, and all of whom were invariably *white.* One of the most progressive representations of Northern free blacks in antebellum sensational fiction appears in Jones's own two novels, *Big Dick, the King of the Negroes,* serialized in Jones's paper and then published as a complete text in 1846, and *Fourpe Tap: or, The Middy of the Macedonian,* a sequel published in 1847. The two texts, class-accented with an inheritance plot indicative of the city-mystery genre emerging in the 1840s, feature a black working-class hero who not only has the physical prowess of Lippard's Devil-Bug, Glow-Worm, Musquito, and Black Sampson, but also serves as the locus of virtue, a role typically reserved for white characters in antebellum popular writing. Although each novel makes an attempt to render a black hero more palatable to Southern readers, Jones's texts emphasize the possibility of cross-racial friendships built on the virtue and mutual respect of the multiracial working classes of Boston. The fact that Boston was a "racially tolerant place" where blacks found jobs and educational opportunities, according to historian James Oliver Horton, helps to account for the expressions of cross-racial sympathy in the city's weekly story paper.[52]

Set in Boston in 1816, *Big Dick* chronicles the efforts of Richard Seaver, nicknamed "Big Dick," to protect the virtuous and punish the wicked, as evidenced in the novel's subtitle, "Virtue and Vice Contrasted." In the preface, Jones, writing under the pseudonym Harry Hazel, sums up the hero's principles: "He was, in truth, a magnanimous and generous man, always to be found advocating the cause of the right, and preventing the strong from trampling upon the weak." In a break from prevailing representations of black masculinity as savage and violent, Seaver is a balance of brains and brawn: "That he was superior to most of his race in intellect and education, cannot be questioned—and this, together with his immense physique gave him a great superiority over the colored population generally" (see figure 4). In the novel, Seaver discovers a newborn abandoned in a basket during a snowstorm, and, after being turned away by a "rich and miserly Frenchman, of sixty," he stops by the Mermaid's Retreat, a "reveling-hall" run by the Dodsells, a British couple marked as foreign by their thick Cockney accents, in contrast to the well-spoken normative black hero. The hall has the "radical democratic" spirit of other sites of multiracial, working-class congregation depicted in city-mysteries: everyone, "high or low—color or country . . . both black and white," dances with abandon to the lively music of the fiddler, Black Pete, and his apprentice, tambourine player Tambo Lum.[53] This homage to Pete Williams's establishment in New York City rewrites Charles

Figure 4. "Fourpe Tap's Encounter with the Giant Negro," from Harry Hazel, *Fourpe Tap* (Boston: Jones's Publishing House, 1847). Courtesy of the Yale Collection of American Literature, Beinecke Rare Book and Manuscript Library.

Dickens's anxiety and moral condemnation of the black-owned bar. Whereas Williams's bar represents the nadir of Five Points depravity in Dickens's *American Notes,* the Mermaid's Retreat, fictionally relocated to Boston, is emblematic of American radical democratic energies.

In *Big Dick,* Jones expresses racial sympathy for Seaver and condemns race prejudice. After Seaver convinces the Dodsells to adopt the baby, he reflects on how the world mistreats him because of his race. "The world calls me rough, and sometimes brutal! but do I not always take the part of the weak? and has not my heart prompted me to protect the child?" Seaver's reasoning and self-defense against Northern race prejudice resonates with the narrator's reflections on the talented fiddler Black Pete, "whose fame would have eclipsed the Vieuxtemps, the Ole Bulls and the Camillo Sivoris who ever drew horse-hair across rosined catgut, had his complexion been of a lighter hue. But, alas! genius never meets its reward under a sable skin!" Seaver, as an honorary member of the local Boston police, befriends the Gray family, "humble but honest people," who had a reversal of fortune due to the duplicity of wealthy villain Mr. Peterson, the father of the young woman whose brother, Philip, had tossed the baby into the snow. Once a successful merchant living in a mansion, Mr. Gray was reduced to working as an honest night watchman and living in a small tenement. The Grays' daughter, Lucy, has been abducted and locked in a brothel by wealthy libertine Philip Peterson, and, in conventional working-class accents, Seaver forces Philip and his co-conspirators, "the two sprigs of aristocracy," to reveal the location. Having rescued and returned Lucy to her parents, Seaver insists on covering Mr. Gray's shift that evening, and "the friends he had made so happy" later return the favor when he is falsely brought up on charges of assault and battery against the men guarding the brothel. In court, the guards' sharp-featured and eloquent attorney, a regular object of class critique in sensational fiction, attempts to exploit Big Dick's blackness and to appeal to popular fears against black men. "He glanced in a cursory manner at the many riots and bloody encounters in which this 'black Sampson'—to use his own expression—had from time to time been engaged, and concluded his harangue by congratulating the court and spectators upon the prospects of speedily getting rid, for a time at least, of this gigantic monster!"[54] Despite the fact that Seaver's involvement in the riots was to break them up, the judge is not persuaded of his innocence until Lucy Gray, timid and veiled, comes to court to testify on his behalf. In a nation rife with race prejudice, a white woman must confirm virtuous Seaver's innocence.

It is significant that Big Dick's personal history includes work as a sailor. According to historian W. Jeffrey Bolster in his book *Black Jacks: African American Seamen in the Age of Sail,* black and white sailors enjoyed cross-racial camaraderie within a hierarchical system of order not based on race. "Although most white sailors did not think of black men as their equals, neither did they accept unquestioningly a hierarchical view of their society or conceive of it in binary terms, as white against black."[55] In *Fourpe Tap,* the sequel to *Big Dick* published a year later, Jones relates that Seaver was born of a Chilean princess, impressed into slavery, rescued by an American vessel, and served valiantly in the American navy against the British during the War of 1812. Seaver's working-class accents as a stalwart sailor, like the gruff engineer of "A Thrilling Incident" published in the *Colored American,* would have appealed to the readers of the *Star Spangled Banner.* By pitting the virtuous sailor Seaver against aristocratic fops, Jones encourages white working-class readers whose whiteness was unstable due to their increasing dependence on "wage slavery," to identify with his black hero. Bolster references this potential for cross racial sympathy among sailors when he writes that "the exploitive system that stigmatized white seamen as dependents influenced and conditioned them to perceive the world from the vantage point of slaves."[56] The fact Frederick Douglass records disguising himself as a sailor to escape to the North is a notable expression of this potential for cross-racial identification among white and black workers. According to Douglass's last autobiography, "In my clothing I was rigged out in sailor style. I had on a red shirt and a tarpaulin hat and black cravat, tied in sailor fashion, carelessly and loosely about my neck. My knowledge of ships and sailor's talk came much to my assistance."[57]

The most dramatic moment in Jones's *Big Dick* comes in his reconceptualization of the Negro Hill Riot in Boston, which, according to conflicting newspaper reports, occurred on either July 14, 1826, or August 26, 1826, and resulted in several houses being torn down in an area that was home to several black families.[58] Jones's description initially calls up white mob violence during urban race riots: "Presently a large body of men, apparently mechanics, sailors and truckmen, followed by an equal number of boys made their appearance, many of them armed with canes, cudgels, and even stones and brickbats; and several were bearing along upon their shoulders fire-hooks, ladders and axes." However, this angry group of working-class mechanics is led by Seaver—"there he stood in all his gigantic majesty"—who insists on the moral rectitude of their actions. In a rallying cry to the rioters, Seaver hopes that the tenements they are about to tear down, which are supposedly sites of vice and sexual assault, will one day be replaced with "hundreds of tenements, occupied by the industrious and virtuous of our young city." In this instance, a multiracial mob of workers descends on an area rife with crime, which, the narrator points out in comparing it to New York's Five Points, was known as "Nigger Hill—as it once was termed in derision—though every shade of human color assembled there."[59] In fact, it turns out that the dissipated aristocrat Philip Peterson is there, and, unbeknownst to him, his sister, Cecile Peterson, has fled there for refuge from a forced wedding to an imposter Frenchman. In this retelling of the 1826 riot on Negro Hill, Jones is careful to represent it not as a race riot, but as a form of vigilante justice that broke along the lines of virtue versus vice, rather than white versus black.

Seaver follows in the footsteps of Lippard's brawny black heroes like Devil-Bug and Black Sampson, who defend the virtue of the lowly from the schemes of aristocrats. When the dissipated and wealthy villain Philip Peterson attempts to stab him during the fracas, Big Dick, like Black Sampson with his scythe on the Revolutionary battlefield, uses the young aristocrat as a human-cudgel to mow down the degraded denizens of Negro Hill. Jones writes, "In another moment, Big Dick seized the assassin, and tossed him above his head, caught him by the ankles, whirled him once around, and rested him as he would have done a billet of wood, upon his shoulders. He now strode toward the thickest of the fight, and using the assassin as a club, swept down his foes at each whirl of this new and powerful weapon!"[60] The fact that Seaver spends the next chapter pondering the moral consequences of having killed Peterson in self-defense further humanizes this black character who serves—in unprecedented fashion—as a popular text's locus of virtue.

Jones based the Big Dick character on a living person in Boston, the renowned African American sailor Richard Crafus, who was also known as Richard Seaver.[61] African American abolitionist and author William Cooper Nell of Boston included Seaver in his 1855 work *The Colored Patriots of the American Revolution,* which included an introduction by Harriet Beecher Stowe. The unattributed entry for Seaver cites an obituary published in the newspaper the *Boston Patriot:* Seaver "was 'a man of mighty mould.' A short time previous to his death he measured six feet five inches in height, and attracted much attention when seen in the street."[62] According to historian W. Jeffrey Bolster, Crafus was taken prisoner by the British navy during the War of 1812 and was known as "King Dick" in the British Admiralty's Dartmoor Prison. Having returned to Boston, Crafus was a hero within the African American community according to local chroniclers: "Dressed in a red vest and white shirt, crowned with 'an old style police cap' and 'swinging an Emmence cane,' long a symbol associated with black leadership, he assembled black Bostonians each Election Day as 'Master of Ceremonies.'"[63] Given Crafus's high profile as an American patriot and a Franklinian leader among men, it is fitting that Jones would feature him as a virtuous defender of the multiracial working classes in *Big Dick*.

Jones, writing again under the pseudonym Harry Hazel, reinforces Seaver's virtue and heroism on behalf of the white working classes in *Big Dick*'s sequel, *Fourpe Tap,* a year later. When a young white carpenter's apprentice, Maurice Melton, is framed for arson and burglary by two spiteful co-workers, one of whom speaks with a Cockney accent, Seaver hides the innocent man from the police and helps to capture the real culprits. The sensational subplot is marked by cross-racial sympathy among the black and white working classes at the expense of newly arrived immigrants. In a scene suggestive of the Underground Railroad, Seaver hides Melton "from the hounds of the law" in an empty building that he owns. Melton trusts Seaver implicitly: "Without making any enquiry into the motives or wishes of Big Dick, Melton followed him into an alley, not far distant, and down the rickety cellar steps of an old uninhabited tenement, when Big Dick, after closing the trap and fastened [*sic*] it with an iron bar upon the inside, led the young man up a flight of steps. There was no door, but the negro raising one of the boards of the floor, they entered a small room." The scene's suggestive critique of chattel slavery and nod toward cross-racial sympathy is strengthened when Jones details his title character's escape from Southern slavecatchers. Fourpe Tap, a slight African American who was kidnapped from an American merchant ship and enslaved by Barbary pirates, is rescued at the beginning of the novel by the USS *Macedonian,* set free for his brave resistance, and lives freely in Boston. His faithful rescuer, the white midshipman Jemmy Gray, inquires what has become of Fourpe Tap "since he was carried off by that southerner who claimed him as a fugitive slave." Seaver explains that Fourpe Tap "slipped through the gentleman's fingers before he left New York, and made tracks for Boston, where he is now in safety. I have no doubt that the planter's claim was a valid one; but little Fourpe is too good a fellow ever to be a bondman." Although Fourpe Tap figures less prominently than Seaver in the sequel and dies abruptly at the end when Big Dick accidentally kills him during a boxing match, the virtuous fugitive slave's harrowing escape from Southern slavecatchers resonates with Melton's evasion of the police's "rogue-catchers."[64] The fact that Melton's chief antagonist, prolific criminal Tim Tatnall, immigrated from London to escape being sent to the penal colony at Botany Bay is a subtle reminder that anti-immigrant nativism could reinforce solidarity among the multiracial, native-born working classes.

Black Ralph and Black Mackey: Racially Liminal Artisan Republican Heroes

In addition to his own *Big Dick* and *Fourpe Tap,* Jones serialized other sensational fiction in his weekly story paper, offering a useful case study of how popular white authors employed blackness to mount a cross-racial economic critique of industrial capitalism for their white and black working-class readers. The recurrent pattern of white protagonist heroes disguising themselves as black men, found in J. H. Robinson's novel *Black Ralph, the Forest Fiend!,* serialized in 1851, and in Edward Carroll's story "Mackey; or, The Black Spy," published in 1852, gestures toward the cross-racial sympathy expressed in white-authored sensational literature of the 1840s and 1850s. Intriguingly, "Edward Carroll" is a likely pseudonym for Ned Buntline, which, if true, would show that even a racist city-mystery writer like Buntline would at times employ cross-racial sympathy for its working-class inflections. Reflecting the racial ambivalence inscribed in the class-accented news items and sketches that surround the serial texts in the pages of the *Star Spangled Banner,* Black Ralph's fierce brand of frontier justice embodies the "charismatic" blackness that historian W. H. Lhamon Jr. claims was popular in early nineteenth century urban youth culture, and Black Mackey's strategic infiltration of the British forces underscores the performativity of race. Although racial hierarchies are reestablished at the end of each text, the title characters' racial liminality—as they transform from one race to another through blackface—unsettles the categories of whiteness and blackness for a working-class audience.

In March 1851, the *Star Spangled Banner* began serializing *Black Ralph, the Forest Fiend!,* which was published as a ninety-seven-page complete text later that year. Its author, J. H. Robinson, published during the 1850s and 1860s at least twenty-four sensational novels boasting such racially inflected titles as *The White Rover* in 1851, *Nightshade; or, The Masked Robber of Hounslow Heath* in 1861, and *Whitelaw* in 1861. This preoccupation with racial signifiers supports Toni Morrison's claim in *Playing in the Dark* that antebellum white authors are *always* ruminating in their works on race and slavery: "It was this Africanism, deployed as rawness and savagery, that provided the staging ground and arena for the elaboration of the quintessential American identity." And yet Robinson's sensational novel is marked with strong racial ambivalences that challenge Morrison's general conclusion that white-authored representations of blackness are largely exploitive. Instead, *Black Ralph* features a series of thrilling incidents and feats of heroism to protect the innocent that are enabled by the character's black disguise, and, in the words of Lhamon Jr., black "charisma." According to Lhamon Jr., who challenges the prevailing view that white minstrel performers knew little of the black experience they were caricaturing on stage, white working-class youths, who increasingly lived among working-class blacks, were deeply attracted to the charisma, swagger, and originality of black culture, and tended to sympathize with the ostracized black characters over their stodgy, white, upper-class antagonists in minstrel songs. "Precisely because middle-class aspirants disdained the black jitterbug [Jim Crow] in every region, the black figure appealed all across the Atlantic as an organizational emblem for workers and the unemployed." The racial liminality in *Black Ralph* and "Mackey" functions in much the same way as Eric Lott contends it does in minstrelsy: "Blackface provided a convenient mask through which to voice class resentments of all kinds . . . occasionally these facts resulted in positive identifications between black and white, however quick the minstrel show usually was to forestall them."[65]

Robinson's *Black Ralph, the Forest Fiend!*—the exclamation point promising a sensational tale—chronicles the actions of a bold and fearless black-disguised white hero who shadows and assists a small group of white pioneers traveling to Utah. Armed with an innovative explosive weapon that silently but mortally tears a small hole in his victims' chests, Black Ralph protects the travelers, who include his nephew, the narrator, Seward, and his lost love, Alice, from hostile bands of Native American Indians and their corrupt white allies. Riding gallantly on a black steed and jumping flaming ramparts, Black Ralph often appears in the nick of time to dispatch the pioneers' enemies. Robinson establishes his hero's blackness in the first chapter, and readers would have assumed for the majority of the novel that they were reading the exploits of a courageous and morally upright African American hero, notwithstanding the "fiend's" seeming otherworldliness and metonymic connection with the devil. After Black Ralph kills a threatening Osage warrior and mysteriously disappears into the woods, Gilmore, a brusque and unrefined trapper, explains what little he knows about the hero and his cognomen: "It's sort of a nickname that he's got by common consent like; but the Ingins say he's black all over, and oncommon ugly in his parsonal appearance, lookin' like nothin' airthly."[66] White working-class readers would have been prepared for an African American hero in the pages of the *Star Spangled Banner* because of Jones's novels *Big Dick* and *Fourpe Tap*.

Defending and preserving women's virtue, whether they are white women or black fugitive slave women, is a standard class-accented subplot in antebellum sensational fiction. Analyzing Lippard's city-mystery novels, Shelley Streeby writes, "For Lippard, the exploitation of 'free' laborers and the seduction or rape of women are analogous forms of oppression that betray revolutionary ideals and contradict republican principles."[67] In *Black Ralph,* working-class protest inheres in the contest between the modest Seward and the boastful Osborne for the hand of young Flora Dale. The rake Osborne, who colludes with the Cherokee Indians to abduct Flora and then plots to rape her, is described in unflattering terms: "He had been one not greatly beloved by the other emigrants, and his reputation as an honest man was far from enviable."[68] Viewed as traitorous, duplicitous, and licentious, Osborne follows in a long line of upper-class villains of sensational fiction, whereas Seward, whose efforts to recover Flora are assisted by Black Ralph, is figured as working-class by his honesty, courage, and probity that make him a worthy husband for Flora. The fact that Black Ralph helps to preserve the virtue of Flora against Osborne's rakish attempts is a significant departure from anxieties about miscegenation that often inform fictional representations of black men and white women in the antebellum period.

The text's working-class accents are most visible in the racial liminality of Black Ralph, a kind of blackface minstrel who does not perform African American caricature, but rather practices principled violence with "ludic transgressive glee."[69] Black Ralph declares his virtue to the pioneers whom he successfully chaperones to the Great Salt Lake: "I have always punished treachery, and befriended the innocent." With his virtue established, Black Ralph gains notoriety by operating outside of middle-class proprieties and enforcing his own brand of frontier justice against rakish libertines, calling up the justified antislavery violence of Lippard's Old Royal and Douglass's Madison Washington. Robinson describes him as a courageous and imposing hero in the climactic battle with Osborne and a group of hostile Utah Indians: "All at once, over the flaming ramparts leaped a mighty steed and a mighty rider . . . As he thundered down among us, [Black Ralph] dealt fatal blows with a weapon which he wielded in his right hand." Consistent with many white-authored sensational novels of the nineteenth century, the text's progressive cultural work explored in the racialized figure of Black Ralph is nevertheless neutralized at the end. Racial hierarchies are restored when Black Ralph reveals himself to be a white man named Forrester who is in search of his lover, Alice, once kidnapped by Native American Indians: "When I wash this dark paint from my face, you will know [Black Ralph] no more. My Alice recovered, my hostility towards the red man dies."[70] Certainly in this instance Robinson is exploiting blackness, which has become a signifier of Forrester's vengeful wrath that only dissipates upon his return to whiteness; however, his transformation into a "charismatic" black hero who defends the virtuous and the innocent through thrilling incidents not only underscores the performativity of race but also appeals to the story paper's working-class audience and encourages the cross-racial sympathy circulating in popular cultural forms of the period.

On March 27, 1852, the *Star Spangled Banner* printed "Mackey; or, The Black Spy" by Edward Carroll, quite possibly Ned Buntline, written expressly for the newspaper.[71] Set during the Revolutionary War, "Mackey" features another instance of blackface minstrelsy that highlights the performativity of race through class-accented melodrama and gestures toward cross-racial identification. In the story, a young rebel lieutenant, Elliot Putnam, disguises himself in blackface and becomes servant Ben Mackey in order to infiltrate and steal the supplies of the British forces occupying the mansion of American loyalist Richard Foster. As in *Black Ralph,* readers are introduced to the title character Ben Mackey after Putnam has already put on blackface, and thus would assume they are reading about the adventures of a black servant who, as the subtitle indicates, is a "Black Spy" for the rebel cause. The precedent had already been set for sympathetic representations of patriotic blacks fighting alongside whites during the Revolutionary War in George Lippard's *The Legends of the American Revolution*. Although Carroll's black war hero Mackey is revealed at the end to be Putnam in blackface, the tale's racial liminality develops a class-accented alliance typical of the period's sensational fiction: the republican virtue of the multiracial working class (Black Mackey and Elliot Putnam) battles the anti-republican schemes of the wealthy (British Colonel Cramer and loyalist Richard Foster).

Consistent with the story's reliance on the working-class popular forms of minstrelsy and melodrama, Carroll's heightened descriptions of Black Mackey draw attention to race as a performance. Putnam, in blackface, mimics black dialect and a stooped gait in order to gain access to the British colonel by claiming to have important news about the rebels' movements: "As they advanced through the lines towards the house, the light of the camp fires shone on the negro, revealing a tall but ungainly and stooped figure, with a face blacker than the night itself. His eyes rolled about with that motion peculiar to his race, and as he strode along with huge strides, his awkward and shambling gait reminded one involuntarily of a dancing bear." With such servile remarks as "Yaw, massa," Elliot, performing as Mackey, the Black Spy, earns the colonel's trust and gives misinformation that the rebels are on the move, when, in fact, they are preparing to ambush the house. As the British soldiers rush off toward where they believe the rebels are amassing, Mackey suddenly transforms into Lieutenant Elliot: "It was strange how his bent form straightened up as they disappeared from his view in the darkness, and while he stood there with his really fine figure thrown into an attitude of scorn, he, with a low, bitter, contemptuous laugh, uttered the single word, '*fools!*' in a tone and voice as unlike his former speech as could be conceived." Carroll exploits caricature from the minstrel show in his racial descriptions that draw distinct contrasts between black Mackey and white Putnam, and yet the ease with which Elliot performs "blackness" points to the permeability of racial categories. Carroll emphasizes race as a cultural performance when he writes, "So well had [Putnam] played his part that he was not for a moment suspected to be other than what he professed."[72]

If Robinson's Black Ralph tends to ease white anxieties about miscegenation by protecting Flora Dale, Carroll's "Mackey" invokes the specter of miscegenation to exploit those same anxieties. The loyalist Foster has a "red hot liberalist" daughter, Ellen, whom he has forbidden from socializing with Putnam and has encouraged to marry British Colonel Cramer. However, when dressed in blackface, Putnam has regular access to the mansion and to Ellen, who is smitten with him. Carroll records the father's shock when, on the night of Putnam's successful plot against the British, he discovers Ellen intimately sharing a sofa in her bedroom with "black" Mackey: "[Foster] peered through the glass with which the upper part of the door was furnished, and was thunderstruck, as it were, by the sight which met his view . . . Upon this sofa was seated the fair form of Ellen, and by her side, holding her hand and apparently in familiar conversation with her, was *the negro, Ben Mackey* . . . When the Black Spy clasped the maiden in his arms and was about to imprint a kiss upon her lips, Foster dashed open the door and with a cry of rage confronted them."[73] Even Carroll's most sympathetic white working-class readers, despite the "miscegenous desires" they might harbor, may have been made anxious by this exploitive scene.[74] Despite the cross-racial sympathy apparent in much sensational fiction, progressive representations of romantic race-mixing are rare: aside from the blissful relationship between the fugitive slave Randolph Royalton and the white expatriate Eleanor Lynn in Lippard's 1850 *The Empire City,* one of the most progressive representations does not appear until 1859 in Harriet E. Wilson's novel *Our Nig*. Although Putnam's whiteness is clearly reestablished in "Mackey," Carroll closes the story with a salacious allusion to miscegenation: "At the close of the war so glorious to the sons of liberty, [Colonel Cramer] sailed for England, and never returned to disturb the joy of the many years of happiness which the Black Spy and his bride enjoyed."[75]

The cross-racial economic critique developed in *Black Ralph, the Forest Fiend!* and "Mackey; or, The Black Spy" is reinforced by news items and advertisements that share the pages of the *Star Spangled*

Banner. In the news report of July 21, 1849, "A Fight Between an Italian and a Negro," free black employee Francis Russell demanded unpaid wages from his Italian employer, Mordecai, who, armed with a sword cane, "stabbed the negro several times in different parts of the body, causing blood to flow profusely," and was arrested for the assault. The account concludes that the Italian was arrested and released by the judge, who ruled "the parties about equally to blame."[76] Such sketches expressing sympathy for wronged black workers, when combined with class-accented columns like "The Printer's Apprentice" and "The Lower Class: Who Are They?," provide important context for understanding the racial liminality in serial fiction. Perhaps the cross-racial context is best summed up in an advertisement from December 14, 1850, for Barnum's American Museum's display about the "Horrors of Slavery," which characterizes chattel slavery for its working-class audience not as a paternalistic and benign institution, but as one replete with the graphic horrors pervading white-authored sensational fiction.

Conclusion

Focusing on early black newspapers and the Boston weekly story paper the *Star Spangled Banner,* this chapter's case study reveals the cross-racial correspondences circulating throughout antebellum popular print culture, and offers a snapshot of the potential—sometimes realized—of white and black authors' efforts to appeal to readers across racial lines. Contrary to the critical consensus that white-authored texts largely exploit blackness, the serial fiction in the *Star Spangled Banner* highlights the performativity of race, unsettles stable notions of whiteness, and encourages cross-racial sympathy among the working classes through racially liminal artisan republican heroes. Similarly, African American newspapers like *Frederick Douglass' Paper* show concern for the material needs of the black working classes, and promote cross-racial class solidarity through favorable reviews of white-authored sensational fiction.

Coda

I close the book with an analysis of Walt Whitman's 1842 temperance novel *Franklin Evans; or The Inebriate,* published just before the advent of the city-mystery genre in America, and Herman Melville's 1849 sea adventure novel *Redburn: His First Voyage,* published during the genre's heyday, to demonstrate how exploring the cross-racial strategies of class protest in white-authored sensational fiction and African American literature not only challenges the American pastime of denigrating the white working classes and disrupts the self-fulfilling meta-narratives of racial and ethnic strife in American life, but also provides a useful context for reassessing canonical figures of American Romanticism. In their popular novels directed at a mass readership and written for quick sales, Whitman and Melville employ sensationalism to interrogate American exceptionalist ideology and highlight the national contradiction of a republic that tolerated chattel slavery. Like city-mystery writers, who I have shown each used artisan republicanism, antislavery protest, and nativism in distinct ways to promote cross-racial class solidarity, Whitman and Melville marshalled the class-accented discourses circulating in popular print culture differently. While Whitman's *Franklin Evans* mounts an artisan republican critique of emergent industrial capitalism and anticipates the "radical democratic" energies of Lippard's writing, the combination of romantic racialism and anti-immigrant nativism forestalls cross-racial class solidarity in a novel that celebrates the working-class temperance society the Washingtonians. However, Melville's *Redburn,* perhaps inspired by the cross-racial strategies in popular city-mysteries like Lippard's *The Quaker City,* which had been published four years earlier, encourages worldwide class solidarity in its critique of global capitalism's beneficiaries and its expression of sympathy for its casualties, namely the English working poor, African Americans, and European immigrants.

Walt Whitman's *Franklin Evans* was first serialized in November 1842 in New York City's *New World* story paper and functions as a forerunner to the city-mystery genre that would not officially begin in America until the appearance of Osgood Bradbury's *Mysteries of Lowell* in 1844, the earliest on record.[1] Whitman's temperance novel was influenced by the sensational mode popularized in penny papers, which included crime reports, and the reform spirit in labor newspapers, in addition to Eugène Sue's urban Gothic exposé *The Mysteries of Paris* that was serialized beginning in June 1842. Whitman and Lippard both did crime reporting for penny papers in the 1840s; literary critic Carl Ostrowski notes their shared sympathetic treatment of criminals: "Though modern readers familiar with Lippard's and Whitman's reputations for social radicalism might find certain insensitive elements of their police reporting distasteful, their attempts to impart basic human dignity to those involved in criminal behavior ultimately should stand out." David S. Reynolds explains that popular writing in the early 1840s was also influenced by the "socialist fervor [that] had by the 1840s become fused with a fierce evangelical emotionalism and a republican rowdiness unknown in Europe." Moreover, the didactic temperance tales of the 1830s had given way to darker stories in the 1840s that were preoccupied with sensationally documenting the ravages of alcoholism and "gloating over the grim details of vice." The Washingtonian Temperance Society, founded in Baltimore in April 1840, catered to the working classes and shared George Lippard's reform emphasis on ameliorating the poor's material needs. According to Sean Wilentz, "Instead of prayers, [the Washingtonians] offered to help the men get back on their feet, by feeding and clothing them and getting them work."[2] It is within this context of class-accented sensationalism and practical reform that we can measure *Franklin Evans*'s influence on city-mysteries' radical employment of artisan republicanism, antislavery protest, and nativism.

Whitman's novel chronicles the trials and tribulations of a greenhorn who comes to New York City "to seek his fortune" after facing economic challenges in the countryside. Evans's initial impression of New York City as a bewildering space full of financial pitfalls and dangerous enticements would be echoed by city-mystery writers over the next decade and by Frederick Douglass in *My Bondage and My Freedom* in 1855. Evans reflects on his arrival, "Here I stood at the entrance of the mighty labyrinth, and with hardly any consciousness of the temptations, doubts, and dangers that awaited me there . . . Some had attained the envied honors—had reaped distinction—and won princely estate; but how few were they, compared with the numbers of failures!"[3] Three years later, Lippard's *The Quaker City* would share *Franklin Evans*'s anxiety about the fickle marketplace, as in when the wealthy libertine Gus Lorrimer laments, "One moment you gather the apple, the next it is ashes. Every thing fleeting and nothing stable, every thing shifting and changing, and nothing substantial! A bundle of hopes and fears, deceits and confidences, joys and miseries, strapped to a fellow's back like Pedlar's wares."[4] Yet while Lippard's working-class characters often leave the city and head west for better fortunes, Whitman's Evans learns to navigate the city successfully, ending the narrative as a wealthy and temperate product of American exceptionalism. Evans balances his anxiety about city life with willful optimism: "Let us rather think of those who, bravely stemming the tide, and bearing up nobly against all opposition, have proudly come off victorious—waving in their hands at last, the symbol of triumph and glory."[5]

Franklin Evans contains passages of artisan republican critique against the corrupt wealthy that are much like what would feature prominently in city-mysteries. Evans works as a clerk for a wealthy banker, Andrews, whom he soon discovers wrests money from the poor through dubious schemes. Whitman's description of the duplicitous banker and his co-conspirator echoes the oxymoronic oppressors of city-mystery fiction: "A person looking on as they parted, would hardly have thought them to be aught else than two respectable citizens—yet were they two most consummate scoundrels." The victims of the failed bank are reminiscent of the desperate and exploited poor for whom George Thompson's the Dead Man exacts fiery revenge in *City Crimes.* Whitman writes, "Widows, left with a narrow competence; young children; sick people, whose cases were hopeless, but who might languish on for many years . . . all these, and hundreds more, had either deposited sums of money in the institution, or were sufferers by its bankruptcy in other ways."[6] Whitman develops the class critique through a mildly nativist representation of Andrew's porter, the Irishman Dennis. Literary critics Christopher Castiglia and Glenn Hendler have documented Whitman's "anti-Catholic journalism, which was aimed particularly against the recently arrived Irish in New York."[7] In *Franklin Evans,* Dennis, who works as a porter and menial servant for Andrews, "had an unfortunate habit of tippling, which sadly interfered with his efficiency at work" and falls to "the very lowest stage of degradation."[8] While Whitman's representation of Dennis associates the Irish with alcoholism, a stereotype that made them targets of temperance reformers and nativists in the 1840s, the narrator expresses sympathy for Dennis by juxtaposing his lonely death in prison with the revels of the scheming businessmen.[9] While the bankers celebrate their crime at a mansion decorated with "the most sumptuous luxury" and "foreign delicacies purchased" for their guests, "the corpse of the *convicted* thief lay cold and clayey upon the prison floors."[10] While *Franklin Evans* mounts an artisan republican critique of the wealthy, it lacks the cross-racial sympathy that I have argued is central to city-mysteries' class protest; the fact Whitman's novel exploits blackness and ultimately reinforces middle-class values aligns it closely with Ned Buntline's and Augustine Duganne's least subversive works.

Whitman's employment of romantic racialism and apology for chattel slavery in *Franklin Evans* is a far cry from Lippard's cross-racial sympathy in *The Quaker City.* During a lengthy subplot, Evans travels to a slave plantation in southern Virginia, where he reports, "by chatting with the slaves, from whose liveliness and cheerful good-humor,

I derived no small share of mirth myself." Characteristic of "white slavery" appeals that lack the racial ambivalence of city-mysteries' appeal to "wage" slavery, Evans defends the plantation owner Bourne's perception that "the merely nominal oppression of [chattel slavery] is overbalanced, so many hundred times, by the stern reality of starvation and despotism in the [Old World]." The potential for cross-racial sympathy inscribed in Evans's impulsive marriage to Margaret, a "luscious and fascinating" Creole slave, is short-lived when he turns his attentions to a Northern white widow, Mrs. Conway, who is subsequently strangled to death by Margaret in a fit of jealous rage. For a time, Margaret is a dynamic and sympathetic multiracial character who defends her virtue by fighting back against a dissolute overseer, vigorously presses her case to the slaveowner Bourne, and loves and protects her younger brother Louis "as a woman might cling to her own child." But this complexity is replaced with racial essentialism after Evans rejects his wife in favor of Mrs. Conway: "with this creature's good traits her heart had still a remnant of the savage."[11] In *Franklin Evans,* which reinforces the myth of the benign slave plantation and depicts the slaves as either jovial or, in Margaret's case, vengeful, race-mixing is not a potential solution to racial strife in America as it would be in the novels of George Lippard and William Wells Brown in 1853.

In a passage that foreshadows and might have inspired Devil-Bug's climactic dream sequence in *The Quaker City,* Evans falls into a trance after Margaret kills Mrs. Conway and dreams of a raucous temperance rally. Like Devil-Bug's apocryphal vision of the republic's collapse in the distant future year of 1950, Evans "knew, that two-score years had elapsed, as I stood amid this mighty nation." Evans does not dream of a Lippardian procession of enchained white and black "wage" and chattel slaves marching under the control of an oppressive monarch, but of "men in the prime of life, with healthy faces and stalwart forms, and every appearance of vigor" because they have taken the temperance pledge.[12] The crowd, that "Army of the Regenerated," shouts and rejoices at the sight of the last intemperate man being brought forth ceremonially to sign the pledge. In Devil-Bug's nightmare, the multiracial poor are "slaves of the cotton Lord and the factory Prince"[13] and can only be saved by the intervention of a wrathful God, whereas Evans's dream focuses on a single man "enslaved" to intemperance and capable of redemption by signing a piece of paper. The man declares, "I throw off the chains, and take upon myself the pleasant bondage of good. It may not be a truth to boast of, that I am the *last* of the serfs of Appetite; yet I joy that I occupy my position before you now, as I do!"[14] The climax of *Franklin Evans*'s reform message is rooted narrowly in the conversion of an individual, and yet the melodramatic procession and mob are inscribed with sensational energies that explode into class-accented jeremiad under the skillful pen of Lippard three years later. The strong resonances between Whitman's and Lippard's passages might be a happy coincidence, but they might also demonstrate that Lippard reworked some of the class-accented scenes in *Franklin Evans* to develop *The Quaker City*'s cross-racial class protest.

Among the major works of Melville, none is more responsive to sensational fiction than *Redburn,* an action-packed bildungsroman that David S. Reynolds notes Melville wrote expressly for popular appeal following the poor reception of his more philosophical *Mardi.*[15] While the protagonist's dream-like excursion into the seedy gambling dens of London has received critical attention for its connection to the city-mystery genre, *Redburn,* as a sensational text concerned with class difference and crimes against the working poor, also resonates with the strategies of cross-racial economic critique discussed in this volume. Through laboring as part of a multiracial and multinational crew, and serving as an eyewitness to abject poverty on the streets of Liverpool, Melville's white protagonist transcends his middle-class myopia as well as his racial and ethnic anxieties that George Lippard and Frederick Douglass understood could splinter class solidarity and sustain socioeconomic inequality in the American North and South.

Told through the perspective of a white youth fallen from middle-class privilege, a character type that frequents the pages of city-mysteries, *Redburn* captures the vulnerability felt by the multiracial lower classes laboring in the capitalist marketplace. The title character, imbued with the aristocratic airs of a city-mystery villain, is forced by necessity to go to sea as a common sailor. Despite his reduced class status, Redburn brings his middle-class pretentions with him to sea, and initially is alienated from his fellow sailors. He is troubled by their cursing and uncouth ways: "And these are the men, I thought to myself, that I must live with so long? these the men I am to eat with, and sleep with all the time?" When he is ordered to clean chicken coops and care for the pigs, Redburn invokes the disingenuous "white slavery" rhetoric that many city-mystery writers and abolitionists eschewed. "Miserable dog's life is this of the sea! commanded like a slave, and set to work like an ass! vulgar and brutal men lording it over me, as if I were an African in Alabama." The irony of Redburn's faulty analogy is heightened by his initial lack of solidarity with and respect for the African American sailors he worked alongside. He is surprised that the black cook Mr. Thompson is semi-literate and a devout Christian, and he is amused with the black steward Lavender, "a handsome, dandy mulatto, that had once been a barber in West-Broadway."[16]

It is during Redburn's stay in Liverpool that his cross-racial working-class consciousness emerges. His description of the docked American ships resonates with city-mysteries' dual critique of capitalism and chattel slavery: "Here lie the noble New York packets, which at home are found at the foot of Wall-street; and here lie the Mobile and Savannah cotton ships and traders." Removed from his usual surroundings in America, Redburn is invigorated and begins to see the world with fresh eyes. Walking the streets of Liverpool, where he sees "poverty, poverty, poverty, in almost endless vistas," Redburn recalls the multiracial American poor. "It was the absence of negroes; who in the large towns in the 'free states' of America, almost always form a considerable portion of the destitute . . . This conveyed a strange feeling; and more than any thing else, reminded me that I was not in my own land." By ironizing the class stratification plaguing the "free states" in the industrial North, Melville's novel echoes the working-class concerns of white-authored city-mysteries and the writing of Douglass, Brown, and Webb. Redburn's education into cross-racial class solidarity is complete when he sympathizes with Lavender's freedom to walk unmolested with a white woman along the streets of Liverpool. "Recognizing [Lavender's] claim to humanity and normal equality,"

Redburn criticizes race prejudice in America, and makes an oblique reference to Thomas Jefferson's rumored affair with Sally Hemings: "In some things, we Americans leave to other countries the carrying out of the principle that stands at the head of our Declaration of Independence."[17] Redburn's view of African Americans progresses from middle-class romantic racialism to cross-racial class solidarity, and echoes the working-class protest found in the white- and black-authored texts of antebellum popular print culture.

Although Redburn carries to sea many assumptions shared by nativists about the non-native-born, the introduction of the virulently nativist sailor Jackson provides a means to trace Redburn's emerging sympathy toward immigrants. Jackson is an Ahab-like misanthrope who wields magnetic influence over the rest of the crew through intimidation and sheer will. Although a native of New York City who wears the "red woolen shirts" characteristic of the working-class Bowery B'hoys and the black laborers championed in city-mysteries, Jackson espouses anti-immigrant nativism and the racist politics of white male suffrage. Redburn's path toward rejecting anti-immigrant nativism is apparent in the fact that he stands in relationship to Jackson as Ishmael would to Captain Ahab in *Moby-Dick* two years later: In the first half of the narrative, Redburn is in awe of Jackson and is affected by Jackson's powerful misanthropy, yet in the same way that Ishmael gravitates toward Ahab's misanthropy before rejecting it in favor of universal fraternity, Redburn ultimately renounces Jackson's nativism.

While exploring the impressive array of ships from around the world docked in port, observing the maimed and emaciated bodies of the poor lining the streets of Liverpool, and engaging with the immigrants who return with the ship to America, Redburn develops sympathy for the casualties of industrialism that stretch across the ocean and recognizes the strength of his native land's diversity. Admiring the well-built ships that "brought together the remotest limits of the earth," Redburn articulates an Ishmael-like faith in humanity: "Here, under the beneficent sway of the Genius of Commerce, all climes and countries embrace; and yard-arm touches yard-arm in brotherly love." The celebration of international commerce informing Redburn's enthusiasm is dampened as he walks among the poor of the city and remarks, "I remember one cripple, a young man rather decently clad, who sat huddled up against the wall, holding a painted board on his knees. It was a picture intending to represent the man himself caught in the machinery of some factory, and whirled about among spindles and cogs, with his limbs mangled and bloody."[18] Melville's attention to the sensational horrors of industrialism is consistent with city-mysteries and the serial fiction in weekly story papers, but *Redburn*'s rejection of nativism, realized after his protagonist witnesses the perilous journey that desperate immigrants risk to reach America, links Melville's novel with the metacritiques of divisive nativism in Lippard's and Douglass's writing.

In one of the most detailed and textured portrayals of the immigrants' passage in antebellum fiction, Melville captures the chaos after a malignant fever sweeps through the ship and describes immigrants' squalid living conditions on the ship. Additionally, Redburn praises the playing of Carlo, an Italian organ-grinder on the ship, which stands in contrast to the anti-immigrant nativism of Buntline's *The Mysteries and Miseries of New York* and Duganne's *The Tenant-House,* which respectively single out Italian fortune-tellers and organ-grinders as public nuisances. In the typically inflated language Melville ironically ascribes to his hero, Redburn reflects, "Reverenced, then, be all street organs; more melody is at the beck of my Italian boy, than lurks in squadrons of Parisian orchestras." When he learns that the wealthy cabin-passengers give Carlo little money for his playing, Redburn expresses class resentment, describing them as "the most finical, miserly, mean men and women, that ever stepped over the Atlantic." Additionally, whereas Jackson takes pleasure in harassing the immigrants and spreads a rumor that they are sailing to Barbary to sell them into slavery, Redburn sympathizes with the "friendless emigrants, stowed away like bales of cotton, and packed like slaves in a slave-ship."[19] It is not only ironic but also symbolic of America's growing plurality that Jackson dies violently and sinks into the ocean just prior to the ship sailing past Staten Island and safely into port. Whereas city-mystery writers and early black writers sometimes employed nativism strategically to develop a dual critique of "wage" and chattel slavery,

Melville, working in *Redburn* with the same themes and within the same sensational mode, demonstrates how canonical Romantic fiction could express powerful class protest and progressive racial ideologies without relying on anti-immigrant nativism.

As class-accented weekly story papers and early black newspapers are rescued from archival obscurity through the ongoing efforts of digital humanities projects, scholars will have increasing opportunities to revise our understanding of historical relations among the multiracial working classes and deepen our appreciation of their dynamic and correspondent cultural expressions. Analyzing the patterns of cross-racial economic critique throughout antebellum print culture highlights the dangers of generalizing about Northern race relations. Over and over again, white authors of sensational fiction draw sympathetic representations of African Americans—in the form of the manly laborer and the fugitive slave—to attack wealthy capitalists in the North and slaveowners in the South. Just as city-mysteries draw on African American literature to mount their economic critique, so, too, did black-authored texts draw on the rhetorical techniques of popular novels. Black-authored texts integrate artisan republicanism, populist appeals to the native-born status of African Americans, and sensational depictions of working life to protest social inequality in the North and chattel slavery in the South. These broad attempts to build cross-racial sympathy and understanding among the multiracial working classes circulated widely in antebellum American literature and deserve our ongoing attention.

NOTES

Introduction

1. George Lippard, *The Empire City; or, New York by Night and Day* (New York: Stringer and Townsend, 1850), 46.
2. Ibid., 47, 54, 54.
3. Nathaniel Hawthorne, *The House of the Seven Gables* (New York: W. W. Norton, 2006), 14.
4. Sean Wilentz, *Chants Democratic: New York City and the Rise of the American Working Class, 1788–1850* (New York: Oxford University Press, 1984), 5.
5. Bruce Laurie, *Working People of Philadelphia, 1800–1850* (Philadelphia: Temple University Press, 1980), 65; David Roediger, *The Wages of Whiteness: Race and the Making of the American Working Class* (New York: Verso, 1991), 13.
6. Nancy Isenberg, *White Trash: The 400-Year Untold History of Class in America* (New York: Viking, 2016), xvi.
7. James Oliver Horton, *Free People of Color: Inside the African American Community* (Washington: Smithsonian Institution Press, 1993), 29, 166; Leslie M. Harris, *In the Shadow of Slavery: African Americans in New York City, 1626–1863* (Chicago: University of Chicago Press, 2003), 7.
8. Dan Schiller, *Objectivity and the News: The Public and the Rise of Commercial Journalism* (Philadelphia: University of Pennsylvania Press, 1981).
9. The term "producing classes" was coined by Philadelphia labor activist William Heighton to designate the manual laborers who produced the country's wealth with their hands, in contrast to what he disparagingly called the "accumulators," the non-producers who "produced nothing [yet] lived in affluence." See Laurie, *Working People*, 76.
10. Sean Wilentz, "Society, Politics, and the Market Revolution, 1815–1848," *The New American History*, ed. Eric Foner (Philadelphia: Temple University Press, 1990), 59.
11. Meredith L. McGill, *American Literature and the Culture of Reprinting, 1834–1853* (Philadelphia: University of Pennsylvania Press, 2003), 3.
12. Lori Merish, *Archives of Labor: Working-Class Women and Literary Culture in the Antebellum United States* (Durham: Duke University Press, 2017), 25, 61, 62.

13. Eric Lott, *Love and Theft: Blackface Minstrelsy and the American Working Class* (New York: Oxford University Press, 1995), 52, 80.
14. Leslie A. Fiedler, *Love and Death in the American Novel,* rev. ed. (1960; repr., Normal, IL: Dalkey Archive Press, 1998), 29, 137; Cathy N. Davidson, *Revolution and the Word: The Rise of the Novel in America* (New York: Oxford University Press, 1986), 314.
15. Nina Baym, "Concepts of the Romance in Hawthorne's America," *Nineteenth-Century Fiction* 38, no. 4 (March 1984): 438; Michael Denning, *Mechanic Accents: Dime Novels and Working-Class Culture in America,* rev. ed. (1987; repr., New York: Verso, 1998), 103.
16. David S. Reynolds, *Beneath the American Renaissance: The Subversive Imagination in the Age of Emerson and Melville* (New York: Oxford University Press, 1988), 201.
17. David S. Reynolds, *George Lippard* (Boston: Twayne Publishers, 1982), 59.
18. Jane Tompkins, *Sensational Designs: The Cultural Work of American Fiction, 1790–1860* (New York: Oxford University Press, 1985), 123; Julia A. Stern, "Excavating Genre in *Our Nig*," *American Literature* 67, no. 3 (September 1995): 439; Naomi Greyser, *On Sympathetic Grounds: Race, Gender, and Affective Geographies in Nineteenth-Century North America* (New York: Oxford University Press, 2018), 3.
19. David S. Reynolds, introduction to *The Quaker City; or, The Monks of Monk-Hall,* by George Lippard (Amherst: University of Massachusetts Press, 1995), xxii; Shelley Streeby, *American Sensations: Class, Empire, and the Production of Popular Culture* (Berkeley: University of California Press, 2002), 33.
20. See Eric Foner, *Free Soil, Free Labor, Free Men: The Ideology of the Republican Party Before the Civil War,* rev. ed. (1970; repr., New York: Oxford University Press, 1995); Jonathan Glickstein, *Concepts of Free Labor in Antebellum America* (New Haven: Yale University Press, 1991).
21. Foner, *Free Soil, Free Labor, Free Men,* 11.
22. Eric Foner, *Politics and Ideology in the Age of the Civil War* (New York: Oxford University Press, 1980), 66.
23. George M. Fredrickson, *The Black Image in the White Mind: The Debate on Afro-American Character and Destiny, 1817–1914* (Middletown, CT: Wesleyan University Press, 1971), 37.
24. Tyler Anbinder, *Nativism and Slavery: The Northern Know Nothings and the Politics of the 1850s* (New York: Oxford University Press, 1992), 106.

Chapter One: Black and White Artisan Heroes

1. Literary critic Isabelle Lehuu reports that the sensational penny paper the *New York Herald,* which would have appealed to the readers of city-mysteries, "reached a broad popularity, even among the black community," and she cites

William Wells Brown's lament about the *New York Herald*'s popularity among black readers. Williams Wells Brown in the *Anglo-African*, August 8, 1863, quoted in Dorothy Sterling, ed., *Speak Out in Thunder Tones: Letters and Other Writings by Black Northerners, 1787–1865* (New York: Da Capo Press, 1973), 233, both quoted in Isabelle Lehuu, *Carnival on the Page: Popular Print Media in Antebellum America* (Chapel Hill: University of North Carolina Press, 2000), 40.

2. Ira Dworkin, introduction to *Narrative of the Life of Frederick Douglass, an American Slave*, by Frederick Douglass, rev. ed. (1845; repr., New York: Penguin, 2014), vii. Literary historian Robert S. Levine concludes that while publishers would inflate the number of editions of a book, "by all accounts the *Narrative* was the most successful slave narrative published in the United States." Robert S. Levine, *The Lives of Frederick Douglass* (Cambridge, MA: Harvard University Press, 2016), 11.
3. W. T. Lhamon Jr., *Raising Cain: Blackface Performance from Jim Crow to Hip Hop* (Cambridge: Harvard University Press, 1998), 73; Eric Lott, *Love and Theft: Blackface Minstrelsy and the American Working Class* (New York: Oxford University Press, 1995), 72.
4. William Lloyd Garrison, "Not to be Trusted," *Liberator,* February 18, 1848; William Wells Brown, *Clotel; or, the President's Daughter,* ed. Robert S. Levine, 2nd ed. (Boston: Bedford/St. Martin's, 2011), 150.
5. *Quaker City Weekly,* June 2, 1849.
6. Although there is no evidence that African Americans joined the Brotherhood of the Union before 1855, historian Mark A. Lause notes that the Brotherhood's annual National Industrial Congresses eventually included African Americans: "The last of these congresses seated a black delegate, representing an African American housing cooperative, and that of 1855 chose a black newspaper editor to serve as one of its officers." Lause, *A Secret Society History of the Civil War* (Urbana: University of Illinois Press, 2011), 32.
7. *Quaker City Weekly,* March 31, 1849.
8. George Lippard, *The White Banner: A Quarterly Miscellany* (Philadelphia: George Lippard Publisher, 1851), 148.
9. Bruce Laurie, *Working People of Philadelphia, 1800–1850* (Philadelphia: Temple University Press, 1980), 139.
10. Michael Denning, *Mechanic Accents: Dime Novels and Working-Class Culture in America,* rev. ed. (1987; repr., New York: Verso, 1998), 97; David S. Reynolds, introduction to *The Quaker City; or, The Monks of Monk-Hall,* by George Lippard (1849; repr., Amherst: University of Massachusetts Press, 1995), xxxviii; David S. Reynolds, *Beneath the American Renaissance: The Subversive Imagination in the Age of Emerson and Melville* (New York: Oxford University Press, 1988), 207.
11. Lippard, *The Quaker City,* 2; Denning, *Mechanic Accents,* 106.
12. Noel Ignatiev, *How the Irish Became White* (New York: Routledge, 1995), 218n1; Dana Nelson, *National Manhood: Capitalist Citizenship and the Imagined Fraternity of White Men* (Durham: Duke University Press, 1998), 148.
13. Playbill, "The Quaker City," November 11, 1844. For more information about the

playbill and the play version that was never performed, see Sari Altschuler and Aaron M. Tobiason, "Playbill for George Lippard's *The Quaker City*," *PMLA* 129, no. 2 (March 2014): 267–73.

14. Lippard, *The Quaker City*, 227.
15. Ibid., 105–6.
16. Douglass, *Narrative of the Life*, 17, 18.
17. Lippard, *The Quaker City*, 52.
18. Sean Wilentz writes, "As it developed, this culture acquired a new ideological significance as well, a sort of republicanism of the streets that connected the workingmen's pride, resentments, and simple pleasures to the language of republican politics. The fire companies were among the first to suggest the connections, in their Fourth of July parades and in their patriotic firehouse icons." See Sean Wilentz, *Chants Democratic: New York City and the Rise of the American Working Class, 1788–1850* (New York: Oxford University Press, 1984), 263.
19. "Literary Notices," *National Era*, July 18, 1850.
20. Augustine Duganne, *The Knights of the Seal: or, The Mysteries of the Three Cities* (Philadelphia: Colon and Adriance, Arcade, 1845), 36, 99.
21. Stephen Rice, *Minding the Machine: Languages of Class in Early Industrial America* (Berkeley: University of California Press, 2004), 8.
22. Lippard, *The Quaker City*, 227.
23. Edgar Allan Poe, "Hop-Frog; or, the Eight Chained Ourang-Outangs" in *The Selected Writings of Edgar Allan Poe* (New York: W. W. Norton, 2004), 423, 422.
24. Lippard, *The Quaker City*, 51.
25. Paul Gilmore, *The Genuine Article: Race, Mass Culture, and American Literary Manhood* (Durham: Duke University Press, 2001), 112–13.
26. Poe, "Hop-Frog," 427.
27. Lippard, *The Quaker City*, 122.
28. Lhamon Jr., *Raising Cain*, 45; Wilentz, *Chants Democratic*, 259; Alexander Saxton, *The Rise and Fall of the White Republic: Class Politics and Mass Culture in Nineteenth-Century America* (New York: Verso, 1990), 176; Lott, *Love and Theft*, 72.
29. Lippard, *The Quaker City*, 55, 40, 114–15, 117, 120.
30. Lhamon Jr., *Raising Cain*, 50–51; Lippard, *The Quaker City*, 307, 326, 367–68; Douglass, *Narrative of the Life*, 26.
31. Lippard, *The Quaker City*, 556.
32. Ibid., 333.
33. Ibid., 389.
34. Eric Foner, *Politics and Ideology in the Age of the Civil War* (New York: Oxford University Press, 1980), 60–61.
35. Denning, *Mechanic Accents*, 108.
36. George Lippard, *The Legends of the American Revolution "1776." Or, Washington and His Generals* (1847; repr., Philadelphia: T. B. Peterson and Brothers, 1876), 361.

37. Ibid., 368, 362, 368, 365, 368.
38. Toni Morrison, *Playing in the Dark: Whiteness and the Literary Imagination* (New York: Vintage Books, 1992), 52.
39. Lippard, *Legends of the American Revolution,* 361–62.
40. Ibid., 372, 374, 374.
41. Matt Cohen and Edlie L. Wong, introduction to *The Killers: A Narrative of Real Life in Philadelphia* by George Lippard (Philadelphia: University of Pennsylvania Press, 2014), 15.
42. Lippard, *The Killers,* 47, 52.
43. Ibid., 63, 64.
44. *Quaker City Weekly,* March 3, 1849.
45. Nathaniel Hawthorne, *The House of the Seven Gables* (New York: W. W. Norton, 2006), 3.
46. Lippard, *The Killers,* 69, 126.
47. Ibid., 86, 94, 95.
48. "Bulgine" appears in the minstrel song "The Fine Old Colored Gentleman" popularized by Dan Emmett of the Virginia Minstrels in the mid-1840s. In the song, the "colored gentleman's" height and strength are indicated by his ability to swallow a "locomotive bulgine." In his essay "Early Minstrel Show Music, 1843–1852," critic Robert S. Winans argues, "As a parody, this song makes fun not only of old black Sambo, but of the English country gentleman who was the subject of the original song." See Winans in *Inside the Minstrel Mask: Readings in Nineteenth-Century Blackface Minstrelsy,* ed. Annemarie Bean, James V. Hatch, and Brooks McNamara (Middletown, CT: Wesleyan University Press, 1996), 155.
49. Dorothy Sterling, ed., *Speak Out in Thunder Tones: Letters and Other Writings by Black Northerners, 1787–1865* (New York: Da Capo Press, 1973), 196.
50. Ibid., 204.
51. Lippard, *The Killers,* 107.
52. Lhamon Jr., *Raising Cain,* 51. Lhamon Jr. also points out that the spelling of "white trach" appears in the early blackface song "De New York Nigga," 48.
53. Lippard, *The Killers,* 163, 135, 160.
54. Ibid., 139, 144.
55. Cohen and Wong, introduction, 27.
56. Lippard, *The Killers,* 162.
57. George Thompson, *City Crimes,* in *Venus in Boston and Other Tales of Nineteenth-Century City Life,* ed. David S. Reynolds and Kimberly R. Gladman (Amherst: University of Massachusetts Press, 2002), 282, 282–83, 283.
58. Lhamon Jr., *Raising Cain,* 3, 22.
59. David S. Reynolds and Kimberly R. Gladman, introduction to *Venus in Boston and Other Tales of Nineteenth-Century City Life,* by George Thompson, ed. David S. Reynolds and Kimberly R. Gladman (Amherst: University of Massachusetts Press, 2002), xi, xiv.
60. Patricia Cline Cohen, Timothy J. Gilfoyle, and Helen Lefkowitz Horowitz, *The*

Flash Press: Sporting Male Weeklies in 1840s New York (Chicago: University of Chicago Press, 2008), 121.

61. See Christopher Looby, "George Thompson's 'Romance of the Real': Transgression and Taboo in American Sensation Fiction," *American Literature* 65, no. 4 (December 1993): 651–72; and Karen J. Renner, "Seduction, Prostitution, and the Control of Female Desire in Popular Antebellum Fiction," *Nineteenth-Century Literature* 65, no. 2 (September 2010): 166–91.
62. Looby, "George Thompson's 'Romance of the Real,'" 656.
63. Thompson, *City Crimes,* 109, 124.
64. Ibid., 309, 150, 125, 152.
65. Harriet E. Wilson, *Our Nig; or, Sketches from the Life of a Free Black* (New York: Penguin, 2005), 8, 9.
66. Thompson, *City Crimes,* 125, 127, 138 (emphasis added).
67. David Roediger, *The Wages of Whiteness: Race and the Making of the American Working Class* (New York: Verso, 1991), 49.
68. Lori Merish, *Archives of Labor: Working-Class Women and Literary Culture in the Antebellum United States* (Durham: Duke University Press, 2017), 153.
69. Thompson, *City Crimes,* 227–28 (emphasis added).
70. Ibid., 185, 185.
71. Carl Ostrowski, "Slavery, Labor Reform, and Intertextuality in Antebellum Print Culture: The Slave Narrative and the City-Mysteries Novel," *African American Review* 40, no. 3 (Fall 2006): 495.
72. Reynolds, *Beneath the American Renaissance,* 181; Thompson, *City Crimes,* 256.
73. Ibid., 234, 234.
74. Ibid., 212, 235.
75. David Anthony, "Class, Culture, and the Trouble with White Skin in Hawthorne's *The House of the Seven Gables,*" in *The House of the Seven Gables,* ed. Robert S. Levine (New York: W. W. Norton, 2006), 439–59, 454–55.
76. Thompson, *City Crimes,* 194.
77. Tyler Anbinder, *Five Points: The Nineteenth-Century New York City Neighborhood That Invented Tap Dance, Stole Elections, and Became the World's Most Notorious Slum* (New York: Plume, 2001), 36.
78. Thompson, *City Crimes,* 194–95.
79. Douglass, *Narrative of the Life,* 92, 93.
80. Reynolds, *Beneath the American Renaissance,* 207; Robert S. Levine, *The Lives of Frederick Douglass,* 11.
81. George M. Fredrickson, *The Black Image in the White Mind: The Debate on Afro-American Character and Destiny, 1817–1914* (Middletown, CT: Wesleyan University Press, 1971), 38n74.
82. *Frederick Douglass' Paper,* January 20, 1854.
83. Robert S. Levine, "*Uncle Tom's Cabin* in *Frederick Douglass' Paper*: An Analysis of Reception," in Harriet Beecher Stowe, *Uncle Tom's Cabin* (New York: W. W. Norton, 2010), 570.

84. Frederick Douglass, *The Heroic Slave* (New Haven, CT: Yale University Press, 2015), 7, 7.
85. Frederick Douglass, *My Bondage and My Freedom* (New York: Penguin, 2003), 12, 13.
86. Douglass, *The Heroic Slave,* 7.
87. Ibid., 34–35.
88. Ibid., 27, 27–28, 28, 32–33.
89. Ibid., 42 and 44, 48, 50–51, and 51.

Chapter Two: The Class Accents of Antislavery Reform

1. Jane Tompkins, *Sensational Designs: The Cultural Work of American Fiction, 1790–1860* (New York: Oxford University Press, 1985), 134.
2. Ann duCille, "Where in the World Is William Wells Brown? Thomas Jefferson, Sally Hemings, and the DNA of African-American Literary History," *American Literary History* 12, no. 3 (Autumn 2000): 451.
3. "The True Remedy for the Fugitive Slave Bill," *Frederick Douglass' Paper,* June 9, 1854.
4. Frederick Douglass, "Do Not Send Back the Fugitive: An Address Delivered in Boston, Massachusetts, on 14 October 1850," *Frederick Douglass Papers Digital Archive,* 245, 245, 245.
5. Ibid., 248, 248.
6. Robert S. Levine, *The Lives of Frederick Douglass* (Cambridge, MA: Harvard University Press, 2016), 116.
7. Douglass, "Do Not Send Back the Fugitive," 247.
8. Frederick Douglass, "The Slaves' Right to Revolt: An Address Delivered in Boston, Massachusetts, on 30 May 1848," *Frederick Douglass Papers Digital Archive,* 130–31.
9. Frederick Douglass, "Slavery, the Slumbering Volcano: An Address Delivered in New York, New York, on 23 April 1849," *Frederick Douglass Papers Digital Archive,* 151, 153, 152.
10. Addison Gayle, *The Way of the New World: The Black Novel in America* (New York: Anchor, 1976), 13; William Wells Brown, *Clotel; or, The President's Daughter,* ed. Robert S. Levine, 2nd ed. (Boston: Bedford and St. Martin's, 2011), 201, 201–2, 202n4.
11. "Meeting in Philadelphia," *National Era,* July 15, 1852.
12. *Literary World* published a Stringer and Townsend advertisement for the first volume (consisting of parts one and two) of *The Empire City* on July 13, 1850. The first Stringer and Townsend advertisement for the complete novel did not appear in the *Literary World* until October 26, 1850.
13. George Lippard, *The Empire City; or, New York by Night and Day* (New York: Stringer and Townsend, 1850), 75, 76, 76.

14. Lippard, *The Empire City,* 105, 7.
15. Jeannine Marie DeLombard, *Slavery on Trial: Law, Abolitionism, and Print Culture* (Chapel Hill: University of North Carolina Press, 2007), 21.
16. Lippard, *The Empire City,* 123, 124.
17. Shelley Streeby, "Opening Up the Story Paper: George Lippard and the Construction of Class," *boundary2* 24, no. 1 (Spring 1997): 199–200.
18. Lippard, *The Empire City,* 130, 131, 205.
19. George Lippard, *New York: Its Upper Ten and Lower Million* (Cincinnati, OH: H. M. Rulison, 1853), 116, 117.
20. In *My Bondage and My Freedom,* Douglass writes, "Within the bounds of his just earnings, I hold that the slave is fully justified in helping himself to the *gold and silver, and the best apparel of his master, or that of any other slaveholder; and that such taking is not stealing in any just sense of that word.* The morality of *free* society can have no application to *slave* society." Frederick Douglass, *My Bondage and My Freedom* (New York: Penguin, 2003), 140.
21. Lippard, *New York,* 117, 117.
22. Paul Gilmore, *The Genuine Article: Race, Mass Culture, and American Literary Manhood* (Durham: Duke University Press, 2001), 47.
23. Brown, *Clotel,* 98, 99.
24. Carl Ostrowski, *Literature and Criminal Justice in Antebellum America* (Amherst: University of Massachusetts Press, 2016), 54.
25. Lippard, *New York,* 121.
26. Douglass, "Do Not Send Back the Fugitive," 248.
27. Lippard, *New York,* 241.
28. Ibid., 122.
29. *Liberator,* December 31, 1841.
30. The complete title of Harriet E. Wilson's 1859 novel is, *Our Nig; or, Sketches from the Life of a Free Black, in a Two-Story White House, North, Showing that Slavery's Shadows Fall Even There.*
31. James Callender, "The President, Again," *Richmond Recorder,* September 1, 1802.
32. "Jefferson's Daughter," *North Star,* March 31, 1848.
33. "Thomas Jefferson and Slavery," *Frederick Douglass' Paper,* April 1, 1852.
34. Robert S. Levine, "Introduction: Cultural and Historical Background," *Clotel,* 16. Also, see Annette Gordon-Reed, *The Hemings of Monticello: An American Family* (New York: W. W. Norton, 2008).
35. Thomas Jefferson Foundation, "Monticello Affirms Thomas Jefferson Fathered Children with Sally Hemings," *Monticello,* accessed May 27, 2019, https://www.monticello.org/thomas-jefferson/jefferson-slavery/thomas-jefferson-and-sally-hemings-a-brief-account/monticello-affirms-thomas-jefferson-fathered-children-with-sally-hemings/.
36. Brown published *Clotel* in London with Partridge and Oakey in November 1853, and Lippard published *New York* in Cincinnati with H. M. Rulison sometime at the end of 1853 before it was reprinted in Cincinnati by E. Mendenhall in 1854.

The title page of Rulison's edition lists 1853, the same year the publisher filed for copyright in the Clerk's Office of the District Court of the United States for the District of Ohio. An 1855 biography of Lippard, titled *The Life and Choice Writings of George Lippard,* states that *New York* "appeared only a few weeks before [Lippard's] decease" on February 9, 1854, and may refer to the Mendenhall edition. See John Bell Bouton, *The Life and Choice Writings of George Lippard* (New York: H. H. Randall, 1855), 128.

37. William Farmer in William Wells Brown, *Three Years in Europe: or, Places I Have Seen and People I Have Met* (London: Charles Gilpin, 1852), xxviii.
38. Brown, *Clotel,* 88, 207.
39. Ibid., 180, 181.
40. Eric Lott, *Love and Theft: Blackface Minstrelsy and the American Working Class* (New York: Oxford University Press, 1995), 79; Streeby, "Opening Up the Story Paper," 196.
41. George Lippard, "Key to The Quaker City; or, The Monks of Monk Hall," appended to *The Quaker City; or, The Monks of Monk-Hall* (Philadelphia: published by the author, 1845).
42. Lippard, *New York,* 79, 79.
43. Ibid., 268, 108.
44. Thomas Jefferson, *Notes on the State of Virginia* (Chapel Hill: University of North Carolina Press, 1982), 138.
45. Lippard, *New York,* 79, 242–43.
46. Levine, "Introduction," 18–19.
47. Lippard, *The Empire City,* 202.
48. Lippard, *New York,* 84.
49. Ibid., 108.
50. Harriet E. Wilson, *Our Nig; or, Sketches from the Life of a Free Black,* ed. P. Gabrielle Foreman and Reginald H. Pitts (New York: Penguin, 2005), 6.
51. P. Gabrielle Foreman and Reginald H. Pitts, introduction to *Our Nig,* xxxvii.
52. David Dowling, "'Other and More Terrible Evils': Anticapitalist Rhetoric in Harriet Wilson's *Our Nig* and Proslavery Propaganda," *College Literature* 36, no. 3 (Summer 2009): 131.
53. Wilson, *Our Nig,* 6.
54. Sheila Post-Lauria, *Correspondent Colorings: Melville in the Marketplace* (Amherst: University of Massachusetts Press, 1996), 167; Herman Melville, "Poor Man's Pudding and Rich Man's Crumbs," *The Piazza Tales and Other Prose Pieces, 1839–1860,* ed. Harrison Hayford and Herschel Parker (Chicago: Northwestern University Press, 1987), 291, 290.
55. Ibid., 296.
56. Notably, *Clotel* also rejects pro-slavery authors who claim the English laboring classes are worse off than American chattel slaves. Insisting that as "bad as are the social evils of England, those of Slavery are immeasurably worse," William Wells Brown denounces the comparison to European "wage slaves" rather than

to American "wage" slaves in the North, thereby preserving a cross-racial appeal to the urban working classes, 150–51.

57. Melville, "Poor Man's Pudding," 296.
58. Katie Frye, "The Case against Whiteness in William Wells Brown's *Clotel*," *Mississippi Quarterly* 62, no. 4 (Fall 2009): 528.
59. Brown, *Clotel,* 110, 116, 117, 117, 117.
60. Lippard, *The Empire City,* 120.
61. George Lippard, *Memoirs of a Preacher; or The Mysteries of the Pulpit* (Philadelphia: T. B. Peterson, 1864), 46. Lippard serialized *Memoirs of a Preacher* in his *Quaker City Weekly* from 1848 to 1849.
62. Frederick Douglass, *The Heroic Slave* (New Haven, CT: Yale University Press, 2015), 21.
63. Henry Louis Gates Jr., introduction to *Our Nig*, xlix.
64. Lippard, *New York,* 108, 108.
65. Brown, *Clotel,* 130.
66. Douglass, *My Bondage and My Freedom,* 29, 30, 81–82.
67. Ibid., 105, 115, 116, 125.
68. Ibid., 136, 152, 157, 157, 157, 162.
69. Ibid., 226, 226, 226.
70. Ibid., 296, 297, 297, 298, 298.
71. "New Story by George Lippard," *National Era,* January 5, 1854.
72. Douglass, *My Bondage and My Freedom,* 238.
73. George Lippard, *Eleanor; or, Slave Catching in the Quaker City,* serialized novel, *Philadelphia Sunday Mercury,* January 29, 1854.
74. Ibid., February 5, 1854.
75. Frederick Douglass, *Narrative of the Life of Frederick Douglass, an American Slave,* rev. ed. (1845; repr., New York: Penguin, 2014), 41.
76. See George Lippard, "The Heart-Broken," *Nineteenth-Century: A Quarterly Miscellany, Vol. I* (Philadelphia: G. B. Zieber and Co., 1848), 19–27.
77. Lippard, *Eleanor, Philadelphia Sunday Mercury,* February 5, 1854.
78. DeLombard, *Slavery on Trial,* 3.
79. Lippard, *Eleanor, Philadelphia Sunday Mercury,* February 12, 1854; Douglass, *Narrative of the Life,* 34.
80. Lippard, *Eleanor, Philadelphia Sunday Mercury,* February 5, 1854.
81. Ibid., February 19, 1854.
82. Ibid., February 26, 1854. David S. Reynolds notes, "[Lippard's] legends and lectures about Paine 'aroused a great deal of attention,' causing 'an increased sale of Paine's works' and impelling a late nineteenth-century historian to praise Lippard for bravely defending Paine when such defense meant ostracism." See David S. Reynolds, *George Lippard* (Boston: Twayne Publishers, 1982), 68.
83. Lippard, *Eleanor, Philadelphia Sunday Mercury,* March 5, 1854.
84. Ibid.
85. Ibid., February 12, 1854.

86. David Roediger, *Colored White: Transcending the Racial Past* (Berkeley: University of California Press, 2002), 120, 120.
87. Lippard, *Eleanor, Philadelphia Sunday Mercury,* February 12, 1854.

Chapter Three: The Cross-Racial Appeal of Nativism

1. *The Rights of All,* September 18, 1829.
2. Nikki M. Taylor, *Frontiers of Freedom: Cincinnati's Black Community, 1802–1868* (Athens: Ohio University Press, 2005), 51, 52; Emil Klauprecht, *German Chronicle in the History of the Ohio Valley and Its Capital City Cincinnati in Particular,* trans. Dale V. Lally Jr., ed. Don Heinrich Tolzmann (1864; Westminster, MD: Heritage Books, 2007), 170.
3. *The Rights of All,* September 18, 1829.
4. "Barbarism in America," *The Rights of All,* August 7, 1829.
5. "Education to Young Men," *Colored American,* March 4, 1837.
6. Ibid.
7. Tyler Anbinder, *Nativism and Slavery: The Northern Know Nothings and the Politics of the 1850s* (New York: Oxford University Press, 1992), 106.
8. *Colored American,* March 4, 1837.
9. See respectively the August 12, 1837, and the November 4, 1837, issues of the *Colored American.*
10. Robert Ernst, *Immigrant Life in New York City, 1825–1863* (New York: Octagon Books, 1979), 102–3.
11. Thomas R. Whitney, "The Colored People," *Republic: A Monthly Magazine of American Literature, Politics and Art,* January 1852, 40.
12. Harriet Beecher Stowe, *Uncle Tom's Cabin; or, Life Among the Lowly* (1852; New York: W. W. Norton, 2010), 395, 394.
13. Susan Ryan, "Errand into Africa: Colonization and Nation Building in Sarah J. Hale's *Liberia,*" *New England Quarterly* 68, no. 4 (December 1995): 561–62.
14. Ibid., 566.
15. Joseph Michael Sommers, "*Godey's Lady's Book:* Sarah Hale and the Construction of Sentimental Nationalism," *College Literature* 37, no. 3 (summer 2010): 45.
16. Isabelle Lehuu, *Carnival on the Page: Popular Print Media in Antebellum America* (Chapel Hill: The University of North Carolina Press, 2000), 102.
17. Sarah Josepha Hale, *Liberia; or, Mr. Peyton's Experiments* (New York: Harper and Brothers, 1853), 56, 59, 68.
18. Ibid., 78.
19. Shane White, *Stories of Freedom in Black New York* (Cambridge, MA: Harvard University Press, 2002), 212.
20. Hale, *Liberia,* 77.
21. Ibid., 83, 83.
22. Ibid., 86, 87.

23. Samuel Otter, *Philadelphia Stories: America's Literature of Race and Freedom* (New York: Oxford University Press, 2010), 217.
24. Hale, *Liberia,* 88.
25. Ibid., 228.
26. "Literary Notices," *Frederick Douglass' Paper,* November 5, 1852.
27. Frederick Douglass, "Slavery, the Slumbering Volcano: An Address Delivered in New York, New York, on 23 April 1849," *Frederick Douglass Papers Digital Archive,* 149–50, 151, 151.
28. Frederick Douglass, *My Bondage and My Freedom* (New York: Penguin, 2003), 277; James McCune Smith, introduction to *My Bondage and My Freedom,* 24.
29. "Letter to Mrs. Stowe," *Frederick Douglass' Paper,* December 2, 1853.
30. "Learn Trades or Starve!," *Frederick Douglass' Paper,* March 4, 1853.
31. "The Industrial College," *Frederick Douglass' Paper,* January 20, 1854.
32. William Wells Brown, *Clotel; or, the President's Daughter,* ed. Robert S. Levine, 2nd ed. (Boston: Bedford/St. Martin's, 2011), 160, 163.
33. Ibid., 183, 183.
34. George Lippard, *New York: Its Upper Ten and Lower Million* (Cincinnati, OH: H. M. Rulison, 1853), 78, 79.
35. See Eric Gardner, "'A Gentleman of Superior Cultivation and Refinement': Recovering the Biography of Frank J. Webb," *African American Review* 50 no. 4 (reprint; winter 2017): 1043–54.
36. Otter, *Philadelphia Stories,* 264.
37. See Anna Engle, "Depictions of the Irish in Frank Webb's *The Garies and Their Friends* and Frances E. W. Harper's *Trial and Triumph,*" *MELUS: The Journal of the Society for the Study of Multi-Ethnic Literature of the United States* 26, no. 1 (spring 2001): 151–71; Elizabeth Stockton, "The Property of Blackness: The Legal Fiction of Frank J. Webb's *The Garies and Their Friends,*" *African American Review* 43, no. 2–3 (summer/fall 2009): 473–86.
38. Otter, *Philadelphia Stories,* 225.
39. Anbinder, *Nativism and Slavery,* 6–7.
40. Frank J. Webb, *The Garies and Their Friends* (Baltimore, MD: Johns Hopkins University Press, 1997), 179–80, 175.
41. Ibid., 111, 111.
42. Ibid., 377, 392.
43. Sean Wilentz, *Chants Democratic: New York City and the Rise of the American Working Class, 1788–1850* (New York: Oxford University Press, 1984), 323; Robert Ernst, "Economic Nativism in New York City During the 1840s," *New York History* 29, no. 2 (1948): 174; Bruce Laurie, "'Nothing on Compulsion': Life Styles of Philadelphia Artisans, 1820–1850," *Labor History* 15, no. 3 (June 1974): 357.
44. Scattered issues of Duganne's the *Iron Man,* once listed as available at the Chester County Historical Society in West Chester, Pennsylvania, have not been located.

45. Albert Johannsen, *The House of Beadle and Adams and Its Dime and Nickel Novels, Vol. II* (Norman: University of Oklahoma Press, 1950), 85–88.
46. Augustine Duganne, *The Daguerreotype Miniature; or, Life in the Empire City* (Philadelphia: G. B. Zieber, 1846), 19, 14.
47. Eric Lott, *Love and Theft: Blackface Minstrelsy and the American Working Class* (New York: Oxford University Press, 1995), 81.
48. Duganne, *The Daguerreotype Miniature,* 26.
49. Augustine Duganne, *Eustace Barcourt; or, The Illegitimate. A Story of Conflict Between Good and Evil* (Philadelphia: G. B. Zieber and Company, 1848), 96, 97, 106.
50. Duganne attended and spoke against the Fugitive Slave Law at the same meeting in Philadelphia as Lippard. See "Meeting in Philadelphia," *National Era,* July 15, 1852.
51. Duganne, *Eustace Barcourt,* 67, 105, 105.
52. See Johannsen, *The House of Beadle and Adams, Vol. II,* 168; see Jay Monaghan, *The Great Rascal: The Life and Adventures of Ned Buntline* (New York: Bantam Books, 1951), 142.
53. Anbinder, *Nativism and Slavery,* 22n.
54. *Ned Buntline's Own,* December 2, 1848.
55. Jay Monaghan indicates that local newspaper accounts reported 34 killed and 141 wounded during the violent suppression of the rioting. Most historical sources on the Astor Place Riot place the number of dead closer to 21. For Monaghan's treatment of Ned Buntline's role in the Astor Place Riot, see his *The Great Rascal: The Life and Adventures of Ned Buntline* (New York: Bantam Books, 1951), 147–59. Also, see Peter G. Buckley's "The Case Against Ned Buntline: The 'Words, Signs, and Gestures' of Popular Authorship," *Prospects* 13 (October 1988): 249–72. Buckley indicates that Buntline was the only person convicted for conspiring to riot, which carried a $600 fine and one year in jail (254).
56. Buckley, "The Case Against Ned Buntline," 253.
57. Ned Buntline, *The Mysteries and Miseries of New York: A Story of Real Life* (New York: Berford and Co., 1848), Part I, 33.
58. Ibid., Part II, 14.
59. Ibid., Part IV, 71.
60. Ibid., Part II, 84–85.
61. Ibid., Part V, 88.
62. Whitney, *Republic,* January 1852, 36–37.
63. Elizabeth Fenton, *Religious Liberties: Anti-Catholicism and Liberal Democracy in Nineteenth-Century U.S. Literature and Culture* (New York: Oxford University Press, 2011), 107.
64. J. Hector St. John de Crèvecoeur, *Letters from an American Farmer* (1782; New York: Penguin Books, 1986), 73; Ray Billington, *The Protestant Crusade 1800–1860: A Study of the Origins of American Nativism* (New York: Macmillan, 1938),

4, 18–19; Robert S. Levine, *Conspiracy and Romance: Studies in Brockden Brown, Cooper, Hawthorne, and Melville* (New York: Cambridge University Press, 1989), 9–10; Ernst, *Immigrant Life in New York City,* 135; Anbinder, *Nativism and Slavery,* 8.

65. "Proposals for Publishing the Freedom's Journal," *Freedom's Journal,* March 16, 1827.
66. Ibid., March 23, 1827.
67. "Trickery Exposed," *Freedom's Journal,* February 14, 1829.
68. Anbinder, *Nativism and Slavery,* 43.
69. "Keeping the Sabbath," *Weekly Advocate,* January 28, 1837.
70. "Sunday Hair Dressers," *Colored American,* April 1, 1837.
71. "Working on the Sabbath," *Star Spangled Banner,* August 21, 1852.
72. Fenton, *Religious Liberties,* 104, 106.
73. Frederick Douglass, *Narrative of the Life of Frederick Douglass, an American Slave,* rev. ed. (1845; repr., New York: Penguin, 2014), 47–48.
74. Robert S. Levine, *The Lives of Frederick Douglass* (Cambridge, MA: Harvard University Press, 2016), 93–94.
75. Anbinder, *Nativism and Slavery,* 106.
76. Douglass, *My Bondage and My Freedom,* 201.
77. Jenny Franchot, *Roads to Rome: The Antebellum Protestant Encounter with Catholicism* (Berkeley: University of California Press, 1994), 101.
78. Bruce Laurie, *Working People of Philadelphia, 1800–1850* (Philadelphia: Temple University Press, 1980), 29.
79. For a fuller discussion of the ethnic politics of the Kensington nativist riots in Philadelphia, see David Montgomery's "The Shuttle and the Cross: Weavers and Artisans in the Kensington Riots of 1844," *Journal of Social History* 5 (summer 1972): 411–46.
80. Shelley Streeby, *American Sensations: Class, Empire, and the Production of Popular Culture* (Berkeley: University of California Press, 2002), 23.
81. "A Thought for the Bigots of All Colours," *Quaker City Weekly,* February 24, 1849.
82. "Words for the People," *Quaker City Weekly,* March 31, 1849.
83. Susan Griffin, *Anti-Catholicism and Nineteenth-Century Fiction* (New York: Cambridge University Press, 2004), 17, 104.
84. Samuel Morse, *Foreign Conspiracy Against the Liberties of the United States* (New York: Arno Press, 1977), 118.
85. Lippard, *New York,* 35, 147.
86. Griffin, *Anti-Catholicism,* 111.
87. Lippard, *New York,* 147.
88. Otter, *Philadelphia Stories,* 170.
89. Lippard, *New York,* 68, 283.
90. Ibid., 85, 85.
91. "The American State Convention," *New York Tribune,* September 16, 1857, 5.
92. Monaghan, *The Great Rascal,* 198.

93. "Augustine Joseph Hickey Duganne," *Dictionary of American Biography, Vol. 3,* ed. Allen Johnson and Dumas Malone (New York: Scribner's, 1937), 492–93.
94. In *Nativism and Slavery,* Anbinder writes that Know Nothing candidates also had success in California, Indiana, and Ohio in 1854: "In every state where they had time to organize, they could claim some sort of victory" (73).
95. W. T. Lhamon Jr., *Raising Cain: Blackface Performance from Jim Crow to Hip Hop* (Cambridge: Harvard University Press, 1998), 76–77.
96. Anbinder, *Nativism and Slavery,* 34.
97. Augustine Duganne, *The Tenant-House; or, Embers from Poverty's Hearthstone* (New York: Robert M. DeWitt, 1857), 226.
98. Robert W. DeForest and Lawrence Veiller, ed., *The Tenement House Problem, including the Report of the New York State Tenement House Commission of 1900* (New York: MacMillan, 1903), 90.
99. Duganne, *The Tenant-House,* 191.
100. Anbinder, *Nativism and Slavery,* 120.
101. Duganne, *The Tenant-House,* 444–45, 456.
102. Ibid., 421, 421–22, 423.
103. Ibid., 423–24, 237.
104. "Notices of New Works," *Southern Literary Messenger,* January 1859, 80.
105. Streeby, *American Sensations,* 22.
106. Augustine Duganne, *The Fighting Quakers* (Farmville, VA: Schroeder, 1995), 15.

Chapter Four: Class-Accented Sensationalism in the Black and Popular Press

1. Frederick Douglass, *The Life and Times of Frederick Douglass* (Mineola, NY: Dover, 2003), 203.
2. "Plan of the American Industrial School," *Frederick Douglass' Paper,* May 5, 1854.
3. Todd Vogel, "The New Face of Black Labor," *The Black Press: New Literary and Historical Essays* (New Brunswick, NJ: Rutgers University Press, 2001), 37.
4. "Learn Trades or Starve!," *Frederick Douglass' Paper,* March 4, 1853.
5. "Letter to Mrs. Stowe," *Frederick Douglass' Paper,* December 2, 1853.
6. Ibid.
7. "Learn Trades or Starve!"
8. "The Industrial College," *Frederick Douglass' Paper,* January 20, 1854.
9. "Letter to Mrs. Stowe," *Frederick Douglass' Paper,* December 2, 1853.
10. Charles Lewis Reason, "Introduction (The Colored People's 'Industrial College')," *Autographs for Freedom* (Rochester, NY: Wanzer, Beardsley, & Co., 1854), 15.
11. "Plan of the American Industrial School," *Frederick Douglass' Paper,* May 5, 1854.
12. Emerson Bennett, *Ellen Norbury; or, The Adventures of an Orphan* (Philadelphia: T. B. Peterson, 1855), 24.
13. David S. Reynolds, introduction to *The Quaker City; or, The Monks of Monk-*

Hall, by George Lippard (Amherst: University of Massachusetts Press, 1995), xiii.

14. *Spirit of the Times,* January 17, 1845.
15. Lippard, *The Quaker City*, 1.
16. *Quaker City Weekly,* January 6, 1849.
17. "Literary Notices," *National Era,* July 18, 1850.
18. See Dan Schiller, *Objectivity and the News: The Public and the Rise of Commercial Journalism* (Philadelphia: University of Pennsylvania Press, 1981).
19. Frankie Hutton, *The Early Black Press in America, 1827 to 1860* (Westport, CT: Greenwood Press, 1993), x.
20. "Education, No. III," *Freedom's Journal,* April 13, 1827.
21. "Good Advice to Young Men," *Freedom's Journal,* January 9, 1829.
22. Nina Baym, *Novels, Readers, and Reviewers: Responses to Fiction in Antebellum America* (Ithaca, NY: Cornell University Press, 1984), 24.
23. "Licentious Literature," *Weekly Advocate,* January 28, 1837.
24. "Means of Elevation No. VI," *Colored American,* November 16, 1839.
25. "A Thrilling Incident," *Colored American,* January 12, 1839. Note that "highly wrought" was used at this time as a synonym for sensational fiction.
26. Ibid.
27. Elizabeth McHenry, *Forgotten Readers: Recovering the Lost History of African American Literary Societies* (Durham, NC: Duke University Press, 2002), 115, 116; Benjamin Quarles, *Frederick Douglass* (Washington, DC: Associated Publishers, 1948), 96.
28. See respectively, "Novel-Reading Monomaniacs," *North Star,* December 3, 1847; "How to Keep Off Old Age," *North Star,* June 9, 1848; and "Tell Your Father," *North Star,* August 31, 1849.
29. "Heads of the Colored People—The Washerwoman," *Frederick Douglass' Paper,* June 17, 1852.
30. "Literary Notices," *Frederick Douglass' Paper,* May 4, 1855. The newspaper's prospectus of December 8, 1854, indicates that Julia Griffiths penned the literary notices. She returned to England in 1855.
31. "Literary Notices." The sentence from Bennett's preface reads, "I wished to write a novel, which might please the general reader, and at the same time call attention to the vices and miseries which exist in every great city, and especially in that quarter of Philadelphia of which mention has more than once been made." See Bennett, *Ellen Norbury,* 20.
32. "Literary Notices."
33. Bennett, *Ellen Norbury,* 11–12, 52.
34. "New Publications," *Liberator,* May 11, 1855.
35. Mary Hayden Green Pike, *Ida May: A Story of Things Actual and Possible,* ed. Jessie Morgan-Owens (1854, New York: Broadview Press, 2017), 164, 164–65.
36. Nancy Isenberg, *White Trash: The 400-Year Untold History of Class in America* (New York: Viking, 2016), 135.

37. Pike, *Ida May,* 165, 165.
38. Ibid., 319–20, 320, 320.
39. For more information about Mary Hayden Green Pike, see Jessie Morgan-Owens, introduction to *Ida May,* 11–37.
40. Pike, *Ida May,* 77–78, 79.
41. Ibid., 70, 71, 74.
42. Ibid., 287–88, 233.
43. Mary Hayden Green Pike was not identified as the author until January 1856, when the *Boston Telegraph* reviewed her second novel, *Caste,* as having been penned by the same author as *Ida May,* which had appeared under the pseudonym "Mary Langdon." The *National Era* reprinted the *Boston Telegraph* review of *Caste* on January 31, 1856.
44. "Literary Notices," *National Era,* November 16, 1854.
45. "Ida May, the Kidnapped White Slave," *Liberator,* November 17, 1854.
46. "Literary Notices," *Frederick Douglass' Paper,* November 17, 1854.
47. "Miscellaneous, an Extract from 'Ida May,'" *Frederick Douglass' Paper,* December 8, 1854.
48. Pike, *Ida May,* 179, 179–80, 179n3, 180.
49. Douglass, *Narrative of the Life,* 75, 75; Pike, *Ida May,* 179.
50. "Ida May," *Frederick Douglass' Paper,* January 12, 1855.
51. Pike, *Ida May,* 240, 240, 240.
52. James Oliver Horton, *Free People of Color: Inside the African American Community* (Washington, D.C.: Smithsonian Institution Press, 1993), 29.
53. Justin Jones, *Big Dick, the King of the Negroes: or, Virtue and Vice Contrasted: A Romance of High and Low Life in Boston* (Boston: Star Spangled Banner Office, 1846), 7, 7, 12.
54. Ibid., 21, 13, 47.
55. W. Jeffrey Bolster, *Black Jacks: African American Seamen in the Age of Sail* (Cambridge, MA: Harvard University Press, 1997), 100.
56. Ibid., 101.
57. Douglass, *The Life and Times,* 139.
58. Jack Tager, *Boston Riots: Three Centuries of Social Violence* (Boston: Northeastern University Press, 2001), 87.
59. Jones, *Big Dick,* 58, 58, 58, 59.
60. Ibid., 60.
61. Bolster, *Black Jacks,* 103.
62. William Cooper Nell, *The Colored Patriots of the American Revolution, with sketches of several distinguished colored persons: to which is added a brief survey of the condition and prospects of colored Americans* (Boston: Robert F. Wallcut, 1855), 27.
63. Bolster, *Black Jacks,* 111.
64. Justin Jones, *Fourpe Tap: or, The Middy of the Macedonian* (Boston: Jones's Publishing House, 1847), 75, 75, 83, 83, 75.

65. Toni Morrison, *Playing in the Dark: Whiteness and the Literary Imagination* (New York: Vintage Books, 1992), 44; W. T. Lhamon Jr., *Raising Cain: Blackface Performance from Jim Crow to Hip Hop* (Cambridge: Harvard University Press, 1998), 44; Eric Lott, *Love and Theft: Blackface Minstrelsy and the American Working Class* (New York: Oxford University Press, 1995), 68.
66. J. H. Robinson, *Black Ralph, the Forest Fiend!* (Boston: National Publishing Company, 1851), 12.
67. Shelley Streeby, "Opening Up the Story Paper: George Lippard and the Construction of Class," *boundary2* 24, no. 1 (Spring 1997): 199.
68. Robinson, *Black Ralph,* 44.
69. Lott, *Love and Theft,* 77.
70. Robinson, *Black Ralph,* 96, 95, 97.
71. Ned Buntline, whose real name was Edward Zane Carroll Judson, published stories under at least twelve additional pseudonyms, according to his biographer Jay Monaghan. See Monaghan, *The Great Rascal: The Life and Adventures of Ned Buntline* (New York: Bantam Books, 1951), 291. Given that Buntline had published a story called "A Race on the Bahama Banks," in the *Star Spangled Banner* in the late 1840s, and that "Edward Carroll" appears in Buntline's full name, it is likely that Buntline wrote "Mackey; or, The Black Spy."
72. Edward Carroll, "Mackey; or, The Black Spy," *Star Spangled Banner,* March 27, 1852.
73. Ibid.
74. Lori Merish, *Archives of Labor: Working-Class Women and Literary Culture in the Antebellum United States* (Durham: Duke University Press, 2017), 7.
75. Carroll, "Mackey."
76. "A Fight Between an Italian and a Negro," *Star Spangled Banner,* July 21, 1849, 3.

Coda

1. Osgood Bradbury's *Mysteries of Lowell* is the earliest city-mystery listed in *Mechanic Accents.* See Michael Denning, *Mechanic Accents: Dime Novels and Working-Class Culture in America,* rev. ed. (1987; New York: Verso, 1998), 85.
2. Carl Ostrowski, "'The Best Side of a Case of Crime': George Lippard, Walt Whitman, and Antebellum Police Reports," *American Periodicals: A Journal of History, Criticism, and Bibliography* 21, no. 2 (2011): 138; David S. Reynolds, *Beneath the American Renaissance: The Subversive Imagination in the Age of Emerson and Melville* (New York: Oxford University Press, 1988), 82, 68; Sean Wilentz, *Chants Democratic: New York City and the Rise of the American Working Class, 1788–1850* (New York: Oxford University Press, 1984), 309.
3. Walt Whitman, *Franklin Evans, or The Inebriate, A Tale of the Times,* ed.

Christopher Castiglia and Glenn Hendler (Durham, NC: Duke University Press, 2007), 22–23.

4. George Lippard, *The Quaker City; or, The Monks of Monk-Hall: A Romance of Philadelphia Life, Mystery, and Crime* (1849; repr., Amherst: University of Massachusetts Press, 1995), 23.
5. Whitman, *Franklin Evans,* 23.
6. Ibid., 37, 37–38.
7. Christopher Castiglia and Glenn Hendler, introduction to *Franklin Evans,* xviii.
8. Whitman, *Franklin Evans,* 35.
9. See Thomas R. Pegram, *Battling Demon Rum: The Struggle for a Dry America, 1800–1933* (Chicago: Ivan R. Dee, 1998), 32–33.
10. Whitman, *Franklin Evans,* 38–39.
11. Ibid., 77, 78, 80, 87, 99.
12. Ibid., 95, 96.
13. Lippard, *The Quaker City,* 389.
14. Whitman, *Franklin Evans,* 97.
15. Reynolds, *Beneath the American Renaissance,* 144.
16. Herman Melville, *Redburn: His First Voyage,* ed. Harrison Hayford, Hershel Parker, and G. Thomas Tanselle (Chicago: Northwestern University Press, 1969), 34, 66, 83.
17. Ibid., 163, 201, 201–2, 202.
18. Ibid., 165, 186.
19. Ibid., 250–51, 261, 241.

INDEX

TIMOTHY HELWIG is professor of English at Western Illinois University. Born in York, Pennsylvania, he completed his PhD in English at the University of Maryland, College Park in 2006, and he was awarded the Carl Bode Prize for the best graduate dissertation in American literature. He has held visiting research fellowships at the American Antiquarian Society and the Library Company of Philadelphia, and he serves as an elected officer for the Research Society for American Periodicals and Sigma Tau Delta International English Honor Society. He has published articles in *American Studies, American Periodicals,* and Cambridge's *A History of American Crime Fiction.* He lives in Illinois with his wife, Magdelyn, and their three mischievous cats.